C-1310   CAREER EXAMINATION SERIES

This is your
PASSBOOK for...

Heavy Equipment Mechanic

Test Preparation Study Guide
Questions & Answers

COPYRIGHT NOTICE

This book is SOLELY intended for, is sold ONLY to, and its use is RESTRICTED to individual, bona fide applicants or candidates who qualify by virtue of having seriously filed applications for appropriate license, certificate, professional and/or promotional advancement, higher school matriculation, scholarship, or other legitimate requirements of education and/or governmental authorities.

This book is NOT intended for use, class instruction, tutoring, training, duplication, copying, reprinting, excerption, or adaptation, etc., by:

1) Other publishers
2) Proprietors and/or Instructors of "Coaching" and/or Preparatory Courses
3) Personnel and/or Training Divisions of commercial, industrial, and governmental organizations
4) Schools, colleges, or universities and/or their departments and staffs, including teachers and other personnel
5) Testing Agencies or Bureaus
6) Study groups which seek by the purchase of a single volume to copy and/or duplicate and/or adapt this material for use by the group as a whole without having purchased individual volumes for each of the members of the group
7) Et al.

Such persons would be in violation of appropriate Federal and State statutes.

PROVISION OF LICENSING AGREEMENTS – Recognized educational, commercial, industrial, and governmental institutions and organizations, and others legitimately engaged in educational pursuits, including training, testing, and measurement activities, may address request for a licensing agreement to the copyright owners, who will determine whether, and under what conditions, including fees and charges, the materials in this book may be used them. In other words, a licensing facility exists for the legitimate use of the material in this book on other than an individual basis. However, it is asseverated and affirmed here that the material in this book CANNOT be used without the receipt of the express permission of such a licensing agreement from the Publishers. Inquiries re licensing should be addressed to the company, attention rights and permissions department.

All rights reserved, including the right of reproduction in whole or in part, in any form or by any means, electronic or mechanical, including photocopying, recording, or by any information storage and retrieval system, without permission in writing from the Publisher.

Copyright © 2024 by
National Learning Corporation

212 Michael Drive, Syosset, NY 11791
(516) 921-8888 • www.passbooks.com
E-mail: info@passbooks.com

PUBLISHED IN THE UNITED STATES OF AMERICA

PASSBOOK® SERIES

THE *PASSBOOK® SERIES* has been created to prepare applicants and candidates for the ultimate academic battlefield – the examination room.

At some time in our lives, each and every one of us may be required to take an examination – for validation, matriculation, admission, qualification, registration, certification, or licensure.

Based on the assumption that every applicant or candidate has met the basic formal educational standards, has taken the required number of courses, and read the necessary texts, the *PASSBOOK® SERIES* furnishes the one special preparation which may assure passing with confidence, instead of failing with insecurity. Examination questions – together with answers – are furnished as the basic vehicle for study so that the mysteries of the examination and its compounding difficulties may be eliminated or diminished by a sure method.

This book is meant to help you pass your examination provided that you qualify and are serious in your objective.

The entire field is reviewed through the huge store of content information which is succinctly presented through a provocative and challenging approach – the question-and-answer method.

A climate of success is established by furnishing the correct answers at the end of each test.

You soon learn to recognize types of questions, forms of questions, and patterns of questioning. You may even begin to anticipate expected outcomes.

You perceive that many questions are repeated or adapted so that you can gain acute insights, which may enable you to score many sure points.

You learn how to confront new questions, or types of questions, and to attack them confidently and work out the correct answers.

You note objectives and emphases, and recognize pitfalls and dangers, so that you may make positive educational adjustments.

Moreover, you are kept fully informed in relation to new concepts, methods, practices, and directions in the field.

You discover that you are actually taking the examination all the time: you are preparing for the examination by "taking" an examination, not by reading extraneous and/or supererogatory textbooks.

In short, this PASSBOOK®, used directedly, should be an important factor in helping you to pass your test.

HEAVY EQUIPMENT MECHANIC

DUTIES
Involve the repair and maintenance of a variety of heavy automotive equipment, including graders, bulldozers, rollers, shovels, cranes, tractors and snow loaders; mounts and dismounts snow plow blades and other auxiliary equipment; repairs and maintains auxiliary equipment on trucks, graders and rollers; repairs or overhauls transmissions, brake systems, water pumps, differentials and front and rear axles; occasionally operates lathes and other machine shop equipment in making and repairing automotive parts.

SCOPE OF THE EXAMINATION
The multiple-choice test will cover knowledge, skills and/or abilities in such areas as:

1. Operation, maintenance and repair of automotive, truck and heavy highway equipment;
2. Tools and test equipment used in the maintenance of motor vehicles; and
3. Maintenance and repair of gasoline and diesel engines.

HOW TO TAKE A TEST

I. YOU MUST PASS AN EXAMINATION

A. *WHAT EVERY CANDIDATE SHOULD KNOW*

Examination applicants often ask us for help in preparing for the written test. What can I study in advance? What kinds of questions will be asked? How will the test be given? How will the papers be graded?

As an applicant for a civil service examination, you may be wondering about some of these things. Our purpose here is to suggest effective methods of advance study and to describe civil service examinations.

Your chances for success on this examination can be increased if you know how to prepare. Those "pre-examination jitters" can be reduced if you know what to expect. You can even experience an adventure in good citizenship if you know why civil service exams are given.

B. *WHY ARE CIVIL SERVICE EXAMINATIONS GIVEN?*

Civil service examinations are important to you in two ways. As a citizen, you want public jobs filled by employees who know how to do their work. As a job seeker, you want a fair chance to compete for that job on an equal footing with other candidates. The best-known means of accomplishing this two-fold goal is the competitive examination.

Exams are widely publicized throughout the nation. They may be administered for jobs in federal, state, city, municipal, town or village governments or agencies.

Any citizen may apply, with some limitations, such as the age or residence of applicants. Your experience and education may be reviewed to see whether you meet the requirements for the particular examination. When these requirements exist, they are reasonable and applied consistently to all applicants. Thus, a competitive examination may cause you some uneasiness now, but it is your privilege and safeguard.

C. *HOW ARE CIVIL SERVICE EXAMS DEVELOPED?*

Examinations are carefully written by trained technicians who are specialists in the field known as "psychological measurement," in consultation with recognized authorities in the field of work that the test will cover. These experts recommend the subject matter areas or skills to be tested; only those knowledges or skills important to your success on the job are included. The most reliable books and source materials available are used as references. Together, the experts and technicians judge the difficulty level of the questions.

Test technicians know how to phrase questions so that the problem is clearly stated. Their ethics do not permit "trick" or "catch" questions. Questions may have been tried out on sample groups, or subjected to statistical analysis, to determine their usefulness.

Written tests are often used in combination with performance tests, ratings of training and experience, and oral interviews. All of these measures combine to form the best-known means of finding the right person for the right job.

II. HOW TO PASS THE WRITTEN TEST

A. NATURE OF THE EXAMINATION

To prepare intelligently for civil service examinations, you should know how they differ from school examinations you have taken. In school you were assigned certain definite pages to read or subjects to cover. The examination questions were quite detailed and usually emphasized memory. Civil service exams, on the other hand, try to discover your present ability to perform the duties of a position, plus your potentiality to learn these duties. In other words, a civil service exam attempts to predict how successful you will be. Questions cover such a broad area that they cannot be as minute and detailed as school exam questions.

In the public service similar kinds of work, or positions, are grouped together in one "class." This process is known as *position-classification*. All the positions in a class are paid according to the salary range for that class. One class title covers all of these positions, and they are all tested by the same examination.

B. FOUR BASIC STEPS

1) Study the announcement

How, then, can you know what subjects to study? Our best answer is: "Learn as much as possible about the class of positions for which you've applied." The exam will test the knowledge, skills and abilities needed to do the work.

Your most valuable source of information about the position you want is the official exam announcement. This announcement lists the training and experience qualifications. Check these standards and apply only if you come reasonably close to meeting them.

The brief description of the position in the examination announcement offers some clues to the subjects which will be tested. Think about the job itself. Review the duties in your mind. Can you perform them, or are there some in which you are rusty? Fill in the blank spots in your preparation.

Many jurisdictions preview the written test in the exam announcement by including a section called "Knowledge and Abilities Required," "Scope of the Examination," or some similar heading. Here you will find out specifically what fields will be tested.

2) Review your own background

Once you learn in general what the position is all about, and what you need to know to do the work, ask yourself which subjects you already know fairly well and which need improvement. You may wonder whether to concentrate on improving your strong areas or on building some background in your fields of weakness. When the announcement has specified "some knowledge" or "considerable knowledge," or has used adjectives like "beginning principles of…" or "advanced … methods," you can get a clue as to the number and difficulty of questions to be asked in any given field. More questions, and hence broader coverage, would be included for those subjects which are more important in the work. Now weigh your strengths and weaknesses against the job requirements and prepare accordingly.

3) Determine the level of the position

Another way to tell how intensively you should prepare is to understand the level of the job for which you are applying. Is it the entering level? In other words, is this the position in which beginners in a field of work are hired? Or is it an intermediate or advanced level? Sometimes this is indicated by such words as "Junior" or "Senior" in the class title. Other jurisdictions use Roman numerals to designate the level – Clerk I, Clerk II, for example. The word "Supervisor" sometimes appears in the title. If the level is not indicated by the title, check the description of duties. Will you be working under very close supervision, or will you have responsibility for independent decisions in this work?

4) Choose appropriate study materials

Now that you know the subjects to be examined and the relative amount of each subject to be covered, you can choose suitable study materials. For beginning level jobs, or even advanced ones, if you have a pronounced weakness in some aspect of your training, read a modern, standard textbook in that field. Be sure it is up to date and has general coverage. Such books are normally available at your library, and the librarian will be glad to help you locate one. For entry-level positions, questions of appropriate difficulty are chosen -- neither highly advanced questions, nor those too simple. Such questions require careful thought but not advanced training.

If the position for which you are applying is technical or advanced, you will read more advanced, specialized material. If you are already familiar with the basic principles of your field, elementary textbooks would waste your time. Concentrate on advanced textbooks and technical periodicals. Think through the concepts and review difficult problems in your field.

These are all general sources. You can get more ideas on your own initiative, following these leads. For example, training manuals and publications of the government agency which employs workers in your field can be useful, particularly for technical and professional positions. A letter or visit to the government department involved may result in more specific study suggestions, and certainly will provide you with a more definite idea of the exact nature of the position you are seeking.

III. KINDS OF TESTS

Tests are used for purposes other than measuring knowledge and ability to perform specified duties. For some positions, it is equally important to test ability to make adjustments to new situations or to profit from training. In others, basic mental abilities not dependent on information are essential. Questions which test these things may not appear as pertinent to the duties of the position as those which test for knowledge and information. Yet they are often highly important parts of a fair examination. For very general questions, it is almost impossible to help you direct your study efforts. What we can do is to point out some of the more common of these general abilities needed in public service positions and describe some typical questions.

1) General information

Broad, general information has been found useful for predicting job success in some kinds of work. This is tested in a variety of ways, from vocabulary lists to questions about current events. Basic background in some field of work, such as sociology or economics, may be sampled in a group of questions. Often these are principles which have become familiar to most persons through exposure rather than through formal training. It is difficult to advise you how to study for these questions; being alert to the world around you is our best suggestion.

2) Verbal ability

An example of an ability needed in many positions is verbal or language ability. Verbal ability is, in brief, the ability to use and understand words. Vocabulary and grammar tests are typical measures of this ability. Reading comprehension or paragraph interpretation questions are common in many kinds of civil service tests. You are given a paragraph of written material and asked to find its central meaning.

3) **Numerical ability**

Number skills can be tested by the familiar arithmetic problem, by checking paired lists of numbers to see which are alike and which are different, or by interpreting charts and graphs. In the latter test, a graph may be printed in the test booklet which you are asked to use as the basis for answering questions.

4) **Observation**

A popular test for law-enforcement positions is the observation test. A picture is shown to you for several minutes, then taken away. Questions about the picture test your ability to observe both details and larger elements.

5) **Following directions**

In many positions in the public service, the employee must be able to carry out written instructions dependably and accurately. You may be given a chart with several columns, each column listing a variety of information. The questions require you to carry out directions involving the information given in the chart.

6) **Skills and aptitudes**

Performance tests effectively measure some manual skills and aptitudes. When the skill is one in which you are trained, such as typing or shorthand, you can practice. These tests are often very much like those given in business school or high school courses. For many of the other skills and aptitudes, however, no short-time preparation can be made. Skills and abilities natural to you or that you have developed throughout your lifetime are being tested.

Many of the general questions just described provide all the data needed to answer the questions and ask you to use your reasoning ability to find the answers. Your best preparation for these tests, as well as for tests of facts and ideas, is to be at your physical and mental best. You, no doubt, have your own methods of getting into an exam-taking mood and keeping "in shape." The next section lists some ideas on this subject.

IV. KINDS OF QUESTIONS

Only rarely is the "essay" question, which you answer in narrative form, used in civil service tests. Civil service tests are usually of the short-answer type. Full instructions for answering these questions will be given to you at the examination. But in case this is your first experience with short-answer questions and separate answer sheets, here is what you need to know:

1) Multiple-choice Questions

Most popular of the short-answer questions is the "multiple choice" or "best answer" question. It can be used, for example, to test for factual knowledge, ability to solve problems or judgment in meeting situations found at work.

A multiple-choice question is normally one of three types—
- It can begin with an incomplete statement followed by several possible endings. You are to find the one ending which *best* completes the statement, although some of the others may not be entirely wrong.
- It can also be a complete statement in the form of a question which is answered by choosing one of the statements listed.

- It can be in the form of a problem – again you select the best answer.

Here is an example of a multiple-choice question with a discussion which should give you some clues as to the method for choosing the right answer:

When an employee has a complaint about his assignment, the action which will *best* help him overcome his difficulty is to
- A. discuss his difficulty with his coworkers
- B. take the problem to the head of the organization
- C. take the problem to the person who gave him the assignment
- D. say nothing to anyone about his complaint

In answering this question, you should study each of the choices to find which is best. Consider choice "A" – Certainly an employee may discuss his complaint with fellow employees, but no change or improvement can result, and the complaint remains unresolved. Choice "B" is a poor choice since the head of the organization probably does not know what assignment you have been given, and taking your problem to him is known as "going over the head" of the supervisor. The supervisor, or person who made the assignment, is the person who can clarify it or correct any injustice. Choice "C" is, therefore, correct. To say nothing, as in choice "D," is unwise. Supervisors have and interest in knowing the problems employees are facing, and the employee is seeking a solution to his problem.

2) True/False Questions

The "true/false" or "right/wrong" form of question is sometimes used. Here a complete statement is given. Your job is to decide whether the statement is right or wrong.

SAMPLE: A roaming cell-phone call to a nearby city costs less than a non-roaming call to a distant city.

This statement is wrong, or false, since roaming calls are more expensive.

This is not a complete list of all possible question forms, although most of the others are variations of these common types. You will always get complete directions for answering questions. Be sure you understand *how* to mark your answers – ask questions until you do.

V. RECORDING YOUR ANSWERS

Computer terminals are used more and more today for many different kinds of exams.

For an examination with very few applicants, you may be told to record your answers in the test booklet itself. Separate answer sheets are much more common. If this separate answer sheet is to be scored by machine – and this is often the case – it is highly important that you mark your answers correctly in order to get credit.

An electronic scoring machine is often used in civil service offices because of the speed with which papers can be scored. Machine-scored answer sheets must be marked with a pencil, which will be given to you. This pencil has a high graphite content which responds to the electronic scoring machine. As a matter of fact, stray dots may register as answers, so do not let your pencil rest on the answer sheet while you are pondering the correct answer. Also, if your pencil lead breaks or is otherwise defective, ask for another.

Since the answer sheet will be dropped in a slot in the scoring machine, be careful not to bend the corners or get the paper crumpled.

The answer sheet normally has five vertical columns of numbers, with 30 numbers to a column. These numbers correspond to the question numbers in your test booklet. After each number, going across the page are four or five pairs of dotted lines. These short dotted lines have small letters or numbers above them. The first two pairs may also have a "T" or "F" above the letters. This indicates that the first two pairs only are to be used if the questions are of the true-false type. If the questions are multiple choice, disregard the "T" and "F" and pay attention only to the small letters or numbers.

Answer your questions in the manner of the sample that follows:

32. The largest city in the United States is
    A. Washington, D.C.
    B. New York City
    C. Chicago
    D. Detroit
    E. San Francisco

1) Choose the answer you think is best. (New York City is the largest, so "B" is correct.)
2) Find the row of dotted lines numbered the same as the question you are answering. (Find row number 32)
3) Find the pair of dotted lines corresponding to the answer. (Find the pair of lines under the mark "B.")
4) Make a solid black mark between the dotted lines.

VI. BEFORE THE TEST

Common sense will help you find procedures to follow to get ready for an examination. Too many of us, however, overlook these sensible measures. Indeed, nervousness and fatigue have been found to be the most serious reasons why applicants fail to do their best on civil service tests. Here is a list of reminders:

- Begin your preparation early – Don't wait until the last minute to go scurrying around for books and materials or to find out what the position is all about.
- Prepare continuously – An hour a night for a week is better than an all-night cram session. This has been definitely established. What is more, a night a week for a month will return better dividends than crowding your study into a shorter period of time.
- Locate the place of the exam – You have been sent a notice telling you when and where to report for the examination. If the location is in a different town or otherwise unfamiliar to you, it would be well to inquire the best route and learn something about the building.
- Relax the night before the test – Allow your mind to rest. Do not study at all that night. Plan some mild recreation or diversion; then go to bed early and get a good night's sleep.
- Get up early enough to make a leisurely trip to the place for the test – This way unforeseen events, traffic snarls, unfamiliar buildings, etc. will not upset you.
- Dress comfortably – A written test is not a fashion show. You will be known by number and not by name, so wear something comfortable.

- Leave excess paraphernalia at home – Shopping bags and odd bundles will get in your way. You need bring only the items mentioned in the official notice you received; usually everything you need is provided. Do not bring reference books to the exam. They will only confuse those last minutes and be taken away from you when in the test room.
- Arrive somewhat ahead of time – If because of transportation schedules you must get there very early, bring a newspaper or magazine to take your mind off yourself while waiting.
- Locate the examination room – When you have found the proper room, you will be directed to the seat or part of the room where you will sit. Sometimes you are given a sheet of instructions to read while you are waiting. Do not fill out any forms until you are told to do so; just read them and be prepared.
- Relax and prepare to listen to the instructions
- If you have any physical problem that may keep you from doing your best, be sure to tell the test administrator. If you are sick or in poor health, you really cannot do your best on the exam. You can come back and take the test some other time.

VII. AT THE TEST

The day of the test is here and you have the test booklet in your hand. The temptation to get going is very strong. Caution! There is more to success than knowing the right answers. You must know how to identify your papers and understand variations in the type of short-answer question used in this particular examination. Follow these suggestions for maximum results from your efforts:

1) Cooperate with the monitor

The test administrator has a duty to create a situation in which you can be as much at ease as possible. He will give instructions, tell you when to begin, check to see that you are marking your answer sheet correctly, and so on. He is not there to guard you, although he will see that your competitors do not take unfair advantage. He wants to help you do your best.

2) Listen to all instructions

Don't jump the gun! Wait until you understand all directions. In most civil service tests you get more time than you need to answer the questions. So don't be in a hurry. Read each word of instructions until you clearly understand the meaning. Study the examples, listen to all announcements and follow directions. Ask questions if you do not understand what to do.

3) Identify your papers

Civil service exams are usually identified by number only. You will be assigned a number; you must not put your name on your test papers. Be sure to copy your number correctly. Since more than one exam may be given, copy your exact examination title.

4) Plan your time

Unless you are told that a test is a "speed" or "rate of work" test, speed itself is usually not important. Time enough to answer all the questions will be provided, but this does not mean that you have all day. An overall time limit has been set. Divide the total time (in minutes) by the number of questions to determine the approximate time you have for each question.

5) Do not linger over difficult questions

If you come across a difficult question, mark it with a paper clip (useful to have along) and come back to it when you have been through the booklet. One caution if you do this – be sure to skip a number on your answer sheet as well. Check often to be sure that you have not lost your place and that you are marking in the row numbered the same as the question you are answering.

6) Read the questions

Be sure you know what the question asks! Many capable people are unsuccessful because they failed to *read* the questions correctly.

7) Answer all questions

Unless you have been instructed that a penalty will be deducted for incorrect answers, it is better to guess than to omit a question.

8) Speed tests

It is often better NOT to guess on speed tests. It has been found that on timed tests people are tempted to spend the last few seconds before time is called in marking answers at random – without even reading them – in the hope of picking up a few extra points. To discourage this practice, the instructions may warn you that your score will be "corrected" for guessing. That is, a penalty will be applied. The incorrect answers will be deducted from the correct ones, or some other penalty formula will be used.

9) Review your answers

If you finish before time is called, go back to the questions you guessed or omitted to give them further thought. Review other answers if you have time.

10) Return your test materials

If you are ready to leave before others have finished or time is called, take ALL your materials to the monitor and leave quietly. Never take any test material with you. The monitor can discover whose papers are not complete, and taking a test booklet may be grounds for disqualification.

VIII. EXAMINATION TECHNIQUES

1) Read the general instructions carefully. These are usually printed on the first page of the exam booklet. As a rule, these instructions refer to the timing of the examination; the fact that you should not start work until the signal and must stop work at a signal, etc. If there are any *special* instructions, such as a choice of questions to be answered, make sure that you note this instruction carefully.

2) When you are ready to start work on the examination, that is as soon as the signal has been given, read the instructions to each question booklet, underline any key words or phrases, such as *least, best, outline, describe* and the like. In this way you will tend to answer as requested rather than discover on reviewing your paper that you *listed without describing*, that you selected the *worst* choice rather than the *best* choice, etc.

3) If the examination is of the objective or multiple-choice type – that is, each question will also give a series of possible answers: A, B, C or D, and you are called upon to select the best answer and write the letter next to that answer on your answer paper – it is advisable to start answering each question in turn. There may be anywhere from 50 to 100 such questions in the three or four hours allotted and you can see how much time would be taken if you read through all the questions before beginning to answer any. Furthermore, if you come across a question or group of questions which you know would be difficult to answer, it would undoubtedly affect your handling of all the other questions.

4) If the examination is of the essay type and contains but a few questions, it is a moot point as to whether you should read all the questions before starting to answer any one. Of course, if you are given a choice – say five out of seven and the like – then it is essential to read all the questions so you can eliminate the two that are most difficult. If, however, you are asked to answer all the questions, there may be danger in trying to answer the easiest one first because you may find that you will spend too much time on it. The best technique is to answer the first question, then proceed to the second, etc.

5) Time your answers. Before the exam begins, write down the time it started, then add the time allowed for the examination and write down the time it must be completed, then divide the time available somewhat as follows:
    - If 3-1/2 hours are allowed, that would be 210 minutes. If you have 80 objective-type questions, that would be an average of 2-1/2 minutes per question. Allow yourself no more than 2 minutes per question, or a total of 160 minutes, which will permit about 50 minutes to review.
    - If for the time allotment of 210 minutes there are 7 essay questions to answer, that would average about 30 minutes a question. Give yourself only 25 minutes per question so that you have about 35 minutes to review.

6) The most important instruction is to *read each question* and make sure you know what is wanted. The second most important instruction is to *time yourself properly* so that you answer every question. The third most important instruction is to *answer every question*. Guess if you have to but include something for each question. Remember that you will receive no credit for a blank and will probably receive some credit if you write something in answer to an essay question. If you guess a letter – say "B" for a multiple-choice question – you may have guessed right. If you leave a blank as an answer to a multiple-choice question, the examiners may respect your feelings but it will not add a point to your score. Some exams may penalize you for wrong answers, so in such cases *only*, you may not want to guess unless you have some basis for your answer.

7) Suggestions
    a. Objective-type questions
        1. Examine the question booklet for proper sequence of pages and questions
        2. Read all instructions carefully
        3. Skip any question which seems too difficult; return to it after all other questions have been answered
        4. Apportion your time properly; do not spend too much time on any single question or group of questions

5. Note and underline key words – *all, most, fewest, least, best, worst, same, opposite,* etc.
6. Pay particular attention to negatives
7. Note unusual option, e.g., unduly long, short, complex, different or similar in content to the body of the question
8. Observe the use of "hedging" words – *probably, may, most likely,* etc.
9. Make sure that your answer is put next to the same number as the question
10. Do not second-guess unless you have good reason to believe the second answer is definitely more correct
11. Cross out original answer if you decide another answer is more accurate; do not erase until you are ready to hand your paper in
12. Answer all questions; guess unless instructed otherwise
13. Leave time for review

b. Essay questions
1. Read each question carefully
2. Determine exactly what is wanted. Underline key words or phrases.
3. Decide on outline or paragraph answer
4. Include many different points and elements unless asked to develop any one or two points or elements
5. Show impartiality by giving pros and cons unless directed to select one side only
6. Make and write down any assumptions you find necessary to answer the questions
7. Watch your English, grammar, punctuation and choice of words
8. Time your answers; don't crowd material

8) Answering the essay question

Most essay questions can be answered by framing the specific response around several key words or ideas. Here are a few such key words or ideas:

M's: manpower, materials, methods, money, management
P's: purpose, program, policy, plan, procedure, practice, problems, pitfalls, personnel, public relations

a. Six basic steps in handling problems:
1. Preliminary plan and background development
2. Collect information, data and facts
3. Analyze and interpret information, data and facts
4. Analyze and develop solutions as well as make recommendations
5. Prepare report and sell recommendations
6. Install recommendations and follow up effectiveness

b. Pitfalls to avoid
1. *Taking things for granted* – A statement of the situation does not necessarily imply that each of the elements is necessarily true; for example, a complaint may be invalid and biased so that all that can be taken for granted is that a complaint has been registered

2. *Considering only one side of a situation* – Wherever possible, indicate several alternatives and then point out the reasons you selected the best one
3. *Failing to indicate follow up* – Whenever your answer indicates action on your part, make certain that you will take proper follow-up action to see how successful your recommendations, procedures or actions turn out to be
4. *Taking too long in answering any single question* – Remember to time your answers properly

IX. AFTER THE TEST

Scoring procedures differ in detail among civil service jurisdictions although the general principles are the same. Whether the papers are hand-scored or graded by machine we have described, they are nearly always graded by number. That is, the person who marks the paper knows only the number – never the name – of the applicant. Not until all the papers have been graded will they be matched with names. If other tests, such as training and experience or oral interview ratings have been given, scores will be combined. Different parts of the examination usually have different weights. For example, the written test might count 60 percent of the final grade, and a rating of training and experience 40 percent. In many jurisdictions, veterans will have a certain number of points added to their grades.

After the final grade has been determined, the names are placed in grade order and an eligible list is established. There are various methods for resolving ties between those who get the same final grade – probably the most common is to place first the name of the person whose application was received first. Job offers are made from the eligible list in the order the names appear on it. You will be notified of your grade and your rank as soon as all these computations have been made. This will be done as rapidly as possible.

People who are found to meet the requirements in the announcement are called "eligibles." Their names are put on a list of eligible candidates. An eligible's chances of getting a job depend on how high he stands on this list and how fast agencies are filling jobs from the list.

When a job is to be filled from a list of eligibles, the agency asks for the names of people on the list of eligibles for that job. When the civil service commission receives this request, it sends to the agency the names of the three people highest on this list. Or, if the job to be filled has specialized requirements, the office sends the agency the names of the top three persons who meet these requirements from the general list.

The appointing officer makes a choice from among the three people whose names were sent to him. If the selected person accepts the appointment, the names of the others are put back on the list to be considered for future openings.

That is the rule in hiring from all kinds of eligible lists, whether they are for typist, carpenter, chemist, or something else. For every vacancy, the appointing officer has his choice of any one of the top three eligibles on the list. This explains why the person whose name is on top of the list sometimes does not get an appointment when some of the persons lower on the list do. If the appointing officer chooses the second or third eligible, the No. 1 eligible does not get a job at once, but stays on the list until he is appointed or the list is terminated.

X. HOW TO PASS THE INTERVIEW TEST

The examination for which you applied requires an oral interview test. You have already taken the written test and you are now being called for the interview test – the final part of the formal examination.

You may think that it is not possible to prepare for an interview test and that there are no procedures to follow during an interview. Our purpose is to point out some things you can do in advance that will help you and some good rules to follow and pitfalls to avoid while you are being interviewed.

What is an interview supposed to test?

The written examination is designed to test the technical knowledge and competence of the candidate; the oral is designed to evaluate intangible qualities, not readily measured otherwise, and to establish a list showing the relative fitness of each candidate – as measured against his competitors – for the position sought. Scoring is not on the basis of "right" and "wrong," but on a sliding scale of values ranging from "not passable" to "outstanding." As a matter of fact, it is possible to achieve a relatively low score without a single "incorrect" answer because of evident weakness in the qualities being measured.

Occasionally, an examination may consist entirely of an oral test – either an individual or a group oral. In such cases, information is sought concerning the technical knowledges and abilities of the candidate, since there has been no written examination for this purpose. More commonly, however, an oral test is used to supplement a written examination.

Who conducts interviews?

The composition of oral boards varies among different jurisdictions. In nearly all, a representative of the personnel department serves as chairman. One of the members of the board may be a representative of the department in which the candidate would work. In some cases, "outside experts" are used, and, frequently, a businessman or some other representative of the general public is asked to serve. Labor and management or other special groups may be represented. The aim is to secure the services of experts in the appropriate field.

However the board is composed, it is a good idea (and not at all improper or unethical) to ascertain in advance of the interview who the members are and what groups they represent. When you are introduced to them, you will have some idea of their backgrounds and interests, and at least you will not stutter and stammer over their names.

What should be done before the interview?

While knowledge about the board members is useful and takes some of the surprise element out of the interview, there is other preparation which is more substantive. It *is* possible to prepare for an oral interview – in several ways:

1) Keep a copy of your application and review it carefully before the interview

This may be the only document before the oral board, and the starting point of the interview. Know what education and experience you have listed there, and the sequence and dates of all of it. Sometimes the board will ask you to review the highlights of your experience for them; you should not have to hem and haw doing it.

2) Study the class specification and the examination announcement

Usually, the oral board has one or both of these to guide them. The qualities, characteristics or knowledges required by the position sought are stated in these documents. They offer valuable clues as to the nature of the oral interview. For example, if the job involves supervisory responsibilities, the announcement will usually indicate that knowledge of modern supervisory methods and the qualifications of the candidate as a supervisor will be tested. If so, you can expect such questions, frequently in the form of a hypothetical situation which you are expected to solve. NEVER go into an oral without knowledge of the duties and responsibilities of the job you seek.

3) Think through each qualification required

Try to visualize the kind of questions you would ask if you were a board member. How well could you answer them? Try especially to appraise your own knowledge and background in each area, *measured against the job sought*, and identify any areas in which you are weak. Be critical and realistic – do not flatter yourself.

4) Do some general reading in areas in which you feel you may be weak

For example, if the job involves supervision and your past experience has NOT, some general reading in supervisory methods and practices, particularly in the field of human relations, might be useful. Do NOT study agency procedures or detailed manuals. The oral board will be testing your understanding and capacity, not your memory.

5) Get a good night's sleep and watch your general health and mental attitude

You will want a clear head at the interview. Take care of a cold or any other minor ailment, and of course, no hangovers.

What should be done on the day of the interview?

Now comes the day of the interview itself. Give yourself plenty of time to get there. Plan to arrive somewhat ahead of the scheduled time, particularly if your appointment is in the fore part of the day. If a previous candidate fails to appear, the board might be ready for you a bit early. By early afternoon an oral board is almost invariably behind schedule if there are many candidates, and you may have to wait. Take along a book or magazine to read, or your application to review, but leave any extraneous material in the waiting room when you go in for your interview. In any event, relax and compose yourself.

The matter of dress is important. The board is forming impressions about you – from your experience, your manners, your attitude, and your appearance. Give your personal appearance careful attention. Dress your best, but not your flashiest. Choose conservative, appropriate clothing, and be sure it is immaculate. This is a business interview, and your appearance should indicate that you regard it as such. Besides, being well groomed and properly dressed will help boost your confidence.

Sooner or later, someone will call your name and escort you into the interview room. *This is it.* From here on you are on your own. It is too late for any more preparation. But remember, you asked for this opportunity to prove your fitness, and you are here because your request was granted.

What happens when you go in?

The usual sequence of events will be as follows: The clerk (who is often the board stenographer) will introduce you to the chairman of the oral board, who will introduce you to the other members of the board. Acknowledge the introductions before you sit down. Do not be surprised if you find a microphone facing you or a stenotypist sitting by. Oral interviews are usually recorded in the event of an appeal or other review.

Usually the chairman of the board will open the interview by reviewing the highlights of your education and work experience from your application – primarily for the benefit of the other members of the board, as well as to get the material into the record. Do not interrupt or comment unless there is an error or significant misinterpretation; if that is the case, do not hesitate. But do not quibble about insignificant matters. Also, he will usually ask you some question about your education, experience or your present job – partly to get you to start talking and to establish the interviewing "rapport." He may start the actual questioning, or turn it over to one of the other members. Frequently, each member undertakes the questioning on a particular area, one in which he is perhaps most competent, so you can expect each member to participate in the examination. Because time is limited, you may also expect some rather abrupt switches in the direction the questioning takes, so do not be upset by it. Normally, a board member will not pursue a single line of questioning unless he discovers a particular strength or weakness.

After each member has participated, the chairman will usually ask whether any member has any further questions, then will ask you if you have anything you wish to add. Unless you are expecting this question, it may floor you. Worse, it may start you off on an extended, extemporaneous speech. The board is not usually seeking more information. The question is principally to offer you a last opportunity to present further qualifications or to indicate that you have nothing to add. So, if you feel that a significant qualification or characteristic has been overlooked, it is proper to point it out in a sentence or so. Do not compliment the board on the thoroughness of their examination -- they have been sketchy, and you know it. If you wish, merely say, "No thank you, I have nothing further to add." This is a point where you can "talk yourself out" of a good impression or fail to present an important bit of information. Remember, *you close the interview yourself.*

The chairman will then say, "That is all, Mr. _____, thank you." Do not be startled; the interview is over, and quicker than you think. Thank him, gather your belongings and take your leave. Save your sigh of relief for the other side of the door.

How to put your best foot forward

Throughout this entire process, you may feel that the board individually and collectively is trying to pierce your defenses, seek out your hidden weaknesses and embarrass and confuse you. Actually, this is not true. They are obliged to make an appraisal of your qualifications for the job you are seeking, and they want to see you in your best light. Remember, they must interview all candidates and a non-cooperative candidate may become a failure in spite of their best efforts to bring out his qualifications. Here are 15 suggestions that will help you:

1) Be natural – Keep your attitude confident, not cocky

If you are not confident that you can do the job, do not expect the board to be. Do not apologize for your weaknesses, try to bring out your strong points. The board is interested in a positive, not negative, presentation. Cockiness will antagonize any board member and make him wonder if you are covering up a weakness by a false show of strength.

2) Get comfortable, but don't lounge or sprawl

Sit erectly but not stiffly. A careless posture may lead the board to conclude that you are careless in other things, or at least that you are not impressed by the importance of the occasion. Either conclusion is natural, even if incorrect. Do not fuss with your clothing, a pencil or an ashtray. Your hands may occasionally be useful to emphasize a point; do not let them become a point of distraction.

3) Do not wisecrack or make small talk

This is a serious situation, and your attitude should show that you consider it as such. Further, the time of the board is limited – they do not want to waste it, and neither should you.

4) Do not exaggerate your experience or abilities

In the first place, from information in the application or other interviews and sources, the board may know more about you than you think. Secondly, you probably will not get away with it. An experienced board is rather adept at spotting such a situation, so do not take the chance.

5) If you know a board member, do not make a point of it, yet do not hide it

Certainly you are not fooling him, and probably not the other members of the board. Do not try to take advantage of your acquaintanceship – it will probably do you little good.

6) Do not dominate the interview

Let the board do that. They will give you the clues – do not assume that you have to do all the talking. Realize that the board has a number of questions to ask you, and do not try to take up all the interview time by showing off your extensive knowledge of the answer to the first one.

7) Be attentive

You only have 20 minutes or so, and you should keep your attention at its sharpest throughout. When a member is addressing a problem or question to you, give him your undivided attention. Address your reply principally to him, but do not exclude the other board members.

8) Do not interrupt

A board member may be stating a problem for you to analyze. He will ask you a question when the time comes. Let him state the problem, and wait for the question.

9) Make sure you understand the question

Do not try to answer until you are sure what the question is. If it is not clear, restate it in your own words or ask the board member to clarify it for you. However, do not haggle about minor elements.

10) Reply promptly but not hastily

A common entry on oral board rating sheets is "candidate responded readily," or "candidate hesitated in replies." Respond as promptly and quickly as you can, but do not jump to a hasty, ill-considered answer.

11) Do not be peremptory in your answers

A brief answer is proper – but do not fire your answer back. That is a losing game from your point of view. The board member can probably ask questions much faster than you can answer them.

12) Do not try to create the answer you think the board member wants

He is interested in what kind of mind you have and how it works – not in playing games. Furthermore, he can usually spot this practice and will actually grade you down on it.

13) Do not switch sides in your reply merely to agree with a board member

Frequently, a member will take a contrary position merely to draw you out and to see if you are willing and able to defend your point of view. Do not start a debate, yet do not surrender a good position. If a position is worth taking, it is worth defending.

14) Do not be afraid to admit an error in judgment if you are shown to be wrong

The board knows that you are forced to reply without any opportunity for careful consideration. Your answer may be demonstrably wrong. If so, admit it and get on with the interview.

15) Do not dwell at length on your present job

The opening question may relate to your present assignment. Answer the question but do not go into an extended discussion. You are being examined for a *new* job, not your present one. As a matter of fact, try to phrase ALL your answers in terms of the job for which you are being examined.

Basis of Rating

Probably you will forget most of these "do's" and "don'ts" when you walk into the oral interview room. Even remembering them all will not ensure you a passing grade. Perhaps you did not have the qualifications in the first place. But remembering them will help you to put your best foot forward, without treading on the toes of the board members.

Rumor and popular opinion to the contrary notwithstanding, an oral board wants you to make the best appearance possible. They know you are under pressure – but they also want to see how you respond to it as a guide to what your reaction would be under the pressures of the job you seek. They will be influenced by the degree of poise you display, the personal traits you show and the manner in which you respond.

ABOUT THIS BOOK

This book contains tests divided into Examination Sections. Go through each test, answering every question in the margin. We have also attached a sample answer sheet at the back of the book that can be removed and used. At the end of each test look at the answer key and check your answers. On the ones you got wrong, look at the right answer choice and learn. Do not fill in the answers first. Do not memorize the questions and answers, but understand the answer and principles involved. On your test, the questions will likely be different from the samples. Questions are changed and new ones added. If you understand these past questions you should have success with any changes that arise. Tests may consist of several types of questions. We have additional books on each subject should more study be advisable or necessary for you. Finally, the more you study, the better prepared you will be. This book is intended to be the last thing you study before you walk into the examination room. Prior study of relevant texts is also recommended. NLC publishes some of these in our Fundamental Series. Knowledge and good sense are important factors in passing your exam. Good luck also helps. So now study this Passbook, absorb the material contained within and take that knowledge into the examination. Then do your best to pass that exam.

EXAMINATION SECTION

EXAMINATION SECTION
TEST 1

DIRECTIONS: Each question or incomplete statement is followed by several suggested answers or completions. Select the one that BEST answers the question or completes the statement. *PRINT THE LETTER OF THE CORRECT ANSWER IN THE SPACE AT THE RIGHT.*

1. When servicing a fleet of Cat D8 tractors, the PROPER method of refueling is to

    A. top off the tanks before each shift
    B. leave some room for expansion when filling at the start of each shift
    C. top off the tanks at the end of each shift
    D. use portable pumps for filling where possible

2. In order to PROPERLY install a flat metal lock, used with a cap screw, the lock should be bent

    A. in two 45-degree bends
    B. over a curved surface
    C. to catch the inside of the cap screw
    D. sharply on a flat surface of the cap screw

3. Bearings which require heat for installation should be heated in

    A. lubricating oil to 250° F
    B. diesel fuel to 300° F
    C. lubricating oil to 400° F
    D. diesel fuel to 400° F

4. A standard torque down test on a bolt, to be used with standard heat treated bolts and stud nuts in assembling Cat equipment, is _____ foot-lbs.

    A. 110 ± 115   B. 265 ± 50   C. 800 ± 400   D. 1500 ± 200

5. When assembling duo-cone floating seals in a Cat D8 tractor, the toric sealing ring SHOULD be assembled with

    A. a thumb and finger
    B. a torque wrench
    C. a 2000 PSI hydraulic press
    D. regular pliers and a screwdriver

6. When servicing the hydraulic system of a Cat D8 tractor and 8S bulldozer, the mechanic SHOULD put the control levers in the _____ position.

    A. hold   B. float   C. release   D. neutral

7. The one of the following conditions that would NOT be a possible direct cause of a Cat diesel engine in a crawler tractor overheating is

    A. low coolant level
    B. low fuel pressure
    C. corroded water pump
    D. leaking precombustion chamber gaskets

8. When a Cat D8 tractor water temperature regulator is being checked for proper opening temperature, the regulator SHOULD start to open at

   A. 120° F B. 144° F C. 152° F D. 164° F

9. In a Cat D8 tractor, the water pump is sealed with a _____ seal.

   A. duo-cone
   B. leather-faced bellows
   C. carbon-faced bellows
   D. O-ring

10. The sealed pressure overflow assembly in a Cat D8 tractor's radiator assembly has the PRIMARY purpose of

    A. maintaining a constant coolant level
    B. preventing air from entering
    C. preventing coolant from leaking out
    D. maintaining a constant pressure during tractor operation

11. The MAIN oil pump on a Cat D8 engine is driven by a

    A. gear from the timing gear train
    B. belt from the fan belt assembly
    C. gear from the flywheel
    D. series of gears from the camshaft

12. The engine oil pump on a Cat D8 tractor is located in the front section of the oil pan and can be worked on by

    A. removing the rear section of the oil pan
    B. removing the timing gear case
    C. removing the oil pan covers
    D. disassembling the bell housing

13. In the case of a Cat D8 power shift tractor transmission failure, a CRITICAL requirement before returning the tractor to operation is to install a new

    A. engine oil cooler
    B. transmission oil cooler core assembly
    C. engine filter element
    D. transmission air cleaner

14. Valve rotation is a term which refers to the

    A. removal and reassembly of all valves
    B. turn of the valves during engine operation
    C. placement of the valves in another location in the firing sequence
    D. normal tune-up procedure for the valves

15. The end gap in a newly-installed piston ring SHOULD be measured with a _____ gage.

    A. feeler B. ring C. plug D. surface

16. Pistons which have been removed from a diesel engine for repair and replacement should be replaced IF

    A. they are scored above the top compressing ring
    B. the ring grooves are carboned up
    C. they are badly scored below the compressing ring
    D. the top ring is worn

17. When adjusting the alternator for proper voltage on a newly-styled power-shift Cat D8 tractor, a mechanic SHOULD use a(n)

    A. ammeter and a pair of pliers
    B. voltmeter and a socket wrench
    C. voltmeter and a screwdriver
    D. voltage regulator and a screwdriver

18. The one of the following phrases that does NOT accurately describe the type of power-shift transmission in a 46A power-shift Cat D8 tractor is

    A. planetary drive
    B. oil actuated
    C. constant mesh
    D. hydraulically engaged

19. When checking to insure proper PSI settings on the steering clutch actuating pistons, the steering clutches of a Cat D8 tractor SHOULD be

    A. *engaged* with the engine at full throttle
    B. *disengaged* with the engine at low idle
    C. *engaged* with the engine at low idle
    D. *disengaged* with the engine at full throttle

20. The hydraulic pump on the Cat D8 tractor power-shift transmission supplies oil to the transmission

    A. only
    B. and torque converter only
    C. , torque converter, and steering clutches only
    D. , torque converter, steering clutches, and brakes

21. When the track on a Cat D8 tractor is being assembled, the pad belts should have a torqued down pressure of AT LEAST _____ PSI.

    A. 50 ± 10   B. 100 ± 20   C. 150 ± 30   D. 250 ± 50

22. The seals between the pin and bushings of the Cat D8 tractor are of the _____ type.

    A. bellows
    B. O-ring
    C. duo-cone
    D. leather-faced

23. As a safety measure, before removing the master pin on the tracks of any track-type tractor, it is BEST to

    A. remove all pressure from the hydraulic track adjustor
    B. have the idler in the up position
    C. have the idler in the down position
    D. remove the duo-cone seals

4 (#1)

24. When tracks on a Cat D8 are properly adjusted to minimize wear, the sag between the carrier-roller and idler should be no more than

    A. ¼" to ½"
    B. ½" to 1½"
    C. 1" to 1½"
    D. 1½" to 2½"

25. To change the front idler on a tractor from the low to the high position, a mechanic MUST rotate the

    A. bearing 180° only
    B. bearing and idler 180°
    C. idler 180° only
    D. shaft 180° only

26. The turbo-charger on any diesel engine performs the BASIC function of _____ air pressure.

    A. *decreasing* the intake
    B. *increasing* the intake
    C. *decreasing* the exhaust
    D. *increasing* the exhaust

27. The PRIMARY reason for removal of carbon from a turbine wheel of an automotive-type turbo-charger is to

    A. prevent hot spots
    B. prevent loss of air pressure
    C. increase manifold temperature
    D. prevent dynamic imbalance

28. If a timing gear has 120 teeth and turns at 700 RPM, the speed that a 420 tooth gear mated to it will turn at is _____ RPM.

    A. 150 B. 200 C. 500 D. 2450

29. The engine hydraulic system and transmission on a certain type of tractor use the same type oil. This oil is delivered in 55 gal. drums.
    How many drums are needed to make all three changes on ten of these tractors whose capacities are the following:
    Engine ....58 quarts
    Transmission .... 70 quarts
    Hydraulic system .... 22 gallons

    A. 100 drums
    B. 50 drums
    C. 54 drums
    D. 10 drums

30. A new shop layout requires the following:
    1,000 sq. ft. for tool room
    3,000 sq. ft. for parts room
    10,000 sq. ft. for service bays
    5,500 sq. ft. for isles
    The building should be AT LEAST _____ yards wide and _____ yards long.

    A. 10; 70 B. 20; 70 C. 25; 70 D. 30; 70

31. After moving a track-type tractor equipped with a bulldozer into an area for servicing, the operator should ALWAYS

   A. lower the blade
   B. ground the scarifier
   C. tilt the blade forward
   D. lower the bowl

32. The diameter of the main journals on the crankshaft of a new series Cat D8 tractor is 4.259 to 4.261 inches.
The MAXIMUM allowable main-bearing clearance should be no more than

   A. .003   B. .005   C. .007   D. .010

33. NORMAL procedure in removing the liners from a wet-type diesel engine would require the use of a

   A. puller ring and 4 lb. hammer
   B. brass puller rod and hammer
   C. manual puller
   D. hydraulic puller

34. When the crankshaft of a Cat D8 is worn sufficiently to require regrinding and standard oversized bearings are used, the shaft should be turned down to EITHER _____ under-size.

   A. .025" or .050"
   B. .010" or .020"
   C. .050" or 0.10"
   D. .001" or .002"

35. To insure MAXIMUM cable life on a crawler-drawn scraper, the mechanic should

   A. grease the cable with engine oil
   B. replace the cable when any part is worn
   C. pull out a few feet of cable when worn
   D. grease the sheave grooves with gear lub

36. PROPER procedure in filling a large earthmoving tire with air should include use of

   A. hand-held air lines
   B. steel hammers
   C. self-attaching air chucks
   D. chains and lifting hooks

37. The bearing journals on a standard six-cylinder diesel engine with a four-stroke firing cycle are spaced _____ apart.

   A. 30°   B. 60°   C. 90°   D. 120°

38. The BASIC advantage of using an alternator over a generator on an automotive diesel engine is that the alternator

   A. provides alternating current
   B. provides full voltage at idle speeds
   C. provides better starting in cold weather
   D. is easier to adjust

39. The normal SAE definition of net flywheel horsepower includes a requirement that the engine be running at rated RPM and that it be equipped with

   A. no attachments
   B. fan, generator and no water pump or radiator
   C. fan, generator, water pump and radiator
   D. fan, generator, water pump and no radiator

40. GENERALLY, a diesel engine in a tractor or loader is operated with its compression ratio _____ as that of a gasoline engine.

   A. four times as great
   B. the same
   C. twice as great
   D. five times as great

KEY (CORRECT ANSWERS)

1. C	11. A	21. D	31. A
2. D	12. C	22. C	32. C
3. A	13. B	23. A	33. D
4. D	14. B	24. C	34. A
5. A	15. A	25. B	35. C
6. A	16. A	26. B	36. C
7. B	17. C	27. D	37. B
8. D	18. C	28. B	38. B
9. C	19. B	29. D	39. C
10. D	20. D	30. D	40. C

TEST 2

DIRECTIONS: Each question or incomplete statement is followed by several suggested answers or completions. Select the one that BEST answers the question or completes the statement. *PRINT THE LETTER OF THE CORRECT ANSWER IN THE SPACE AT THE RIGHT.*

1. In a normal automotive and earthmoving application, a STANDARD commercial diesel engine ignites the fuel at   1.____

    A. 450° F B. 900° F C. 1450° F D. 212° F

2. The one of the following that is NOT normally used as a starting system for automotive and earthmoving diesel engines in mobile equipment is   2.____

    A. a gasoline starting engine
    B. a direct electric starting motor
    C. air pressure
    D. a hydraulic motor

3. A four-cycle diesel engine has a firing sequence BEST described as   3.____

    A. power, scavenging, compression, stroke, and firing
    B. intake, compression, firing, power, and exhaust
    C. exhaust, compression, firing, and power
    D. exhaust, intake, firing, and power

4. When a diesel engine is equipped with a gasoline starting engine, the compression release control is opened   4.____

    A. *after* the main engine is turning over
    B. *before* the main engine is turning over
    C. *after* the starting engine is at full RPM
    D. *after* the starting engine is turning the diesel engine

5. The one of the following that is NOT a normal method used to help start a diesel engine in cold weather is   5.____

    A. dip stick heaters
    B. glow plugs
    C. manifold heating
    D. ethylene glycol injection

6. The BASIC reason for cam grinding a diesel engine cylinder is so that   6.____

    A. the piston rings will seat better
    B. the piston will not stick in the lines
    C. it will become more nearly round when running hot
    D. it will not be as hard to turn over when starting

7. The turbo-charger used on a GM diesel engine is BEST described as _____ driven.   7.____

    A. exhaust-gas
    B. intake-gas
    C. mechanically
    D. hydraulically

8. When removing an 8S hydraulic bulldozer from a Cat D8 tractor for tractor servicing, the bulldozer lift cylinders SHOULD be secured with

    A. hanger link, bolt, nut, and lockwasher
    B. master pin and link
    C. bracket and hose coupler
    D. J bolt clamps and pins

9. On an earthmoving machine, the hydraulic crossover valve has a function of being able to use

    A. two circuits with one valve
    B. one circuit with two valves
    C. both circuits at the same time
    D. varying pressures in the same circuit

10. When making adjustments on a clutch of a double-drum cable control mounted on a Cat D8 tractor used for pulling a scraper, a mechanic should ALWAYS

    A. disengage the clutch
    B. shut off the engine
    C. loosen the clamp nut and clutch-engaging nut lock bolt
    D. move the clutch-engaging rod one inch beyond the *clutch engaged* mark

11. The engine oil that should be used for a Cat D8 tractor using a Cat engine is

    A. superior lubricant Series 1
    B. superior lubricant Series 3
    C. standard multiviscosity Series 2
    D. standard multiviscosity Series 1

12. The engine oil that should be used for a Cummins diesel engine is

    A. superior lubricant Series 1
    B. superior lubricant Series 3
    C. standard multiviscosity Series 2
    D. standard multiviscosity Series 1

13. When the sulphur content of the diesel fuel used in a Cat diesel engine goes above 0.4%, the oil change period should be changed from _____ to _____ Service Meter Hours.

    A. 500; 300   B. 250; 125   C. 500; 100   D. 250; 100

14. In a four-stroke diesel engine, each piston fires every _____ of the crankshaft.

    A. revolution   B. 2 revolutions
    C. 4 revolutions   D. ½ revolution

15. In an automotive engine, when the alternator is functioning properly and a low charging rate is experienced, the mechanic should check the

    A. magneto   B. generator
    C. regulator   D. battery cables

16. The PROPER equipment to use in removing a sprocket from a Cat D8 tractor is a 16.____

    A. hydraulic puller   B. chain hoist and fall
    C. socket wrench   D. bar and rubber hammer

17. The PROPER amount of pressure for installation of a Cat D8 sprocket on its splines 17.____
    is _____ to _____ tons.

    A. 10; 20   B. 20; 25   C. 35; 40   D. 60; 65

18. Segmented sprocket teeth on a tractor makes it EASIER to 18.____

    A. make pin contact   B. make bushing contact
    C. clean the tracks   D. assemble the tracks

19. The one of the following that is NOT an OSHA requirement while working on heavy con- 19.____
    struction machinery is wearing

    A. safety glasses   B. safety shoes
    C. a hard hat   D. loose clothing

20. The one of the following that is the BEST way to store oily rags is 20.____

    A. in a closed metal container
    B. piled in a corner of the repair shop
    C. in a covered wooden box
    D. piled under a work bench

21. The reason for NOT going to full throttle immediately when starting a turbo-charged auto- 21.____
    motive-type diesel engine is to

    A. allow the bearings to warm up
    B. prevent the engine oil from diluting
    C. ensure bearing lubrication
    D. ensure equal heating of the turbine blades

22. A Cummins diesel engine model designated as NTA-370 is BEST described as 22.____

    A. naturally aspirated, torque adjusted, and 370 max. horsepower
    B. four valve head, turbo-charged, after cooled, and 370 max. horsepower
    C. naturally aspirated, turbo-charged, after cooled, and 370 max. horsepower
    D. 16 valve turbo-charged intercooled and 370 max. horsepower

23. Of the following phrases, the one that does NOT describe a common arrangement com- 23.____
    mon in a V-type automotive diesel engine is

    A. two cam shafts   B. two timing gear trains
    C. one crankshaft   D. two exhaust manifolds

24. The normal oil temperature range for a Cummins diesel engine is MOST NEARLY 24.____

    A. 140 to 160° F   B. 140 to 220° F
    C. 180 to 290° F   D. 180 to 225° F

25. The one of the following that is NOT a safety requirement when using ether as a cold weather starting aid on a diesel engine is never

    A. spray directly into the manifold
    B. use near an open flame
    C. use with a preheater
    D. use with a flame-thrower

Questions 26-28.

DIRECTIONS: Questions 26 through 28, inclusive, are to be answered in accordance with the following paragraph.

The following is a set of instructions on engine shut-down procedure: When an engine equipped with an electric shut-down valve is used, the engine can be shut down completely by turning off the switch key on installations equipped with an electric shut-down valve, or by turning the manual shut-down valve lever. Turning off the switch key which controls the electric shut-down valve always stops the engine unless the override button on the shut-down valve has been locked in the open position. If the manual override on the electric shut-down valve is being used, turn the button full counterclockwise to stop the engine.

CAUTION: Never leave the switch key or the override button in the valve open or run position when the engine is not running. With overhead tanks, this would allow fuel to drain into the cylinder, causing hydraulic lock.

26. According to the above paragraph, it becomes apparent that if an engine does not stop when the electric shut-down valve switch key is shut off,

    A. an open manual switch is present
    B. the override button is locked in the closed position
    C. a closed manual switch is functioning
    D. the override button is locked in the open position

27. When using an engine equipped with an electric shut-down valve,

    A. no alternate method is available
    B. a manual method is not present
    C. a manual override can shut the engine down
    D. a manual override will not work

28. As a matter of caution, the switch key in the closed position or the override button in the stop position will

    A. assist in keeping fuel in the cylinders
    B. prevent fuel from flooding the cylinder cavities
    C. assist in producing hydraulic lock
    D. aid fuel dilution

29. A detroit diesel engine with the designation of 8V-53N is BEST described as an _____ with a cubic inch displacement of _____ cu. in.

    A. 8 cylinder V-type; 212   B. 16 cylinder V-type; 424
    C. 8 cylinder N-type; 848   D. 8 cylinder V-type; 424

30. Diesel engine fuels are rated by number from 1 to 4. The relationship between the flash point of a fuel and its number is that, as the flash point

    A. *increases,* the numbers either increase or decrease, depending on the volatility of the fuel
    B. *increases,* the numbers increase
    C. *decreases,* the numbers increase
    D. *decreases,* the numbers decrease

31. In order to locate a misfiring cylinder in a GM diesel engine, the valve cover should be removed and each cylinder checked by

    A. holding down the injector follower
    B. using a pressure gage
    C. regapping the plugs
    D. increasing the fuel to each cylinder one at a time

32. When a GM diesel engine is being serviced, the NORMAL interval for cleaning the cooling system is _____ hours or _____ miles.

    A. 200; 600
    B. 500; 15,000
    C. 1000; 30,000
    D. 1500; 60,000

33. The one of the following situations that will NOT cause the automatic electrical shutdown system on a GM engine to stop the engine is

    A. a loss of coolant
    B. a loss of oil pressure
    C. overspeeding
    D. a decrease in R.P.M.

34. A medium range thermostat for a Cummins diesel engine NORMALLY has a range of

    A. 170 to 185° F
    B. 140 to 160° F
    C. 180 to 195° F
    D. 120 to 145° F

35. When filling a diesel engine cooling system, the mix required is 80% antifreeze and 20% water. You are required to fill seven systems containing 30 gals. each.
    The number of 5 gal. cans of antifreeze that are required is MOST NEARLY

    A. 210   B. 168   C. 34   D. 26

36. When changing a *throw-away* type fuel filter element on a Cummins diesel engine, the housing should be tightened

    A. with a torque wrench
    B. with a socket wrench
    C. with a hand clamp and a screwdriver
    D. by hand

37. Hydraulic hoses are NORMALLY rated by _____ rating.

    A. cord ply
    B. stul mesh
    C. P.S.I.
    D. C.F.M.

38. The starting system of a diesel engine is actuated by two 12-volt batteries in parallel. 38.___
The electric current produced is _____ volt _____.

    A. 12; D.C.   B. 24; D.C.   C. 12; A.C.   D. 24; A.C.

39. Fan belt checks and adjustments, using the suggested A,B,C Cummins maintenance 39.___
manual method, are FIRST required at the _____ interval.

    A. A   B. B   C. C   D. D

40. When two 12-volt 450-ampere-hour batteries are installed in series, the system is rated 40.___
as _____ volt-_____ amp hour.

    A. 24; 450   B. 12; 900   C. 12; 450   D. 24; 900

KEY (CORRECT ANSWERS)

1. C	11. B	21. C	31. A
2. D	12. A	22. B	32. C
3. B	13. B	23. B	33. D
4. B	14. B	24. D	34. A
5. D	15. C	25. A	35. C
6. C	16. A	26. D	36. D
7. C	17. D	27. C	37. C
8. A	18. D	28. B	38. A
9. A	19. D	29. D	39. B
10. B	20. A	30. B	40. A

EXAMINATION SECTION
TEST 1

DIRECTIONS: Each question or incomplete statement is followed by several suggested answers or completions. Select the one that BEST answers the question or completes the statement. *PRINT THE LETTER OF THE CORRECT ANSWER IN THE SPACE AT THE RIGHT.*

1. The proper operation and maintenance of any crane, shovel, or dragline is CHIEFLY the responsibility of the

    A. foreman B. oiler C. mechanic D. operator

    1.____

2. The *angle indicator* on a power-operated crane measures the

    A. angle of the boom to the horizontal
    B. angle of the boom to the vertical
    C. tilt of the housing which covers the rotating operator's station
    D. angle between the boom and the whipline

    2.____

3. On a power-operated crane, the device used to prevent the boom from being pulled over the top of the cab is the

    A. brake
    C. boom point
    B. boom stop
    D. base

    3.____

4. The block and sheave arrangement on the boom point to which the topping lift cable is reeved for lowering and raising the boom is called the

    A. boom harness
    C. axle
    B. cableway
    D. bogie

    4.____

5. The extension attached to the boom point of a crane to provide added length for lifting is known as a

    A. folding boom
    C. mast
    B. lay
    D. jib

    5.____

6. The *Load Rating Chart* of a mobile crane makes no allowance for

    A. range of crane load ratings
    B. operating radii and boom angles
    C. permissible boom lengths
    D. operating speeds

    6.____

7. The WEAKEST part of any crane hoist or sling should be the

    A. clip B. link C. hook D. clamp

    7.____

8. Of the following types of equipment, the one which is MOST often used for excavation operations where extended reach (40 to 60 feet) is an important factor is the

    A. pay loader
    C. dragline
    B. power shovel
    D. backhoe

    8.____

9. Assume that a man is reeling wire onto a smooth-faced drum. With the man facing the drum, the wire is going from the man over the top of the drum, starting with that part of the drum at the man's right side.
   The procedure being followed by this man is

   A. *correct* as described
   B. *wrong* because the wire should be reeled under the drum
   C. *wrong* because the reeling should start at the man's left side
   D. *wrong* because wire should not be reeled onto a smoothfaced drum

10. The point at which vibration will cause the GREATEST weakness in a wire rope used on rapid hoisting rigs is, approximately, _____ to _____ feet above the load attachment.

   A. 5; 20   B. 30; 45   C. 50; 65   D. 70; 85

11. The efficiency of a clipped attachment depends on the manner in which the clips are put on the wire rope, the tightness of nuts on the clips, *and* the _____ the wire rope.

   A. diameter of
   B. construction of
   C. number of clips used on
   D. manufacturer of

12. Of the following types of end connections, the one which is NOT generally used for attaching a wire rope to a clamshell bucket is the

   A. socket attachment
   B. spliced eye attachment
   C. clipped attachment
   D. wedge socket

13. A Langlay wire rope should be used ONLY with a load that

   A. is relatively light
   B. cannot rotate as it is being lifted
   C. is supported on a float
   D. will keep the rope tight

14. Of the following materials, the one MOST commonly used to make crane brake linings is

   A. cotton fabric
   B. bakelite
   C. neoprene
   D. asbestos fabric

15. The MAIN reason why an operator of a diesel-powered rig must not permit the diesel engine to run out of fuel is to prevent

   A. condensation in the fuel tank
   B. damage to the fuel injection system
   C. an increase in coolant temperature
   D. damage to the oil pressure regulating valve

16. If a power shovel, equipped with an electric power plant that has a single electric motor drive, is operating sluggishly due to lack of power, it would be BEST to check the motor with a

   A. tachometer and a rheostat
   B. dwell meter
   C. voltmeter and an ammeter
   D. Bailey meter

17. An operator of a gasoline-powered rig permits the engine to idle unnecessarily for long periods of time. Of the following, the MOST probable result of this practice is that the   17._____

   A. rig will operate more smoothly
   B. lubricating oil will be diluted
   C. radiator water temperature will rise too high
   D. clutch controls will freeze

18. Before fully engaging the engine clutch to set a piece of machinery in operation, the operator should   18._____

   A. partially engage and then disengage the engine clutch to test its operation
   B. check the operating controls to be sure that the clutches are in neutral
   C. examine the gears for proper lubrication
   D. examine the main machinery, making certain that no obstruction prevents its normal operation

19. An operator of a crane wished to change over from dragline operation to a clamshell operation.   19._____
    Assuming there is no boom change, the minimum amount of time it would take three men to make the conversion would be, MOST NEARLY, in the range of _____ to _____ hours.

   A. 2; 3   B. 6; 7   C. 8; 9   D. 10; 11

20. The PRIMARY function of outrigging on a truck crane is to   20._____

   A. extend the boom length
   B. avoid wear of the hoist wire rope
   C. give side support to the truck body
   D. strengthen the structural members of the boom

21. The lowering of a load by a direct-current-powered crane is controlled by _____ braking.   21._____

   A. hydraulic   B. mechanical
   C. dynamic   D. double disc

22. The shaft which operates the valves of a gasoline engine is the _____ shaft.   22._____

   A. crank   B. distributor
   C. valve   D. cam

23. Of the following, the BEST practical way to prevent a lead plate storage battery from freezing in cold weather is to   23._____

   A. turn off all the auxiliaries when not in use
   B. keep the specific gravity of the electrolyte below 1.150
   C. keep it well charged
   D. disconnect the battery cables when the machine is not in use

24. Grades in excavation work are usually designated by   24._____

   A. degree   B. percent   C. height   D. elevation

25. Of the following, the one that is a positive mechanical device for engaging or disengaging power is the

   A. universal
   B. clutch
   C. brake
   D. unloader

26. Of the following, the tool or device that is commonly used to check the firing of spark plugs in a gasoline engine is a(n)

   A. tachometer
   B. ammeter
   C. screw driver with an insulated handle
   D. feeler gauge

27. If the power fails when hoisting a load, the FIRST thing an operator should do is to

   A. land the load under brake control
   B. communicate with the appointed individual in charge of operations
   C. move all clutch or other power controls to the *off* position
   D. set all brakes and locking devices

28. In a 4-stroke-cycle, full-diesel engine, the fuel is ignited by

   A. a jump spark
   B. special spark plugs
   C. highly compressed air
   D. hot exhaust gases

29. The function of the pre-combustion chamber on a diesel engine is to

   A. eliminate pre-ignition
   B. obtain higher compression pressures
   C. pre-cool the lubricating oil
   D. assure complete combustion of the fuel

30. The PRIMARY reason for including a thermal overload device in an electrical circuit containing a 40-horsepower A.C. motor is to

   A. increase the motor's efficiency
   B. control the speed of the motor
   C. protect the motor from overheating
   D. decrease the torque of the motor

31. The MAIN function of the intercooler in a two-stage air compressor is to

   A. cool the lubricating oil
   B. cool the air between stages of compression
   C. permit the expansion of combustion products
   D. remove impurities from the air

32. The relief valve on a gasoline-powered portable air compressor is located on the

   A. oil reserve tank
   B. suction side of the air compressor
   C. discharge side of the air compressor
   D. combustion exhaust manifold

33. In a diesel engine, the injection pump and the nozzle are lubricated by

    A. an SAE 30 oil
    B. the diesel fuel itself
    C. heat-resistant grease
    D. mineral oil

34. The SAE number is an index of a diesel lubricating oil's

    A. specific gravity
    B. film strength
    C. viscosity
    D. anti-foaming ability

35. Excessive lubrication of diesel cylinders may cause

    A. condensation in the cylinders
    B. dangerous vapors in the cylinders
    C. pre-ignition in the cylinders
    D. sticking piston rings

36. The method by which water generally enters the lubricating oil system of a diesel engine is through

    A. rain dripping down into the vents
    B. condensation of the combustion products
    C. a leaky crankcase cover
    D. radiator spill-over

37. In an operator's manual, a lubricant is designated as SUMMER SAE-140 E.P. This lubricant would MOST probably be

    A. an easy-pour lubricant
    B. a grease
    C. an extreme-pressure lubricant
    D. interchangeable with chassis grease

38. A sudden change in the color of a lubricating oil in an operating engine would MOST probably be caused by a(n)

    A. dirty filter
    B. clogged oil breather
    C. overfill of lubricating oil
    D. severe overload and heat

39. The air cleaner of an air compressor is of the oil bath type.
    Of the following substances, the one that it is BEST to use to clean the filter element of this cleaner is

    A. gasoline
    B. oil
    C. water spray
    D. wood alcohol

40. The shipper shaft of a shovel boom is generally located close to the boom's

    A. mid-point
    B. top
    C. bottom
    D. drum

KEY (CORRECT ANSWERS)

1. D	11. C	21. C	31. B
2. A	12. A	22. D	32. C
3. B	13. B	23. C	33. B
4. A	14. D	24. B	34. C
5. D	15. B	25. B	35. D
6. D	16. C	26. C	36. B
7. C	17. B	27. D	37. C
8. C	18. D	28. C	38. D
9. A	19. A	29. D	39. B
10. A	20. C	30. C	40. A

TEST 2

DIRECTIONS: Each question or incomplete statement is followed by several suggested answers or completions. Select the one that BEST answers the question or completes the statement. *PRINT THE LETTER OF THE CORRECT ANSWER IN THE SPACE AT THE RIGHT.*

1. A friction-type clutch is preferable to a positive-type clutch in crane applications because a   1.____

    A. positive clutch can be applied only at high speeds
    B. friction clutch needs no maintenance
    C. positive clutch cannot take loads as well as a friction clutch
    D. friction clutch can be engaged at any speed

2. Of the following types of pumps, the one which is NOT generally found on power-driven mobile machinery is the _____ pump.   2.____

    A. piston-type rotary
    B. reciprocating type
    C. gear-type
    D. balanced vane-type

3. The term *CFM*, as applied to the capacity of air compressors, is an abbreviation for   3.____

    A. compressor feed mechanism
    B. centrifugal force meter
    C. compression fuel machine
    D. cubic feet per minute

4. In a certain crane, a horizontal roller chain drive provides power to the jack shaft. In order that there be proper tension in the roller chain, the chain should be adjusted so that there is   4.____

    A. no sag
    B. a small amount of sag
    C. sufficient sag to allow the chain to droop at its midpoint to the level of the center line of the driving sprocket
    D. sufficient sag so that the top chain and the bottom chain will make an angle of 60° at the driving sprocket

5. Of the following, a switch operated by the motion of a moving part of an electrically powered machine is usually called a _____ switch.   5.____

    A. disconnect
    B. remote-control
    C. limit
    D. service

6. The BEST type of torch to use for cutting wire rope used on a land-based construction site is the   6.____

    A. oxy-acetylene torch
    B. oxy-hydrogen lance
    C. air-propane torch
    D. oxy-butane torch

7. Of the following gear types, the one that would NOT be used to transmit power between two parallel shafts is the _____ gear.   7.____

    A. spur
    B. herringbone
    C. helical
    D. bevel

19

8. The cylinder of a 2-stroke-cycle diesel engine is scavenged by the

   A. mixture of fuel oil and exhaust gases
   B. mixture of fuel oil and intake air
   C. intake fuel
   D. combustion air

9. A COMMON cause of engine back pressure in a gasoline engine is a

   A. rusted muffler
   B. blocked muffler passage
   C. loose exhaust pipe
   D. corroded muffler bracket

10. A grease with a consistency number of 2 is classified as

    A. semifluid   B. hard   C. very hard   D. medium

11. The one of the following to which a micron rating would be assigned is a(n)

    A. grease
    B. oil filter
    C. strainer
    D. magnetic plug

12. An oil is rated as SAE 20W.
    The number *20* refers to the oil's

    A. viscosity at 0° F
    B. detergent factor
    C. specific volume
    D. rate of deterioration

13. Crane machinery and equipment is BEST lubricated

    A. whenever it is needed
    B. when severe vibration occurs
    C. when out of service
    D. at scheduled times

14. Of the following parts of an electric motor, the one which should be checked for proper lubrication is the

    A. bearings
    B. commutator
    C. rotating field
    D. windings

15. Of the following liquids, the one which is used as an electrolyte in a lead-plate storage battery is

    A. hydrochloric acid
    B. salt water
    C. sulphuric acid
    D. ammonia water

16. A battery hydrometer is used mainly to determine a battery's

    A. specific gravity
    B. temperature
    C. resistance
    D. salinity

17. The BEST method to use to remove a stuck gear from a shaft is to

    A. use a wheel puller
    B. use heavy hammer blows to loosen the gear
    C. heat the shaft and then remove the gear
    D. apply oil and rotate the gear slowly

18. Internal leakage in the hydraulic oil line piping system of a mobile unit will

    A. provide lubrication for such parts as shafts and pistons
    B. result in an oil loss from the lubrication system
    C. not cause a power loss
    D. decrease with normal wear of the parts of the unit

19. A preventive maintenance program is a program in which

    A. machinery is serviced whenever required
    B. maintenance of machinery is performed on a regular schedule
    C. the machines are maintained in such a way that there is never any down-time
    D. inspection of machinery is performed only during slack periods

20. An external gear pump consists essentially of

    A. two meshed gears in a closely fitted housing
    B. one gear which is activated by the moving fluid
    C. a piston turning a gear in an enclosed housing
    D. an inlet and outlet reciprocating valve

21. The MINIMUM width of each seizing that is wrapped around a wirerope that is to be cut should be _____ the diameter of the rope.

    A. equal to   B. 1 1/2 times
    C. 2 times   D. 3 times

22. Before cutting a 1" diameter non-preformed regular-lay 6x19 wire rope, the MINIMUM number of seizings that should be placed on each side of the spot where the wire rope is to be cut is

    A. 1   B. 2   C. 3   D. 4

23. When seizing a wire rope, a *seizing iron* is mainly used to

    A. measure the length of seizing wire
    B. straighten the seizing wire
    C. loosen a badly made seizing
    D. wrap the seizing tightly

24. Of the following materials, the one from which seizing wire is made is

    A. copper   B. annealed iron
    C. nylon   D. aluminum

25. Oil used on wire rope which goes through the sheaves and over the drum of a crane will generally

    A. cause the drum to slip
    B. increase the life of the rope
    C. gum up the sheaves
    D. cause the wire to have a slimy surface

26. As a result of insertion of a steel thimble into a spliced eye attachment of a wire rope, the

    A. load will be equally distributed to the wire rope
    B. wire rope will flatten out of shape
    C. wire strands of the rope will tend to break when load is applied
    D. holding power of the attachment will be increased

27. Wedge sockets are MOST frequently used to

    A. temporarily attach wire rope to a piece of equipment
    B. make permanent attachments of wire rope to a piece of equipment
    C. connect two different sizes of wire rope to each other
    D. adjust the length of wire rope to fit the job

28. A *left-lay, regular-lay* wire rope has

    A. the wires laid right-handed and the strands left-handed
    B. the wires laid left-handed and the strands right-handed
    C. both wires and strands laid right-handed
    D. both wires and strands laid left-handed

Questions 29 - 33.

DIRECTIONS: Questions 29 through 33 inclusive are to be answered in accordance with the following paragraphs.

Exhaust valve clearance adjustment on diesel engines is very important for proper operation of the engine. Insufficient clearance between the exhaust valve stem and the rocker arm causes a loss of compression and, after a while, burning of the valves and valve seat inserts. On the other hand, too much valve clearance will result in noisy operation of the engine.

Exhaust valves that are maintained in good operating condition will result in efficient combustion in the engine. Valve seats must be true and unpitted and valve stems must work smoothly within the valve guides. Long valve life will result from proper maintenance and operation of the engine.

Engine operating temperatures should be maintained between 160° F and 185° F. Low operating temperatures result in incomplete combustion and the deposit of fuel lacquers on valves.

29. According to the above paragraphs, too much valve clearance will cause the engine to operate

    A. slowly   B. noisily   C. smoothly   D. cold

30. On the basis of the information given in the above paragraphs, operating temperatures of a diesel engine should be between _____ F and _____ F.

    A. 125°; 130°
    C. 160°; 185°
    B. 140°; 150°
    D. 190°; 205°

31. According to the above paragraphs, the deposit of fuel lacquers on valves is caused by

    A. high operating temperatures
    B. insufficient valve clearance
    C. low operating temperatures
    D. efficient combustion

32. According to the above paragraphs, for efficient operation of the engine, valve seats must

    A. have sufficient clearance
    B. be true and unpitted
    C. operate at low temperatures
    D. be adjusted regularly

33. According to the above paragraphs, a loss of compression is due to insufficient clearance between the exhaust valve stem and the

    A. rocker arm   B. valve seat
    C. valve seat inserts   D. valve guides

34. The BEST of the following ways to deal with a helper assigned to you who is a chronic complainer is to

    A. tell him to stop complaining so much
    B. treat each complaint as if it were valid
    C. walk away from him when he starts to complain
    D. tell him his complaints are senseless

35. An oiler assigned to service your crane has always performed his duties diligently, but for the past several weeks he has been lax.
    Of the following actions, the BEST one to take would be to

    A. recommend his transfer
    B. report him to your superior
    C. re-assign him to office work
    D. ask him if there is anything wrong

36. Of the following, the BEST procedure for an operator to follow when breaking in a new oiler on the job is to

    A. assign work that he is capable of performing
    B. give him minor work assignments to do until he proves he is capable of doing the job
    C. praise him even though his work is not satisfactory
    D. criticize the man in a loud manner when he makes an error

37. An operator of a crane working a short distance from where you are operating, is rendered unconscious when the boom of his crane hits an electric power line.
    Of the following, after safely securing your machine, the FIRST procedure for you to follow would be to

    A. immediately apply artificial respiration to the unconscious operator
    B. call a physician
    C. determine if an electrical hazard still exists aboard the crane
    D. administer a stimulant to the unconscious operator

38. A crane engineman is operating a gasoline-powered crane and sees smoke coming from the engine.
   In this situation, the operator should FIRST

   A. call his helper for assistance
   B. get the fire extinguisher
   C. shut the engine off
   D. wait for flames to appear

39. Assume that a helper has fallen off the crane and is unable to move.
   The BEST procedure to follow in this instance would be to

   A. seek medical aid, letting him lie where he is
   B. place him in a sitting position
   C. give him a stimulant to drink
   D. call the other workers to remove him from the work site

40. Of the following types of fire extinguishing agents, the one that should NOT be used on an oil fire in an oil storage area is

   A. foam
   B. dry chemical
   C. carbon dioxide
   D. soda acid

KEY (CORRECT ANSWERS)

1.	D	11.	B	21.	A	31.	C
2.	B	12.	A	22.	C	32.	B
3.	D	13.	D	23.	D	33.	A
4.	B	14.	A	24.	B	34.	B
5.	C	15.	C	25.	B	35.	D
6.	A	16.	A	26.	D	36.	A
7.	D	17.	A	27.	A	37.	C
8.	D	18.	A	28.	A	38.	C
9.	B	19.	B	29.	B	39.	A
10.	D	20.	A	30.	C	40.	D

EXAMINATION SECTION
TEST 1

DIRECTIONS: Each question or incomplete statement is followed by several suggested answers or completions. Select the one that BEST answers the question or completes the statement. *PRINT THE LETTER OF THE CORRECT ANSWER IN THE SPACE AT THE RIGHT.*

1. Of the following lubricating greases, the one that is generally known as a heat-resisting grease is _____ grease.   1._____

   A. soda (sodium) soap
   B. lime (calcium) soap
   C. aluminum soap
   D. mixed (soda and lime)

2. The chassis grease recommended for MOST pieces of construction equipment is generally   2._____

   A. lime base-water resistant
   B. SAE-140 E.P.
   C. number 3 cup
   D. number 2 cup

3. The PRIMARY advantage that a friction clutch has over a positive clutch is that the friction clutch   3._____

   A. runs at lower speeds
   B. requires less maintenance
   C. can be engaged at either low or high speeds
   D. runs at high speeds

4. Of the following makes of power plants for cranes, the one which uses diesel fuel is the   4._____

   A. Allis-Chalmers L-525
   B. G.M. 4055-C
   C. Waukesha 140 GKU
   D. Waukesha 140 GKU (with torque converter)

5. In a 2-stroke cycle diesel engine, the cylinder is scavenged by   5._____

   A. the combustion air
   B. the exhaust gases
   C. the injected fuel oil
   D. a mixture of fuel oil and air

6. In a 6 x 19 Seale wire rope, the wires in one strand are   6._____

   A. always of the same size
   B. of different diameters
   C. meshed with soft cores
   D. of the flattened strand type

7. Of the following metals, the one that is USUALLY used for socketing wire ropes is   7._____

   A. lead
   B. tin
   C. zinc
   D. 50-50 solder

8. On the suction stroke of a four-stroke cycle full diesel engine, _____ drawn into the cylinder.

   A. fuel oil only is
   B. air and a full charge of fuel oil are
   C. air only is
   D. air and a one-half charge of fuel oil are

9. The PRIMARY purpose of crossing a belt when connecting two pulleys is to

   A. rotate the shafts in opposite directions
   B. decrease the belt friction contact
   C. be able to use a thinner belt
   D. increase the overall belt efficiency

10. Double-base safety clips having corrugated jaws when used on wire rope in making up an eye develops approximately _____ of the strength of the rope.

    A. 60%   B. 70%   C. 80%   D. 95%

11. The number of ropes usually used on the movable block of a 4 part fall is MOST NEARLY

    A. 6   B. 4   C. 3   D. 2

12.

   In the above sketch, the left P, in pounds, required to raise the 1200 pound block from the ground is MOST NEARLY

   A. 200   B. 160   C. 144   D. 96

13. In the common rail system of solid fuel injection in a diesel engine, a control wedge is generally used to

    A. control the lift of the mechanically operated spray valve
    B. meter the fuel oil at the transfer pump
    C. control the fuel oil level in the fuel tank
    D. fix the fuel oil pressure in the *common rail*

14. In the fuel system for a 4-stroke cycle full diesel engine, the oil travels in sequence from the fuel tank to the

   A. filters, transfer pump, pre-combustion chamber, injection pump, and injection valve
   B. filters, transfer pump, pre-combustion chamber, injection valve, and injection pump
   C. transfer pump, filters, injection pump, injection valve, and pre-combustion chamber
   D. filters, injection pump, transfer pump, injection valve, and pre-combustion chamber

15. The camshaft operating the valves of a 4-stroke cycle diesel engine rotates at _____ speed of the crankshaft.

   A. the same   B. half the
   C. double the   D. four times the

16. The speed of a crane trolley motor is 1200 r.p.m.
    If the motor pinion has 24 teeth and the driven gear has 92 teeth, the speed of the gear shaft is MOST NEARLY

   A. 250   B. 300   C. 350   D. 3600

17. In a 4-stroke cycle full diesel engine, the fuel is ignited by means of

   A. special spark plugs
   B. hot exhaust gases
   C. highly compressed air in the cylinder
   D. glow plugs in the cylinder heads

18. The proper gap on a spark plug can be MOST accurately set by use of a _____ gage.

   A. dial   B. conventional flat feeler
   C. square wire feeler D. round wire feeler

19. A considerable amount of water in the crankcase of a gasoline engine would NOT be likely due to

   A. a cylinder head crack   B. cylinder head gasket leaks
   C. cylinder block cracks   D. condensation

20. A good program of preventive maintenance would NOT require

   A. having the work done in an off shift
   B. periodic inspection
   C. cleaning the equipment before servicing
   D. accurate records of the servicing done

21. The MAXIMUM ampere rating of the fuse to be used in an existing circuit depends upon the

   A. size of wire in the circuit   B. connected load
   C. voltage of the line   D. rating of the switch

22. On a truck mounted portable air compressor, the differential assembly is located in the

   A. truck transmission housing   B. air compressor crankcase
   C. truck rear housing   D. air regulating equipment

23. In operation, a gasoline driven air compressor is said to be unloaded when the

    A. air compressor is driven at low speed
    B. discharge valves on the air compressor are held in the open position
    C. safety valve on the air compressor is engaged in the open position
    D. inlet valves on the air compressor are held in the open position

24. In reference to air controlled machines operating in mid-winter, the reservoir of the anti-freezer or evaporator should be filled with

    A. methyl alcohol
    B. ethyl alcohol
    C. an alcohol containing an inhibitor
    D. prestone

25. A grade of 1 in 20 is approximately the same as a _____ rise in a _____ run.

    A. 1 foot; 200 inch   B. 1 yard; 125 yard
    C. 10 inch; 200 yard   D. 12 inch; 7 yard

26. The minimum factor of safety of a wire rope that is used for grab buckets should be NOT less than

    A. 4   B. 6   C. 8   D. 10

27. Whenever possible, it is BEST to remove a gear from a shaft by means of

    A. heating the gear with a flame
    B. heavy but uniform blows with a hammer
    C. cooling the shaft with dry ice
    D. an appropriate wheel puller

28. For digging open cuts, drainage ditches, and gravel pits, where the material is to be moved from 20 to 3000 feet before dumping, one would use a _____ Excavator.

    A. Crawler Crane   B. Gantry Crane
    C. Drag-line   D. Diesel Shovel

29. If a bucket capable of carrying 5 3/4 cubic yards is loaded to 3/4 of its capacity, it will be carrying, in cubic yards, APPROXIMATELY

    A. 3 1/2   B. 4 1/4   C. 4 7/8   D. 5 1/4

30. A guy line is generally used with a

    A. diesel driven scraper   B. stiff leg derrick
    C. truck mounted clamshell   D. gantry crane

31. The point shaft on a boom is usually located near the

    A. top of the boom   B. bottom of the boom
    C. dead end cable socket   D. hoist drum

32. Assume that a horizontal roller chain drive is used to transmit power to the jack shaft of a crane.
For proper tension in the roller chain,

    A. there should be a small amount of sag in the chain
    B. the sag should bring the chain down to the center line of the driving sprocket
    C. there should be no sag in the chain
    D. the chain should make an angle of at least 50 when leaving the driving sprocket

32.____

33.

[Diagram: shaft with pulleys of 16" dia., 9" dia., 12" dia., 8" dia., and 6" dia. with 100# belt pull]

In reference to the above sketch, in order to balance the 100 lbs. belt pull on the 6" diameter pulley, a belt pull of approximately 67 lbs. should be attached to which one of the following pulleys?

    A. 16"   B. 12"   C. 9"   D. 8"

33.____

34. Of the following statements concerning torque converter equipped machines, the one which is MOST NEARLY CORRECT is that

    A. the torque converter is a transmission with a limited number of ratios
    B. at normal speeds, the line pulls are less than on a standard mechanical drive machine
    C. the shock loading is increased during shovel operations
    D. at stall conditions, the engine is *putting out* its maximum power

34.____

35. To transmit power between two shafts that are in the same plane but 90° to each other, it is BEST to use _____ gear(s).

    A. spur   B. worm and spur
    C. bevel   D. herringbone

35.____

36. Under normal operations, the oil pressure regulating valve piston on a torque converter should be removed and cleaned once

    A. a day   B. a week
    C. a month   D. every three months

36.____

37. The operating oil pressure in a torque converter usually has a range of approximately _____ to _____ psi.

    A. 15; 20   B. 35; 40   C. 50; 65   D. 70; 85

37.____

38. For successful operation of a machine equipped with a torque converter, the operator should

    A. watch the load or bucket
    B. listen to the engine
    C. vary the output, shaft governor setting
    D. vary the engine governor setting

39. The clutch torque delivered by a fluid coupling is APPROXIMATELY _____ the engine torque.

    A. the same as
    B. twice that of
    C. three times that of
    D. four times that of

40. The type of knot that can be used for shortening a rope which does not have free ends, without cutting the rope, is called a

    A. sheet bend
    B. hawser bend
    C. sheepshank
    D. clove hitch

KEY (CORRECT ANSWERS)

1. A	11. B	21. A	31. A
2. A	12. C	22. C	32. A
3. C	13. A	23. D	33. C
4. B	14. C	24. A	34. D
5. A	15. B	25. D	35. C
6. B	16. B	26. B	36. B
7. C	17. C	27. D	37. B
8. C	18. D	28. C	38. A
9. A	19. D	29. B	39. A
10. D	20. A	30. B	40. C

TEST 2

DIRECTIONS: Each question or incomplete statement is followed by several suggested answers or completions. Select the one that BEST answers the question or completes the statement. *PRINT THE LETTER OF THE CORRECT ANSWER IN THE SPACE AT THE RIGHT.*

1. The purpose of the hand-operated choke on a gasoline engine is to 1.____

    A. provide an excess amount of air for easy starting
    B. provide a rich mixture for starting
    C. increase the jet opening for more gasoline
    D. provide a lean mixture for starting

2. In reference to gasoline engines, a common cause of engine back pressure is a 2.____

    A. corroded muffler   B. corroded exhaust pipe
    C. loose muffler   D. clogged muffler passage

3. A *right* lang lay wire rope has 3.____

    A. wires and strands laid opposite to one another
    B. the wires laid left and the strands laid right
    C. both wires and strands laid to the right
    D. the wires laid right and the strands laid left

4. An ambidextrous operator during his working hours will MOST likely 4.____

    A. handle his controls with ease
    B. handle his controls slowly
    C. be handicapped in lifting loads
    D. understand instructions easily

5. Assume that a two leg bridle sling with hooks and 5/8 inch diameter ropes has a safe load capacity of 4.4 tons when the legs are in a vertical position.
   If the legs are set at 90% to each other, the safe load capacity, in tons, of this sling is MOST NEARLY 5.____

    A. 6.2   B. 4.4   C. 3.1   D. 2.2

6. Fires in and around electrical equipment are BEST extinguished by using 6.____

    A. water
    B. sand
    C. carbon dioxide
    D. soda acid chemical solution

7. A dipper trip assembly is USUALLY found on a _____ boom. 7.____

    A. shovel   B. crane
    C. drag-line   D. clamshell

8. A convenient practical method of checking if the spark plugs in a gasoline engine are firing is to

    A. use a high tension voltmeter
    B. short them with an insulated handle screwdriver
    C. replace the spark plugs one at a time in the order of firing
    D. use a high tension ammeter across each spark plug

8.___

9. In a two-stage air compressor, if numbers are given to components as follows: 1st stage cylinder (1), 2nd stage cylinder (2), receiver tank (3), and intercooler (4); the path of the air when compressor is operating would be

    A. 1, 2, 4, 3   B. 4, 1, 2, 3
    C. 1, 3, 2, 4   D. 1, 4, 2, 3

9.___

10. When a lead acid type battery is fully charged, the hydrometer reading should be APPROXIMATELY

    A. 1.280   B. 1.190   C. 1.150   D. 1.000

10.___

11. If battery acid comes into contact with the skin, the BEST thing to do is

    A. wipe the contact area with a piece of cloth
    B. wash away with large quantities of water
    C. wash away with a salt solution
    D. place a tourniquet above the contact area

11.___

12.

Assume that a section of a sand barge is uniformly loaded with sand as shown above.
The total number of cubic yards of sand in this section is MOST NEARLY

    A. 120   B. 790   C. 1170   D. 2260

12.___

13. With reference to a gasoline-driven air compressor, the tern *CFM* refers to the

    A. gasoline consumption of the engine
    B. type of unloader used on the compressor
    C. capacity of the compressor
    D. maximum revolutions of the compressor

13.___

14. Backfiring through the carburetor of a gasoline engine may MOST likely be caused by

    A. an advanced spark
    B. a blown cylinder head gasket
    C. poor combustion
    D. a defective condenser

15. Vapor-lock in a gasoline engine is MOST likely due to

    A. fuel forming bubbles in the gas line
    B. the carburetor being clogged with dirt
    C. an over rich gas-air mixture
    D. a break in the fuel pump diaphragm

16. Of the following lubricating greases, the one that is water-resistant and can be used where the operating temperature does not exceed 175° F is _____ grease.

    A. lime (calcium) soap
    B. soda (sodium) soap
    C. aluminum soap
    D. mixed (soda and lime)

17. The speed regulation of an A.C. wound rotor induction motor is BEST obtained by

    A. using a diverter
    B. varying the resistance in the rotor circuit
    C. varying the stator voltage
    D. rotating the brushes on the slip rings

18. The type of A.C. motor commonly used for powering electric cranes is the _____ motor.

    A. slip ring type induction
    B. synchronous
    C. squirrel-cage type induction
    D. universal

19. A dash pot arrangement on a circuit breaker or motor starter USUALLY provides for

    A. under-voltage protection
    B. short-circuit protection
    C. absorbing mechanical stresses or vibration when the device is closed
    D. delayed-time action

20. The PRIMARY importance of outrigging on a truck crane is

    A. to prevent the load from swinging
    B. to operate the bucket
    C. for lateral support of truck body
    D. to hold the boom in position

21. A shovel equipped with a dual crowd will MOST likely

    A. handle more cubic yards of material per hour
    B. require superior operators
    C. stall under harder digging
    D. have less tension in the crowd cable

22. The quotation, *When an assembly is removed from a crane for replacement of a bushing, gear, or any individual part, it is an excellent practice to completely recondition the entire assembly.*
Following the advice in this quotation, the crane engineman will MOST likely learn that

    A. it is cheaper to buy two or more different parts
    B. repetition of work on repairs can be eliminated
    C. replacement parts will wear less than original parts
    D. replacement of one part in an assembly is less costly in the long run

23. In reference to overhead traveling bucket cranes, the term dynamic braking means MOST NEARLY

    A. actuating a trustor brake
    B. energizing a magnetic type brake
    C. closing a magnetic contactor which permits the brake to close
    D. a method of reducing the speed of hoisting motors when lowering a load

24. The type of lubricant commonly used for a bridge motor gear case at low temperature (below 32° F) is

    A. S.A.E. 90
    B. S.A.E. 160
    C. S.A.E. 250
    D. dip-gear grease

25. A gear-type transfer pump is one that USUALLY contains

    A. hydraulic plungers
    B. rollers and pinions
    C. twin gear elements
    D. poppet type valves

26. On a shovel boom, the shipper shaft is USUALLY located near the

    A. top of the boom
    B. bottom of the boom
    C. jack shaft drum
    D. mid-point of the boom

27. The characteristic of a series motor which makes its use desirable for cranes is that a large increase in torque is obtained

    A. with a large increase in voltage
    B. with a moderate increase in current
    C. when lowering a load
    D. with a moderate decrease in current

28. The compression ratio of a modern diesel engine has an approximate range of (with no starting ignition device)

    A. 3-5
    B. 6-8
    C. 9-11
    D. 12-22

29. If you were to instruct an oiler to do a sequence of jobs and operations, he would MOST likely do them

    A. in any order
    B. without regards to specifications
    C. when the machine is down
    D. in the prescribed order

30. The lifting ability of a crawler-mounted crane PRIMARILY depends upon the   30.____

    A. gearing   B. engine power
    C. balance of the crane   D. strength of the cables

31. The breaking strength of a new 1/2" diameter 6 x 19 fiber core wire rope made of plow   31.____
    steel is APPROXIMATELY _____ tons.

    A. 2   B. 3   C. 5   D. 10

32. Of the following tools for cutting wire rope used on construction equipment, the one that   32.____
    is BEST is a(n)

    A. hacksaw   B. standard bolt cutter
    C. oxyacetylene torch   D. cold chisel

33. The purpose of adding a jib boom to the regular boom of a crane is to   33.____

    A. act as a counterweight when lifting
    B. prevent overloading
    C. shift the center of gravity
    D. obtain greater reach

34. When a crane is equipped with a jib boom, the lifting capacity of the boom is APPROXI-   34.____
    MATELY _____ the crane load.

    A. 1/2 of   B. 3/4 of
    C. the same as   D. 1 1/2 times

35. Of the following bell or whistle hoist signals, the one that is customarily used to signal the   35.____
    lowering of a load is _____ quick signal(s).

    A. two   B. three
    C. one   D. a series of

36. An authorized signalman working in conjunction with the crane operator has his arm   36.____
    extended, fingers clenched, and thumb upward while moving his hand up and down.
    The signalman is signalling the crane operator to

    A. lift the boom up
    B. lower the load
    C. hoist the load
    D. stop immediately (emergency)

Questions 37-40.

DIRECTIONS: Questions 37 through 40, inclusive, are to be answered in accordance with the
              paragraph below.

Operators spotting loads with long booms and working around men need the smooth, easy operation and positive control of uniform pressure swing clutches. There are no jerks or grabs with these large disc-type clutches because there is always even pressure over the entire clutch lining surface. In the conventional band-type swing clutch, the pressure varies between dead and live ends of the band. The uniform pressure swing clutch has excellent provision for heat dissipation. The driving elements, which are always rotating, have a great number of fins cast in them. This gives them an impeller or blower action for cooling, resulting in longer life and freedom from frequent adjustment.

37. According to the above paragraph, it may be said that conventional band-type swing clutches have

    A. even pressure on the clutch lining
    B. larger contact area
    C. smaller contact area
    D. uneven pressure on the clutch lining

38. According to the above paragraph, machines equipped with uniform pressure swing clutches will

    A. give better service under all conditions
    B. require no clutch adjustment
    C. give positive control of hoist
    D. provide better control of swing

39. According to the above paragraph, it may be said that the rotation of the driving elements of the uniform pressure swing clutch is always

    A. continuous   B. constant
    C. varying   D. uncertain

40. According to the above paragraph, freedom from frequent adjustment is due to the

    A. operator's smooth, easy operation
    B. positive control of the clutch
    C. cooling effect of the rotating fins
    D. larger contact area of the bigger clutch

KEY (CORRECT ANSWERS)

1.	B	11.	B	21.	A	31.	D
2.	D	12.	C	22.	B	32.	C
3.	C	13.	C	23.	D	33.	D
4.	A	14.	B	24.	A	34.	A
5.	C	15.	A	25.	C	35.	B
6.	C	16.	D	26.	D	36.	A
7.	A	17.	B	27.	B	37.	D
8.	B	18.	A	28.	D	38.	D
9.	D	19.	D	29.	D	39.	A
10.	A	20.	C	30.	C	40.	C

EXAMINATION SECTION
TEST 1

DIRECTIONS: Each question or incomplete statement is followed by several suggested answers or completions. Select the one that BEST answers the question or completes the statement. *PRINT THE LETTER OF THE CORRECT ANSWER IN THE SPACE AT THE RIGHT.*

NOTE: In this examination, wherever the word HOURS is used in reference to maintenance service, it shall NOT refer to the normal clock hours, but to HOUR-METER hours.

1. After long, continuous operation, the *jar* of the diesel air pre-cleaner in a late model D8 Caterpillar tractor usually contains 1.____

   A. frozen water
   B. dirt and dust
   C. lube oil
   D. gasoline leakage from the starting engine

2. The starting engine clutch shift collar in a late model D8 Caterpillar tractor is lubricated by means of a(n) 2.____

   A. hydrostatic oiling device
   B. splash-type oiling system
   C. forced feed lubricator
   D. oil cup

3. The capacity of the diesel fuel tank in a late model D8 Caterpillar tractor is MOST NEARLY _____ gallons. 3.____

   A. 5   B. 15   C. 70   D. 150

4. The *hour meter* in a late model D8 Caterpillar tractor is located 4.____

   A. in the operator's cab
   B. on the right side of the engine at the rear of the fuel injection pump housing
   C. on the left side of the engine near the air cleaner
   D. next to the drawbar pin

5. The clearance between the fuel injection pump plunger and the barrel in a late model D8 Caterpillar tractor is APPROXIMATELY 5.____

   A. .01"   B. .05"   C. .025"   D. .0001"

6. In the SAE classification of oils, the lower numbered oils are 6.____

   A. heavier
   B. lighter
   C. vegetable oils exclusively
   D. oils with a graphite additive

7. The diesel engine in a late model D8 Caterpillar tractor is a(n)

   A. *in-line* job
   B. *V*-type engine
   C. radial type engine
   D. opposed cylinder type engine

8. When operating in extremely dusty conditions, the final drive in a late model D8 Caterpillar tractor should be washed and refilled every _____ hours.

   A. 240   B. 480   C. 900   D. 1,280

9. The device or material used to determine the specific gravity of a battery is

   A. Nessler's solution   B. barometer
   C. hydrometer   D. thermometer with wet bulb

10. The generator and starting engine electric starter should be removed, disassembled, washed, and parts replaced (if necessary) in a late model D8 Caterpillar tractor after APPROXIMATELY _____ hours.

    A. 2,000   B. 400   C. 4,000   D. 800

11. In operation on a job, the blade of a modern bulldozer is raised by means of

    A. hydraulic pressure   B. air pressure
    C. hand crank   D. block and tackle

12. The fuel tank of the diesel engine on a late model D8 Caterpillar tractor should be inspected regularly for

    A. lube oil leakage   B. rust
    C. dust   D. water

13. To obtain the wattage rating of a generator which is used for the lighting system of a tractor,

    A. *multiply* volts by amperes
    B. *divide* volts by amperes
    C. *divide* amperes by volts
    D. *add* volts and amperes

14. Grousers are used on late model D8 Caterpillar tractors to

    A. eliminate icing in the operator's cab
    B. heat the diesel fuel
    C. afford better traction
    D. keep the battery warm

15. The diesel engine of a late model D8 Caterpillar tractor is cooled primarily by

    A. air   B. water
    C. a synthetic coolant   D. circulating oil

16. The front end of the late model D8 Caterpillar tractor is supported by

    A. the front axle   B. a heavy leaf spring
    C. a heavy helical spring   D. hydraulic *snubbers*

17. The standard track shoe in a late model D8 Caterpillar tractor is about _____ wide.   17.____

    A. 8"   B. 15"   C. 22"   D. 32"

18. The brake pedals on a late model D8 Caterpillar tractor are adjustable for   18.____

    A. angle *only*
    B. length *only*
    C. neither angle nor length
    D. both angle and length

19. The steering clutches in a late model D8 Caterpillar tractor are designed to operate   19.____

    A. wet
    B. with a heavy oil lubricant
    C. dry
    D. with a light oil lubricant

20. In a late model D8 Caterpillar tractor, the starting engine crankcase oil level should be checked APPROXIMATELY every _____ hours.   20.____

    A. 60   B. 100   C. 200   D. 10

21. If there is sludge or foreign matter evident on the metallic strainer of the transmission oil filter, on a late model D8 Caterpillar tractor, the strainer element should be   21.____

    A. washed off with a non-inflammable cleaning fluid
    B. washed off with saturated calcium chloride solution
    C. cleaned off with a wood rasp
    D. soaked in *white* gas

22. In starting the starting engine in cold weather in a late model D8 Caterpillar tractor, it is advisable to crank it several revolutions with the ignition switch _____ and the starting engine _____ .   22.____

    A. off; clutch disengaged   B. on; cluth disengaged
    C. on; pinion engaged   D. off; pinion engaged

23. The gasoline starting engine of a late model D8 Caterpillar tractor is a _____ -cylinder engine.   23.____

    A. one   B. two   C. six   D. four

24. The gasoline starting engine of a late model D8 Caterpillar tractor is a _____ cycle engine.   24.____

    A. uni   B. 4   C. 2   D. 3

25. After operating in extremely dusty conditions, a diesel engine air cleaner on a late model D8 Caterpillar tractor should be filled with   25.____

    A. transmission oil
    B. crankcase lubricating oil
    C. track roller lubricant
    D. ball and roller bearing lubricant

26. An operator is preparing to replace the transmission oil. He takes a sufficient amount of SAE 80 and dilutes it properly with kerosene.
Assuming that the operator is following instructions correctly, then it can be said that the late model D8 Caterpillar tractor is being used when outside temperatures are APPROXIMATELY _____ ° F.

   A. 70 B. 35 C. 95 D. 0

27. When running a late model D8 Caterpillar tractor, the operator notes that the *free motion* at the top of the steering clutch levers is very nearly six (6) inches.
The operator should know that this free motion should

   A. be adjusted to 7"
   B. be adjusted to 5"
   C. be adjusted to 3"
   D. not be changed

28. To properly adjust the flywheel clutch lever on a late model D8 Caterpillar tractor so that the lever engages with a distinct snap, it is necessary to

   A. remove the clutch and make adjustments while out of the unit
   B. leave transmission gears engaged and turn collar clockwise
   C. first wash clutch engaging linkage in kerosene, then make necessary adjustments
   D. leave the clutch engaged and tighten adjusting collar to proper adjustment

29. The purpose of the pre-combustion chamber in a late model D8 Caterpillar tractor is to

   A. heat and volatilize the diesel oil
   B. heat the combustion air
   C. give direction to the burning fuel into the cylinder head
   D. filter the disel fuel immediately before combustion

30. On a late model D8 Caterpillar tractor, the track adjustment is correct when the track may be raised above the track carrier roller a distance of

   A. 1/4" to 3/4"
   B. 3" to 4"
   C. 1 1/2" to 2"
   D. 4" to 5"

31. The fuel recommended for use in the diesel engine of a late model D8 Caterpillar tractor is _____ oil.

   A. #6 bunker B. #5 bunker C. #2 fuel D. #1 fuel

32. If sludge is noticeable when draining the diesel crankcase on a late model D8 Caterpillar tractor,

   A. no immediate action need be taken
   B. a complete engine overhaul should be made
   C. the engine valves should be readjusted
   D. the oil pump suction bell screen should be removed and cleaned

33. When the diesel engine on a late model D8 Caterpillar tractor is running irregularly and smoking, it may be caused by

   A. a misfiring spark plug
   B. worn ignition wiring
   C. a faulty fuel spray
   D. poor timing setting

34. A loose fan belt on the diesel engine of a late model D8 Caterpillar tractor will PROBA-   34.____
    BLY cause

    A. a broken fan blade
    B. an overheated engine
    C. no effect on engine performance
    D. excessive wear of the starting engine battery

35. The starting engine crankcase on a late model D8 Caterpillar tractor should be drained   35.____
    every

    A. 120 to 240 hours   B. 8 to 12 hours
    C. day   D. 1,000 hours

36. When operating in deep mud or water, the track roller frame outer bearings on a late   36.____
    model D8 Caterpillar tractor should be lubricated every

    A. 2,000 hours since it is practically self-lubricating
    B. 100 hours
    C. 50 hours
    D. 5 hours

37. On a late model D8 Caterpillar tractor, when the diesel fuel is transferred from the tank to   37.____
    the injection pumps, it is

    A. aerated   B. filtered
    C. atomized   D. warmed slightly

38. The area of ground contact (with standard track shoes) of a late model D8 Caterpillar   38.____
    tractor is 4,296 sq.in. Expressed in sq.ft., this is MOST NEARLY

    A. 358   B. 29.8   C. 159.3   D. 21.37

39. A towing winch develops a bare drum line pull of 11.8 tons. This force represents, in   39.____
    pounds,

    A. 23,850   B. 28,300   C. 23,800   D. 23,600

40. A power take-off is available for a late model D8 Caterpillar tractor with a *splined* shaft.   40.____
    Splined means MOST NEARLY

    A. laminated   B. annealed
    C. slotted   D. chrome-plated

41. Failure of the starting engine to start on a late model D8 Caterpillar tractor may be   41.____
    caused MOST likely by

    A. faulty magneto
    B. faulty injection pump
    C. clogged oil pressure line
    D. no water in the radiator

42. When an acid-type storage battery is in good operating condition, the electrolyte should   42.____
    have a specific gravity of

    A. 1.100   B. 1.200   C. 1.000   D. 1.300

43. The brake lock control on a late model D8 Caterpillar tractor, when applied, is provided to   43.____

    A. prevent the tractor from backing up a grade
    B. keep the tractor moving in a straight line
    C. hold the tractor on a grade
    D. control engine speed when climbing grades

44. On a late model D8 Caterpillar tractor, if the starting engine is not capable of turning the   44.____
    diesel engine fast enough because of the diesel engine compression, it is good practice
    to

    A. move the compression release lever to half position
    B. open the throttle of the starting engine
    C. advance the spark of the starting engine
    D. readjust the starting engine carburetor

45. In order to steer a late model D8 Caterpillar tractor going down grade when the load is   45.____
    pushing the tractor, it is necessary to

    A. reverse the operation of the steering clutches
    B. put all gears in neutral
    C. turn off the diesel fuel
    D. steer in the usual manner

46. When fuel lines on the diesel engine of a late model D8 Caterpillar tractor are opened for   46.____
    any purpose and air enters the fuel system, an operator should

    A. readjust the fuel nozzles
    B. prime the fuel system
    C. clean the injector pumps
    D. set the compression release lever on *start* for 5 minutes

47. The CORRECT order of events in the cylinder of the 4-stroke cycle diesel engine is: 47.____
    Intake,

    A. power, compression, exhaust
    B. compression, power, exhaust
    C. exhaust, compression, power
    D. power, exhaust, compression

48. In normal operation, the diesel engine fuel is injected into a cylinder _____ stroke of the   48.____
    piston.

    A. at the start of the intake
    B. at the end of the exhaust
    C. at the start of the compression
    D. very close to the end of the compression

49. In order to properly shut off a diesel engine of a late model D8 Caterpillar tractor, the   49.____
    operator should

    A. choke the air intake to the engine
    B. inject a fine spray of water into each cylinder

C. set the injection pump control lever to the extreme forward position
D. set the compression release lever at half

50. When an operator short-circuits a spark plug on an operating starting engine on a late model D8 Caterpillar tractor, he essentially is checking to find out if the

    A. engine timing is correct
    B. plug is misfiring
    C. battery is sufficiently charged to properly fire the plugs
    D. fuel air ratio is correct

50.____

51. Servicing of the diesel crankcase lubricating oil filters on a late model D8 Caterpillar tractor should be performed

    A. only when the engine is overhauled
    B. only when the oil becomes dirty
    C. each time the crankcase is drained
    D. when the engine starts to misfire

51.____

52. If a late model D8 Caterpillar tractor persists in tending to turn to the right when all controls are set for a straight forward direction, it may be due to

    A. slipping clutch for the right track
    B. main engine clutch not properly disengaged
    C. starting engine clutch not engaged
    D. a loose brake on the right track

52.____

53. Failure of the generator to properly charge the storage battery may MOST likely be caused by

    A. a burned out headlight bulb
    B. a faulty voltage regulator
    C. too low a specific gravity of battery electrolyte
    D. burned out light fuse

53.____

54. The proper way to clean corrosion from the storage battery terminals is to

    A. scrub them with a strong soap solution
    B. brush them with a weak acid solution
    C. scrub them with a weak solution of bicarbonate of soda and water
    D. scrape them with a knife

54.____

55. The diesel fuel filter housing of a late model D8 Caterpillar tractor should be drained of sediment and water at least every _____ hours.

    A. 120 B. 180 C. 60 D. 250

55.____

56. A poor spark at the spark plug of the gasoline starting engine may MOST likely be caused by

    A. a frozen battery
    B. a weak condenser in magneto
    C. a weak battery
    D. advanced timing

56.____

57. The fan belts used on the late model D8 Caterpillar tractor are properly adjusted if they can be pushed inward at the center APPROXIMATELY _____ inch(es).

    A. 3   B. 1 1/2   C. 6   D. 1/4

58. The diesel engine valve clearance adjustment on a late model D8 Caterpillar tractor should be made while the engine is

    A. cold   B. warm   C. hot   D. dismantled

59. The diesel engine valve clearance adjustment and the compression release clearance adjustment on a late model D8 Caterpillar tractor should be made with the

    A. compression release lever in the *Run* position
    B. compression release lever in the *Start* position
    C. throttle control lever disconnected
    D. compression release lever in the *Half* position

60. The proper valve clearance for the inlet valves on the diesel engine of a late model D8 Caterpillar tractor should be set at MOST NEARLY

    A. .050"   B. .101"   C. .250"   D. .012"

61. The inlet valve clearance of the gasoline starting engine on a late model D8 Caterpillar tractor should be set at MOST NEARLY

    A. .030"   B. .008"   C. .0008"   D. .020"

62. The spark plug gap in the gasoline starting engine of a late model D8 Caterpillar tractor should be set at MOST NEARLY

    A. .038"   B. .050"   C. .025"   D. .010"

63. Contact points of the starting engine magneto breaker on a late model D8 Caterpillar tractor should be set MOST NEARLY at

    A. .010" to .011"   B. .050" to .060"
    C. .009" to .010"   D. .014" to .020"

64. On tractors equipped with lighting systems without batteries when additional electrical devices are to be added, it is necessary to FIRST

    A. check generator capacity
    B. check the lighting system in use
    C. check the light switch
    D. lubricate the generator bearings

65. On a late model D8 Caterpillar tractor, air cleaner screens used on diesel engines operated on jobs where dust conditions are severe should be cleaned MOST NEARLY every _____ hours.

    A. 120   B. 480   C. 60   D. 240

66. The SAE number of diesel crankcase oil, when used at temperatures above freezing on a late model D8 Caterpillar tractor, should be

    A. 30   B. 60   C. 40   D. 80

67. On a late model D8 Caterpillar tractor, in order to keep rain and snow from entering the exhaust pipes of the tractor which is to stand idle without shelter, those pipes should be fitted with

    A. rubber caps
    B. cork plugs
    C. rain traps
    D. cotton waste

68. If a late model D8 Caterpillar tractor must stand without shelter, it is advisable to

    A. remove the seat cushions and place them under the engine
    B. tilt the seat cushion so that moisture will not enter the padding under the cushion covering
    C. turn seat cushions upside down
    D. leave the seat cushions as they are

69. The length of track on each side of a tractor is very nearly 22 1/2 feet.
    If this tractor is driven in a straight line for a distance of 1/2 mile (2,640 feet), the number of revolutions which the driving tracks must make is MOST NEARLY

    A. 11.7   B. 117   C. 120.5   D. 334

70. A tractor is operated on a given landfill operation during the following time intervals in one day: from 8:15 A.M. to 11:45 A.M.; from 12:30 P.M. to 6:00 P.M.; from 6:45 P.M. to 11:30 P.M.
    The total net operating time, expressed in hours and minutes, is MOST NEARLY _____ hours, _____ minutes.

    A. 13; 30   B. 13; 15   C. 13; 45   D. 12; 45

71. The type of valve which is generally found in a 4-cycle diesel engine to control the admission of air to the cylinder is commonly known as a _____ valve.

    A. ported sleeve
    B. piston type
    C. poppet type
    D. weighted

72. On an earth landfill operation, a tractor operator will generally tamp the fill MOST efficiently by proper use of a

    A. root ripper
    B. gradebuilder blade
    C. brush cutter
    D. sheepsfoot roller

73. In operating a bulldozer over hard ground or obstacles, the operator can BEST keep the blade from bobbing up and down by means of

    A. pneumatic back pressure
    B. weighting the lower blade platform with bags full of sand
    C. an oil shock absorber
    D. a positive lock

74. On a late model D8 Caterpillar tractor, to absorb end shock on the front idler and to provide smooth track operation, _____ provided.

    A. a rubber bumper is
    B. an oil shock absorber is
    C. two recoil springs are
    D. a semi-elliptical leaf spring is

75. To *make a pass* with the bulldozer means to
    A. test the blade lifting equipment
    B. attach auxiliary equipment to the drawbar
    C. use the set bulldozer blade to perform a specific work unit once
    D. disconnect the bulldozer blade

76. On a late model D8 Caterpillar tractor, the maximum travel speed at rated engine R.P.M. (governed at full load) when the transmission is set in the 6th forward position is APPROXIMATELY _____ M.P.H.
    A. 2   B. 5   C. 7   D. 10

77. The fluid which is commonly used in the hydraulic system to position the bulldozer blade is
    A. water
    B. alcohol
    C. kerosene
    D. a lightgrade lubricating oil

78. The positioning of the bulldozer blade is controlled by the operator in the cab of a late model D8 Caterpillar tractor by means of a
    A. gang of pushbuttons
    B. pawled foot pedal
    C. hand-operated lever
    D. wheel with a notched rim

79. Late model D8 Caterpillar tractors are equipped with a drawbar which allows an operator to position it easily. The MAXIMUM number of non-swinging positions in which the drawbar may be locked is
    A. 6   B. 5   C. 4   D. 3

80. On a late model D8 Caterpillar tractor, for a particular job, the tractor operator finds it necessary to use the rear power take-off.
    At constant engine speed and by proper setting of the levers, he can operate this power take-off at any of _____ speeds.
    A. 2   B. 3   C. 4   D. 5

KEY (CORRECT ANSWERS)

1. B	21. A	41. A	61. B
2. D	22. A	42. D	62. C
3. C	23. B	43. C	63. D
4. B	24. B	44. A	64. A
5. D	25. B	45. A	65. C
6. B	26. D	46. B	66. A
7. A	27. C	47. B	67. C
8. B	28. B	48. D	68. B
9. C	29. A	49. C	69. B
10. C	30. C	50. B	70. C
11. A	31. C	51. C	71. C
12. D	32. D	52. A	72. D
13. A	33. C	53. B	73. D
14. C	34. B	54. C	74. C
15. B	35. A	55. C	75. C
16. B	36. D	56. B	76. B
17. C	37. B	57. B	77. D
18. D	38. B	58. C	78. C
19. C	39. D	59. A	79. B
20. D	40. C	60. D	80. A

48

EXAMINATION SECTION

TEST 1

DIRECTIONS: Each question or incomplete statement is followed by several suggested answers or completions. Select the one that BEST answers the question or completes the statement. *PRINT THE LETTER OF THE CORRECT ANSWER IN THE SPACE AT THE RIGHT.*

1. Front stabilizer bars on automotive vehicles are set in such a manner that they　　1.____
   A. apply force opposite to that of the springs when the springs are deflected equally
   B. normally connect to both lower control arms
   C. are adjustable in order to level the vehicle
   D. have one end attached to the lower control arm and the other end attached to the frame

2. Ignition point contact alignment is BEST adjusted by bending the　　2.____
   A. movable point arm　　　　　B. pivot post
   C. breaker plate　　　　　　　　D. stationary point bracket

3. When disc brakes are retracted so as not to be touching the braking disc, the amount of retraction　　3.____
   A. is affected by the piston return springs
   B. must be a minimum of 1/32 of an inch
   C. is affected by the piston seals
   D. is limited by the metering valve

4. A PROPERLY operating positive crankcase ventilation valve will　　4.____
   A. control air flow as a direct function of engine speed
   B. increase air flow in direct proportion to the increase in manifold vacuum
   C. shut off air flow at high intake manifold vacuum
   D. reduce air flow at high intake manifold vacuum

5. The air-fuel ratio, by weight, in a properly functioning gasoline automotive engine is MOST NEARLY　　5.____
   A. 15:1　　　B. 30:1　　　C. 600:1　　　D. 9000:1

6. Cam ground pistons are distinguished by　　6.____
   A. being ground perfectly round
   B. having a larger diameter across the piston pin faces
   C. having a larger diameter parallel to the crankshaft centerline
   D. having a larger diameter perpendicular to the crankshaft centerline

7. In an automotive engine, the intake valves USUALLY open _____ TDC and close _____ BDC of the intake stroke.　　7.____
   A. after; after　　　　　　B. after; before
   C. before; before　　　　D. before; after

49

8. In an automotive engine, the exhaust valves USUALLY open _____ BDC of the power stroke and _____ TDC of the intake stroke.
   A. after; before
   B. before; before
   C. before; after
   D. after; after

9. The PRIMARY function of a blower on a two-cycle diesel engine is to
   A. provide air for scavenging
   B. increase the compression ratio
   C. blow in the fuel-air mixture
   D. cool the oil after compression in the injector pump

10. Excessive free travel of the clutch pedal would be indicated if the
    A. transmission was hard to shift smoothly
    B. clutch slipped when fully engaged
    C. throwout bearing failed prematurely
    D. release levers were worn

11. Vacuum is usually referred to in inches of mercury.
    The number of pounds per square inch pressure above zero (absolute pressure) of a 20 inch vacuum is MOST NEARLY
    A. 4.9   B. 7.4   C. 9.6   D. 11.8

12. Only a portion of the heat energy released by the gasoline in an automotive engine is transmitted to the wheels for driving purposes.
    In an automobile in good condition and with an efficiently operating engine, this portion is MOST NEARLY
    A. 90%   B. 50%   C. 20%   D. 2%

13. An adjustment is made to the right front wheel of a vehicle equipped with shims at the junction of the upper suspension arm and the frame support by moving the upper suspension arm away from the frame a greater amount in the front than in the rear. This is done to
    A. increase the steering knuckle angle
    B. adjust the caster in a negative direction
    C. adjust the camber in a negative direction
    D. adjust the caster in a rotary direction

14. In an automotive rear axle in which the pinion gear engages the ring gear below the centerline of the axle, the cut of the pinion and ring gear is
    A. spiral bevel
    B. spur bevel
    C. double helical
    D. hypoid

15. Of the following statements concerning the operation in low gear of a fully synchronized (in forward gears) three-speed transmission, the one that is NOT correct is that
    A. both clutch sleeves must engage gears
    B. power is being transmitted through the countershaft gears
    C. one clutch sleeve must be engaged
    D. the reverse idler gear is being driven by a countershaft gear

Questions 16-17.

DIRECTIONS: Questions 16 and 17 are to be answered in accordance with the following paragraph.

Steam cleaners get their name from the fact that steam is used to generate pressure and is also a by-product of heating the cleaning solution. Steam itself as little cleaning power. It will melt some soils, but it does not dissolve them, break them up, or destroy their clinging power. Rather surprisingly, good machines generate as little steam as possible. Modern surface chemistry depends on a chemical solution to dissolve dirt, destroy its clinging power, and hold it in suspension. Steam actually hinders such a solution, but heat helps its physical and chemical action. Cleaning is most efficient when a hot solution reaches the work in heavy volume.

16. In accordance with the above paragraph, for MOST efficient cleaning,
    A. a heavy volume of steam is needed
    B. hot steam is needed to break up the soils
    C. steam is used to dissolve the surface dirt
    D. a hot chemical solution should always be used

17. When reference to the above paragraph, the steam in a steam cleaner is used to
    A. generate pressure
    B. create by-product chemicals
    C. slow down the chemical action of the cleaning solution
    D. dissolve accumulations of dirt

18. An electromechanical regulator for an automotive alternator differs from a DC generator in that the alternator regulator
    A. has a current regulator unit
    B. has a reverse current relay
    C. does not have a current regulator unit
    D. does not have a voltage regulator unit

19. Of the following statements concerning the charging of lead acid batteries, the one MOST NEARLY correct is that
    A. a fast charge (40-50 amp, 2V) can safely be used if the battery temperature does not exceed 185° F
    B. heavily sulphated batteries respond best to a slow charging rate
    C. a battery on trickle charge cannot be damaged by overcharging
    D. the higher the battery temperature, the smaller the charging current with constant applied voltage

20. The ignition points of a conventional ignition system are adjusted to increase the point gap.
    This adjustment will
    A. increase the dwell angle
    B. retard the ignition timing
    C. advance the ignition timing
    D. decrease the dwell angle with no change in ignition timing

21. A single diaphragm distributor vacuum advance unit 21.____
    A. advances the spark under part throttle operation
    B. is connected to the intake manifold
    C. advances the spark in proportion to engine speed
    D. advances the spark during acceleration or full throttle operation

22. The part of a conventional ignition system that could properly be considered 22.____
    part of BOTH the primary and secondary circuits would be the
    A. condenser   B. distributor rotor
    C. coil   D. ignition points

23. As compared to a conventional type of spark plug, a resistor type of spark 23.____
    plug will
    A. reduce the inductive portion of the spark
    B. lengthen the capacitive portion of the spark
    C. require a higher voltage to function properly
    D. have an auxiliary air gap

24. If the criterion that limits the yearly major repair expenses to 30% of the current 24.____
    value of equipment were reduced to 15% and the depreciation rate of 20% of
    original cost each year were increased to 25%, the expenses for major repairs
    in a shop handling a constant flow of equipment of the same type and age
    would
    A. increase slightly   B. remain the same
    C. increase slightly   D. increase markedly

Question 25.

DIRECTIONS: Question 25 is to be answered in accordance with the following paragraph.

   The storage battery is a lead-acid, electrochemical device used for storing energy in its chemical form. The battery does not actually store electricity, but converts an electrical charge into chemical energy which is stored until the battery terminals are connected to a closed external circuit. When the circuit is closed, the chemical energy inside the battery is transformed back into electrical energy through a chemical action, and, as a result, current flows through the circuit.

25. According to the above paragraph, a lead-acid battery stores 25.____
    A. current   B. electricity
    C. electrical energy   D. chemical energy

26. A cam is to be fashioned from a circular disc with a hole drilled eccentrically 26.____
    on a diameter of the disc but perpendicularly to the surface of the disc. A
    keyed shaft is to be fitted into the hole so that the disc may be rotated in order
    to function as a cam. If the disc is 5 inches in diameter and ½ inch thick and
    the hole is to be 1 inch in diameter, the distance from the center of the disc to
    the center of the hole to be drilled in order for the disc to act as a cam with a 2
    inch lift should be _____ inch(es).
    A. 2   B. 1½   C. 1   D. ½

27. Sparks and open flames should be kept away from batteries that are being charged because of the danger of explosion or fire resulting from the ignition of the generated _____ gas.
    A. fluorine   B. nitrogen   C. hydrogen   D. argon

28. Safety standards indicate that the use of any motor vehicle equipment having an obstructed view to the rear
    A. requires a reverse signal alarm audible above the surrounding noise level
    B. requires the use of two back-up lights of at least 45 watt capacity each
    C. requires the use of a safety contact alarm rear bumper audible above the surrounding noise level
    D. is prohibited

29. In the performance of a compression test, it is found that the addition of a tablespoon of SAE 40 motor oil causes no significant increase in the low compression pressure.
    The low compression pressure is most probably NOT caused by
    A. a broken piston   B. a leaking head gasket
    C. sticking valves   D. worn piston rings

30. Automotive exhaust gas analyzers, as generally used in emission control maintenance, will normally indicate the percentage of
    A. NO   B. SO_2 C. CO_2 D. CO

Questions 31-33.

DIRECTIONS: Questions 31 through 33 are to be answered in accordance with the information given below.

For most efficient utilization of funds and facilities, the rule has been established that the repair cost of a part cannot exceed 50% of the vendor's price for a new part and that a part cannot be made in-house if the cost would be more than 70% of the vendor's price for a new one.

You have found that the average removed sprocket shaft, as shown below, requires both bearing sections to be built up and remachined and one sprocket section to be built up and remachined. The foreman of the machine shop has given you the following information relative to the manufacture or repair of the shafts:

	Time	Rate
Weld 1 bearing section	1.2 hours	$40/hr.
Weld 1 keyway and sprocket section	2.0 hours	$40/hr.
Turn 1 bearing section	0.6 hours	$40/hr.
Turn 1 sprocket section	0.7 hours	$40/hr.
Cut 1 keyway	0.5 hours	$40/hr.

Purchasing has quoted shaft material at $60/ft. and new shafts at $800 each.

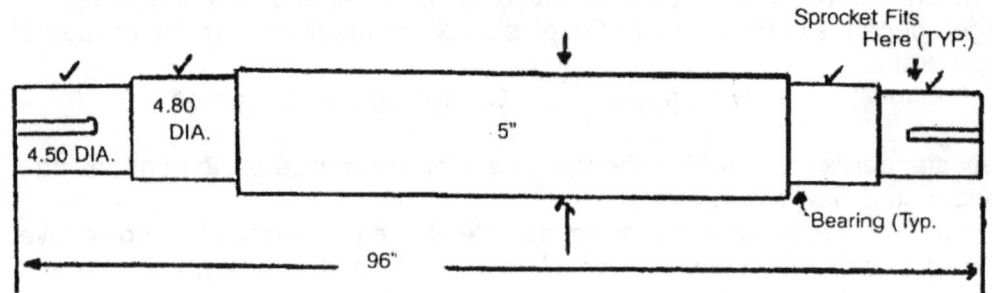

31. In accordance with the information given above, the cost for in-house manufacture of one shaft is
    A. $552.00   B. $560.00   C. $624.00   D. $663.00

32. In accordance with the information given above, the cost of in-house repair of one shaft is
    A. $342.00   B. $272.00   C. $152.00   D. $72.00

33. In accordance with the information given above, the PROPER procedure to follow, under the given rules, is to
    A. repair old shafts and buy new shafts
    B. repair old shafts and make new shafts
    C. make no repairs but make new shafts
    D. make no repairs but buy new shafts

34. The series of small vertical oscillations in the area of the center of a superimposed pattern on the screen of a properly adjusted oscilloscope showing the secondary circuit of a properly tuned automotive engine directly follows the instant at which the
    A. spark plugs fire   B. points open
    C. points close   D. coil starts to discharge

35. A rectangularly shaped repair facility for light trucks is 160 feet wide and 260 feet long. A 10 foot space is provided along each wall for benches and equipment. A 60 foot wide area in the middle of the floor is to remain clear for its entire 260 foot length. The entrance to the shop is at one end of this open area.
    Assuming that there are no columns to contend with, the MAXIMUM area available for parking of trucks is _____ square feet.
    A. 15,600   B. 19,200   C. 26,000   D. 42,600

36. A criterion is established that limits the early major repair expenses to 30% of the current value of the equipment. Equipment is depreciated at a rate of 20% of its original cost each year. A truck purchased on January 1, 2020 for $9,000 had a reconditioned engine installed in February 2023 at a total cost of $900. The amount of money available for additional major repairs on this truck in 2023 was
    A. none   B. $180   C. $360   D. $720

37. Twenty fuel injectors are ordered for your shop by the purchasing department. The terms are list, less 30%, less 10%, less 5%.
If the list price of a fuel injector is $70 and all terms ae met upon delivery, the charges to your budget will be
   A. $1,359.60   B. $1,085.40   C. $837.90   D. $630.80

37.____

38. The cylinders of an 8 cylinder automotive engine have a bore of 4 inches and the pistons have a stroke of 4 inches.
If the clearance volume in each cylinder is 6.0 cubic inches, the cubic inch displacement of the engine is MOST NEARLY
   A. 306   B. 354   C. 402   D. 450

38.____

39. An automotive engine cylinder has a bore of 4 inches and its pistons have a stroke of 4 inches.
If the clearance volume in the cylinder is 6.0 cubic inches, the compression ratio is MOST NEARLY
   A. 10.62:1   B. 9.37:1   C. 8.37:1   D. 7.62:1

39.____

40. Of the following deficiencies found during the inspection of passenger car brakes for issuance of a State Certificate of Inspection, the one that would be cause for REJECTION of the car brakes is that
   A. there is less than 3/64 in. of lining remaining above the drum brake shoe lining rivet heads
   B. the master cylinder brake fluid level is anything less than full
   C. the brake drums have been found to be more than .020 inches oversize
   D. the brake pedal reserve is less than one-half the total possible travel

40.____

41. When checking a fuel pump for proper operation, it is ALWAYS necessary to
   A. connect a vacuum gage to the fuel line between the pump and the carburetor
   B. make the vacuum test before the pressure test
   C. set the gages at floor level to maintain a consistent reference point
   D. make a vacuum test if the pressure or volume test results are not up to specification

41.____

42. On a single cylinder 4 stroke cycle internal combustion engine equipped with a flywheel magneto, the ignition points open at the end of the _____ strokes.
   A. intake and the compression   B. compression and the exhaust
   C. power and the compression   D. intake and the power

42.____

43. An impulse coupling is MOST usually found in
   A. an automatic transmission
   B. a limited slip differential
   C. the front axle of 4 wheel drive vehicles
   D. a magneto

43.____

Questions 44-45.

DIRECTIONS: Questions 44 and 45 are to be answered in accordance with the following paragraph.

You have been instructed to expedite the fabrication of four special salt spreader trucks using chassis that are available in the shop. All four trucks must be delivered before the opening of business on December 1, 2021. Based on workload and available hours, the foreman of the body shop indicates that he could manufacture one complete salt spreader body in five weeks, with one additional week required for mounting and securing each body to the available chassis. No work could begin on the body until the engines and hydraulic components, which would have to be purchased, were available for use. The purchasing department has promised delivery of engines and hydraulic components three months after the order is placed. (Assume that all months have four weeks and the same crew is doing the assembling and manufacturing.)

44. With reference to the above paragraph, assuming that the purchasing department placed the order at the beginning of the first week in February 2020 and ultimate delivery of the firs salt spreader truck would be CLOSEST to the end of the _____ week in _____, 2021.
    A. fourth; July
    B. second; August
    C. fourth; August
    D. first; September

45. With reference to the above paragraph, the LATEST date that the engines and associated hydraulic components could be requisitioned in order to meet the specified deadline would be CLOSEST to the beginning of the _____ week in _____, 2021.
    A. first; February
    B. first; March
    C. third; March
    D. first; April

46. In an OHV internal combustion engine, excessive inlet valve guide clearance manifests itself initially by
    A. lowered cylinder compression pressure
    B. excessive oil consumption
    C. increased manifold vacuum
    D. fluffy black deposits on spark plugs

47. One of your mechanics has performed an automotive fuel system test and reports a fuel flow of ½ pint/minute at 500 rpm, a static fuel pump discharge pressure of 6 psi, and a 15 in.Hg vacuum at the pump inlet flex line.
    These results should suggest to the mechanic that
    A. the system was operating properly
    B. he should check for a leaking pump inlet flex line
    C. he should replace the defective fuel pump
    D. check for a plugged inlet fuel line

48. An electrician is wiring a light switch on a light truck. The light switch will operate the following lamp bulbs:

Quantity	No.	Description	Current (Each)
2	194	Marker	.3
3	67	Clearance	.4
2	1157	Stop/Tail	2.1/.6
2	1141	Front Park	1.5
2	6012	Headlamp	4.2/3.4

The parking lamps are to be on when the headlamps are on.
If the permissible current capacities of wire are
   16 gage   0 – 6 amp
   14 gage   6 – 15 amp
   12 gage   15 – 20 amp
   10 gage   20 – 25 amp,
the smallest size wire that the electrician should use to supply power to the switch would be a _____ gage wire.
   A. 16   B. 14   C. 12   D. 10

49. In an automotive cooling system, the bypass passage or bypass valve
   A. permits a small amount of coolant to pass around the thermostat to maintain circulation
   B. permits the circulation of coolant through the engine block when the thermostat is closed
   C. directly connects the pump inlet to the pump discharge to prevent cavitation in the pump
   D. prevents the coolant in the system from developing excessive pressure

50. When adjusting a recirculating ball worm-and-nut steering gear, it is IMPROPER procedure to
   A. remove the pitman arm before making adjustments
   B. loosen the lash adjustment before checking bearing preload
   C. make the pitman shaft gear over center adjustment with the steering wheel in the center of travel position
   D. adjust the bearing preload with the steering wheel in the center of travel position

KEY (CORRECT ANSWERS)

1. B	11. A	21. A	31. C	41. D
2. D	12. C	22. C	32. B	42. B
3. C	13. B	23. A	33. A	43. D
4. D	14. D	24. A	34. C	44. A
5. A	15. A	25. D	35. B	45. B
6. D	16. D	26. C	36. B	46. B
7. D	17. A	27. C	37. C	47. D
8. C	18. C	28. A	38. C	48. B
9. A	19. B	29. D	39. B	49. B
10. A	20. C	30. D	40. B	50. D

EXAMINATION SECTION
TEST 1

DIRECTIONS: Each question or incomplete statement is followed by several suggested answers or completions. Select the one that BEST answers the question or completes the statement. *PRINT THE LETTER OF THE CORRECT ANSWER IN THE SPACE AT THE RIGHT.*

1. Of the following, the one that is a grease fitting is a _____ fitting.   1._____

    A. Morse
    B. Brown and Sharpe
    C. Zerk
    D. caliper

2. In an automobile equipped with an ammeter, the ammeter is used to   2._____

    A. indicate current flow
    B. regulate current flow
    C. act as a circuit breaker
    D. measure engine r.p.m.

3. The ignition points in the distributor of a gasoline engine are opened by means of a   3._____

    A. spring
    B. vacuum
    C. cam with lobes
    D. gear

4. MOST automobile engines that use gasoline as fuel operate as _____ engines.   4._____

    A. single cycle
    B. single stroke, single cycle
    C. two-stroke, two-cycle
    D. four-stroke, two-cycle

5. For a shop manager, the MOST important reason that equipment which is used infrequently should be considered for disposal is that   5._____

    A. such equipment may cause higher management to think that your shop is not busy
    B. the time required for its maintenance could be better used elsewhere
    C. the men may resent having to work on such equipment
    D. such equipment usually has a higher breakdown rate in operation

6. The PRIMARY function of the thermostat in the cooling system of an automobile engine is to   6._____

    A. control the operating temperature of the engine
    B. keep the operating temperature of the engine as low as possible
    C. provide the proper amount of heat for the heater
    D. retain engine heat when the engine gets hot

7. The PRIMARY purpose of the condenser in the ignition circuit of a gasoline engine is to   7._____

    A. boost the ignition voltage
    B. rectify the ignition voltage
    C. adjust the coil voltage
    D. reduce arcing at the distributor breaker points

8. The PRIMARY purpose of the differential in the rear drive train of an automotive vehicle is to allow each of the rear wheels to

   A. rotate at different speeds
   B. go in reverse
   C. rotate with maximum torque
   D. absorb road shocks

9. When an automobile engine does not start on a damp day, the trouble is MOST likely in the _____ system.

   A. ignition   B. cooling
   C. fuel   D. lubricating

10. The battery of an automobile is prevented from discharging back through the alternator by the blocking action of the

    A. commutator   B. diodes
    C. brushes   D. slip rings

11. The master cylinder in an automobile is actuated by the

    A. steering column   B. brake pedal
    C. clutch plate   D. cam shaft

Questions 12-17.

DIRECTIONS: Questions 12 through 17 are to be answered SOLELY on the basis of the following passage.

The basic hand-operated hoisting device is the tackle or purchase, consisting of a line called a fall, reeved through one or more blocks.

To hoist a load of given size, you must set up a rig with a safe working load equal to or in excess of the load to be hoisted. In order to do this, you must be able to calculate the safe working load of a single part of line of given size; the safe working load of a given purchase which contains a line of given size; and the minimum size of hooks or shackles which you must use in a given type of purchase to hoist a given load. You must also be able to calculate the thrust which a given load will exert on a gin pole or a set of shears inclined at a given angle; the safe working load which a spar of a given size, used as a gin pole or as one of a set of shears, will sustain; and the stress which a given load will set up in the back guy of a gin pole, or in the back guy of a set of shears, inclined at a given angle.

12. The above passage refers to the lifting of loads by means of

    A. erected scaffolds   B. manual rigging devices
    C. power-driven equipment   D. conveyor belts

13. It can be concluded from the above passage that a set of shears serves to

    A. absorb the force and stress of the working load
    B. operate the tackle
    C. contain the working load
    D. compute the safe working load

14. According to the above passage, a spar can be used for a   14.____

    A. back guy   B. block   C. fall   D. gin pole

15. According to the above passage, the rule that a user of hand-operated tackle MUST follow is to make sure that the safe working load is AT LEAST   15.____

    A. equal to the weight of the given load
    B. twice the combined weight of the block and falls
    C. one-half the weight of the given load
    D. twice the weight of the given load

16. According to the above passage, the two parts that make up a tackle are   16.____

    A. back guys and gin poles   B. blocks and falls
    C. rigs and shears   D. spars and shackle

17. According to the above passage, in order to determine whether it is safe to hoist a particular load, you MUST   17.____

    A. use the maximum size hooks
    B. time the speed to bring a given load to a desired place
    C. calculate the forces exerted on various types of rigs
    D. repeatedly lift and lower various loads

18. If you do not understand the operation of some special tool which is used in your work, your BEST procedure would be to   18.____

    A. study up on its operation at home
    B. ask a maintainer to explain its operation
    C. ask another helper to explain its operation
    D. bother nobody and expect to pick up a little more knowledge each time you use the tool

19. For winter servicing of a gasoline engine, it is BEST to use an oil that   19.____

    A. has a low SAE number
    B. has a high SAE number
    C. has a very heavy consistency
    D. contains few additive detergents

20. If a wheel has turned through an angle of 180°, then it has made _____ revolution(s).   20.____

    A. 1/4   B. 1/2   C. 1/8   D. 18

21. The crankshaft in a gasoline engine is PRIMARILY used to   21.____

    A. change reciprocating motion to rotary motion
    B. operate the valve lifters
    C. supply power to each cylinder
    D. function as a flywheel

22. Assume that a mechanic is using a powder-actuated tool and the cartridge misfires. According to recommended safe practices regarding a misfired cartridge, the FIRST course of action the mechanic should take is to
    A. place the misfired cartridge carefully into a metal container filled with water
    B. carefully reload the tool with the misfired cartridge and try it again
    C. immediately bury the misfired cartridge at least two feet in the ground
    D. remove the wadding from the misfired cartridge and empty the powder into a pail of sand

23. The purpose of the ignition coil in a gasoline engine is PRIMARILY to
    A. smooth the voltage
    B. raise the voltage
    C. raise the current
    D. smooth the current

24. Vapor lock in a vehicle with a gasoline engine is caused by excessive heat. To prevent vapor lock, it may be necessary to relocate
    A. the ignition system
    B. the cooling system
    C. the starter motor
    D. a part of the fuel line

25. To accurately measure the small gap between relay contacts, it is BEST to use a(n)
    A. depth gauge
    B. *GO-NO GO* gauge
    C. feeler gauge
    D. inside caliper

KEY (CORRECT ANSWERS)

1.	C	11.	B
2.	A	12.	B
3.	C	13.	A
4.	D	14.	D
5.	B	15.	A
6.	A	16.	B
7.	D	17.	C
8.	A	18.	B
9.	A	19.	A
10.	B	20.	B

21.	A
22.	A
23.	B
24.	D
25.	C

TEST 2

DIRECTIONS: Each question or incomplete statement is followed by several suggested answers or completions. Select the one that BEST answers the question or completes the statement. *PRINT THE LETTER OF THE CORRECT ANSWER IN THE SPACE AT THE RIGHT.*

1. Of the following, the MOST important reason for having a vehicle preventive maintenance and history card is

    A. for use in making vehicle assignments
    B. to check whether the drivers are completing their assignments
    C. for use as a control device in scheduling maintenance
    D. as a means for projecting future maintenance expenses

2. In his efforts to maintain standards of performance, a shop manager uses a system of close supervision to detect or catch errors.
In OPPOSITE method of accomplishing the same objective is to employ a program which

    A. instills in each employee a pride of workmanship to do the job correctly the first time
    B. groups each job according to the importance to the overall objectives of the program
    C. makes the control of quality the responsibility of an inspector
    D. emphasizes that there is a *one* best way for an employee to do a specific job

3. Assume that after taking over a repair shop, a shop manager feels that he is taking too much time maintaining records.
He should

    A. temporarily assign this job to one of his senior repair crew chiefs
    B. get together with his supervisor to determine if all these records are needed
    C. stop keeping those records which he believes are unnecessary
    D. spend a few additional hours each day until his records are current

4. In order to apply performance standards to employees engaged in repair shop activities, a shop manager must FIRST

    A. allow workers to decide for themselves the way to do the job
    B. determine what is acceptable as satisfactory work
    C. separate the more difficult tasks from the simpler tasks
    D. stick to an established work schedule

5. The term *preventative maintenance* is used to identify a plan whereby

    A. equipment is serviced according to a regular schedule
    B. equipment is serviced as soon as it fails
    C. equipment is replaced as soon as it becomes obsolete
    D. all equipment is replaced periodically

63

6. The ratio of air to gasoline in an automobile engine is controlled by the

   A. gas filter
   B. fuel pump
   C. fuel injector
   D. intake manifold

7. *Energizer* is another name given to the

   A. automobile battery
   B. fluorescent fixture ballast
   C. battery charger
   D. generator shunt field

8. Wearshoes may be found on

   A. circuit breakers
   B. automobile brake systems
   C. snow plows
   D. door sills

9. An oscilloscope is an instrument used in

   A. measuring noise levels
   B. displaying waveforms of electrical signals
   C. indicating the concentrations of pollutants in air
   D. photographing high-speed events

10. Assume that a brake pedal of a truck goes to the floorboard when depressed. The one of the following that could cause this condition is

    A. a leak in the hydraulic lines
    B. a clogged hydraulic line
    C. scored drums
    D. glazed linings

11. The universal joints of an automobile are located on the

    A. suspension springs
    B. steering linkages
    C. wheel cylinders
    D. drive shaft

12. The MAIN purpose of a flexible coupling is to connect two shafts which are

    A. of different diameters
    B. of different shapes
    C. not in exact alignment
    D. of different material

13. When using a standard measuring micrometer, starting with a zero reading, one complete counterclockwise revolution of the sleeve will give a reading of _____ inch.

    A. .001   B. .010   C. .025   D. .250

14. If a nut is to be tightened to an exact specified value of inch-lbs., the wrench to use is a _____ wrench.

    A. spanner   B. box   C. lock-jaw   D. torque

15. Common permanent type anti-freezes for automobile cooling systems are MAINLY

    A. alcohol
    B. methanol
    C. ethylene glycol
    D. trichloroethylene

16. The function of the fuel injector on a gasoline engine is to	16._____

    A. mix the air and gasoline properly
    B. filter the fuel
    C. filter the air to engine
    D. pump the gasoline into the cylinder

17. If a car owner complains that the battery in his car is constantly running dry, the item that should be checked FIRST is the	17._____

    A. fan belt   B. generator
    C. voltage regulator D. relay

18. On MOST modern automobiles, foot brake pressure is transmitted to the brake drums by	18._____

    A. air pressure   B. mechanical linkage
    C. hydraulic fluid   D. electromagnetic force

19. Assume that the engine of a car remains cold even though it is run for a period of time. The part that is MOST likely at fault is the	19._____

    A. heat bypass valve B. thermostat
    C. heater control   D. choke

20. A rectifier changes	20._____

    A. DC to AC
    B. AC to DC
    C. single-phase power to three-phase power
    D. battery power to three-phase power

21. Continuity in a de-energized electrical circuit may be checked with a(n)	21._____

    A. voltmeter   B. ohmmeter
    C. neon tester   D. rheostat

22. Of the following crankcase oils, the one that should be used in sub-zero weather is SAE	22._____

    A. 10W   B. 20W   C. 20   D. 30

23. Caster in an automobile is an adjustment in the	23._____

    A. ignition system   B. drive-shaft
    C. rear differential D. front suspension

24. If the spark plugs in an engine run too hot, the result is MOST likely that	24._____

    A. oil and carbon compounds will accumulate on the insulators
    B. the electrodes will wear rapidly
    C. the timing will be retarded
    D. the ignition coil may become damaged

25. A low reading on the oil pressure gauge of a gasoline engine may mean that the

    A. engine bearings are too tight
    B. crankcase oil level is too low
    C. transmission oil level is too low
    D. transmission oil needs changing

KEY (CORRECT ANSWERS)

1.	C	11.	D
2.	A	12.	C
3.	B	13.	C
4.	B	14.	D
5.	A	15.	C
6.	C	16.	A
7.	A	17.	C
8.	C	18.	C
9.	B	19.	B
10.	A	20.	B

21.	B
22.	A
23.	D
24.	B
25.	B

TEST 3

DIRECTIONS: Each question or incomplete statement is followed by several suggested answers or completions. Select the one that BEST answers the question or completes the statement. *PRINT THE LETTER OF THE CORRECT ANSWER IN THE SPACE AT THE RIGHT.*

1. To remove a slotted collar having internal threads from a shaft, the BEST of the following wrenches to use is a(n) _____ wrench.

    A. Allen B. Stillson C. socket D. spanner

2. When using a heavy jack placed on the ground to raise a heavy load, it is important to place a sturdy, flat board under the jack PRIMARILY in order to

    A. facilitate placing the jack under the load
    B. reduce the jacking effort
    C. prevent the jack from slipping out from under the load
    D. decrease the jacking height

3. The pulley wheels of a block and tackle are commonly called

    A. stocks B. swivels C. sheaves D. guides

4. If the diameter of a machined part must be 1.035 ± 0.003", then it is ACCEPTABLE if it measures

    A. 1.031" B. 1.032" C. 1.039" D. 1.335"

5. The type of threads for ordinary screws are USUALLY the _____ type.

    A. square B. buttress C. V D. Acme

6. Of the following actions a repair shop manager can take to determine if the vehicles used in his shop are being utilized properly, the one which will give him the LEAST meaningful information is

    A. conducting an analysis of vehicle assignments
    B. reviewing the number of miles travelled by each vehicle with and without loads
    C. recording the unloaded weights of each vehicle
    D. comparing the amount of time vehicles are parked at job sites with the time required to travel to and from job sites

7. For a shop manager, the MOST important reason that equipment which is used infrequently should be considered for disposal is that

    A. the time required for its maintenance could be better used elsewhere
    B. such equipment may cause higher management to think that your shop is not busy
    C. the men may resent having to work on such equipment
    D. such equipment usually has a higher breakdown rate in operation

8. In an automotive gasoline engine, the camshaft is used PRIMARILY to

   A. drive the transmission
   B. operate the valve lifters
   C. change the reciprocating motion of the pistons to rotary motion
   D. operate the choke mechanism

9. A magnetic motor starter is to be controlled with momentary start-stop pushbuttons at two locations.
   The number of control wires required, respectively, in the conduit between the controller and the first station and in the conduit between the two stations is _____ and _____.

   A. 3; 3   B. 4; 4   C. 3; 4   D. 2; 4

10. If the scale on a shop drawing is 1/2 inch to the foot, then the length of a part which measures 4 1/2 inches long on the drawing has a length of APPROXIMATELY _____ feet.

    A. 2 1/8   B. 4 1/4   C. 8 1/2   D. 10 3/4

11. It is important to use safety shoes PRIMARILY to guard the feet against

    A. tripping hazards   B. heavy falling objects
    C. shock hazards   D. mud and dirt

12. When using a wrench to tighten a bolt, it is considered bad practice to extend the handle of the wrench with a pipe for added leverage PRIMARILY because

    A. the pipe may break
    B. the bolt head may be broken off
    C. more space will be needed to turn the wrench with the pipe on it
    D. no increase in leverage is obtained in this manner

13. The liquid solution in an electrical storage battery MOST commonly is

    A. alkali   B. acid
    C. pure distilled water   D. copper sulphate

14. Manifolds on an internal combustion engine are used

    A. to mount the engine to the frame
    B. for cooling the engine
    C. in the carburetor
    D. to conduct gases into and out of the engine

15. The energy stored by a storage battery is commonly given in

    A. volts   B. amperes
    C. ampere-hours   D. kilowatts

16. Vapor lock occurs in automobile

    A. gas tanks   B. crankcases
    C. transmissions   D. carburetors

17. The instrument generally used to determine the specific gravity of a lead-acid storage battery is the

    A. ammeter
    B. voltmeter
    C. ohmmeter
    D. hydrometer

17.____

18. A tachometer is an instrument that is used to measure

    A. horizontal distances
    B. radial distances
    C. current in electric circuits
    D. motor speed

18.____

19. A material that is commonly used as a lining for bearings in order to reduce friction is

    A. magnesium
    B. cast iron
    C. babbitt
    D. carborundum

19.____

20. In a motor having sleeve bearings, bearing wear can be checked by measuring the air-gap clearance between the armature and the

    A. pole pieces
    B. commutator
    C. bearing
    D. brushes

20.____

21. A revolution counter applied to the end of a rotating shaft reads 100 when a stopwatch is started and 850 after 90 seconds.
    The shaft is rotating at a speed of _____ rpm.

    A. 500   B. 633   C. 750   D. 950

21.____

22. If a kink develops in a wire rope, it would be BEST to

    A. hammer out the kink with a lead hammer
    B. straighten out the kink by putting it in a vise and applying sufficient pressure
    C. discard the portion of rope containing the kink
    D. keep the rope in use and allow the kink to work itself out

22.____

23. The one of the following flat drive-belts that gives the BEST service in dry places is a(n) _____ belt.

    A. rawhide
    B. oak-tanned
    C. chrome-tanned
    D. semirawhide

23.____

24. The letter representing the standard V-belt section which has the lowest horsepower-per-belt rating is

    A. E   B. C   C. B   D. A

24.____

25. The criteria governing preventive maintenance of vehicles require that all of the following be done at certain intervals.
    The one which must be done MOST frequently is

    A. changing the engine oil
    B. changing the engine oil filter
    C. checking the radiator coolant level
    D. rotating the tires

25.____

26. The one of the following that should NOT be lubricated is a(n)

    A. spur gear train	B. motor commutator
    C. roller chain drive	D. automobile axle

27. The one of the following oils that has the LOWEST viscosity is S.A.E.

    A. 70	B. 50	C. 20	D. 10W

28. The one of the following V-belt sections which has the HIGHEST horsepower-per-belt rating is _____ section.

    A. A	B. B	C. C	D. D

29. The one of the following transmission devices which should be oiled MOST often is the

    A. V-belt	B. roller chain
    C. rigid coupling	D. clutch plate

30. The one of the following statements concerning lubricating oil which is CORRECT is:

    A. SAE 10 is heavier and more viscous than SAE 30
    B. Diluting lubricating oil with gasoline increases its viscosity
    C. Oil reduces friction between moving parts
    D. In hot weather, thin oil is preferable to heavy oil

KEY (CORRECT ANSWERS)

1.	D	16.	D
2.	C	17.	D
3.	C	18.	D
4.	B	19.	C
5.	C	20.	A
6.	C	21.	A
7.	A	22.	C
8.	B	23.	B
9.	C	24.	D
10.	C	25.	C
11.	B	26.	B
12.	B	27.	D
13.	B	28.	D
14.	D	29.	B
15.	C	30.	C

ARITHMETICAL REASONING
EXAMINATION SECTION
TEST 1

DIRECTIONS: Each question or incomplete statement is followed by several suggested answers or completions. Select the one that BEST answers the question or completes the statement. *PRINT THE LETTER OF THE CORRECT ANSWER IN THE SPACE AT THE RIGHT.*

1. The sum of the fractions 3/32, 3/16, 3/8, and 3/4 is equal to
   A. 1 13/32   B. 1 5/16   C. 1 7/8   D. 3

2. If a maintainer earns $11.52 per hour, and time and one-half for overtime, his gross salary for a week in which he works 5 hours over his regular 40 hours should be
   A. $460.80   B. $518.80   C. $547.20   D. $578.80

3. If the diameter of a shaft must be 2.620 inches plus or minus .002 inches, the shaft will be SATISFACTORY if it has a diameter of _____ inches.
   A. 2.518   B. 2.600   C. 2.617   D. 2.621

4. A bus part costs $275 per 100 when purchased from a vendor. The bus part could be made in the bus machine shop at a labor cost of $60 for 50 units, with material and other costs amounting to $25 for 25 units.
   If 100 such parts were made in the bus shop, there would be a saving of
   A. $55   B. $95   C. $140   D. $165

5. The sum of 9/16", 11/32", 15/64", and 1 3/32" is MOST NEARLY
   A. 2.234"   B. 2.134"   C. 2.334"   D. 2.214"

6. The diameter of a circle whose circumference is 14.5" is MOST NEARLY
   A. 4.62"   B. 4.81"   C. 4.72"   D. 4.51"

7. A bus part cost $90 per 100 when purchased from a vendor. The bus part could be made in the bus machine shop at a labor cost of $20 for 50 units and material and other costs amounting to $10 for 25 units.
   If 100 such parts are made in the bus stop, there would be a saving of
   A. $10   B. $30   C. $40   D. $60

8. A bus storage battery having a 300 ampere-hour capacity is 50% discharged. If the bus running schedule for the day is such that the battery will be charging at an average rate of 30 amperes for 2½ hours and discharging at an average rate of 9 amperes for 5 hours, then at the end of the day, the battery will be APPROXIMATELY
   A. at full charge   B. 75% charged
   C. 60% charged   D. 50% charged

2 (#1)

9. If the total time allowance for replacing the glass in a broken bus window is 75 minutes, how many jobs of this kind would a maintainer be expected to do in 40 hours of work?
   A. 32 B. 40 C. 60 D. 72

9.____

10. A certain rod is tapered so that it changes diameter at a rate of ¼ inch per foot of length.
    If the tapered rod is 3 inches long, then the difference in diameter between the two ends is MOST NEARLY
    A. 0.250" B. 0.187" C. 0.135" D. 0.062"

10.____

11. How many 9½ inch long pieces of copper tubing can be cut from a 20-foot length of tubing?
    A. 24 B. 25 C. 26 D. 27

11.____

12. Two splice plates must be cut from a piece of sheet steel that has an overall length of 14 3/8 inches. The plates are to be 7 5/8 inches and 5 1/4 inches long. If $1/16$ inch is allowed for each saw cut, then how much material would be left?
    A. 1 3/8" B. 1 1/2" C. 1 5/8" D. 1 3/4"

12.____

13. A maintainer requires several lengths of tubing for oil lines as follows: $12^{7}/_{16}$ inches, 5/16 inches, 9 3/16 inches, 9 1/8 inches, 6 1/4 inches, and 5 inches. The TOTAL length of tubing required is MOST NEARLY _____ feet.
    A. 2 B. 3 C. 4 D. 5

13.____

14. Two-thirds of 10 feet is MOST NEARLY
    A. 6'2" B. 6'8" C. 6'11" D. 7'1"

14.____

15. You are directed to pick up a tray load of brake shoes. The combined weight of tray and brake shoes is 4,000 pounds. Assume that each brake shoe weighs 40 pounds and the tray weighs 240 pounds.
    The number of brake shoes in the tray is MOST NEARLY
    A. 88 B. 94 C. 100 D. 106

15.____

16. A maintainer earns $37.32 per hour, and time and one-half for overtime over 40 hours. Each week, 15 percent of his total salary is deducted for social security and taxes. Also, each week a $54.00 deduction is made for a savings bond and a $27.00 deduction is made for a charitable organization.
    If he works a total of 46 hours in a week, his take-home pay for that week is
    A. $1,828.50 B. $1,554.30 C. $1,473.38 D. $1,232.10

16.____

17. A rectangularly-shaped repair facility for light trucks is 160 feet wide and 260 feet long. A 10-foot space is provided along each wall for benches and equipment. A 60-foot wide area in the middle of the floor is to remain clear for its entire 260 foot length. The entrance to the shop is at one end of this open area.
    Assuming that there are no columns to contend with, the MAXIMUM area available for parking of trucks is _____ sq. ft.
    A. 15,600 B. 19,200 C. 26,000 D. 41,600

17.____

18. A criterion is established that limits the yearly major repair expenses to 30% of the current value of the equipment. Equipment is depreciated at a rate of 20% of its original cost each year. A truck purchased on January 1, 2017 for $27,000 had a reconditioned engine installed in February 2020 at a total cost of $2,700. The amount of money available for additional major repairs on this truck in 2020 is
    A. none   B. $540   C. $1,080   D. $2,160

19. Twenty carburetors are ordered for your shop by the Purchasing Department. The terms are list, less 30% less 10% less 5%.
    If the list price of a carburetor is $210 and all terms are met upon delivery, the charges to your budget will be
    A. $4,078.80   B. $3,256.20   C. $2,513.70   D. $1,892.40

20. The sum of the fractions 7/16", 11/16", 5/32", and 7/8" is MOST NEARLY
    A. 2.1753"   B. 2.1563"   C. 1.9522"   D. 1.9463"

21. If 750 feet of wire weighs 60 lbs., the number of pounds that 150 feet will weigh is MOST NEARLY
    A. 12   B. 10   C. 8   D. 6

22. A steel rod 19.750" long is to have three pieces cut from its length. One piece is to be 3.250" long, the second 6.500" long, and the third piece 5.375".
    If .125" is allowed for each cut, the length of the material left over is
    A. 3.750"   B. 4.250"   C. 4.500"   D. 5.150"

23. If the distance between the north and south terminals is 10.8 miles and a train makes six roundtrips, then the total mileage would be NEAREST _____ miles.
    A. 22   B. 65   C. 130   D. 145

24. If the thickness of material worn from a car wheel is approximately 1/16 inch off the diameter in 20,000 miles of travel, the wheel diameter will be reduced from 33 inches to 32 3/4 inches after _____ miles.
    A. 60,000   B. 80,000   C. 100,000   D. 120,000

25. If the distance between north and south terminals is 11.3 miles and a train makes five roundtrips, then the total travel mileage would be NEAREST _____ miles.
    A. 23   B. 55   C. 115   D. 130

KEY (CORRECT ANSWERS)

1.	A		11.	B
2.	C		12.	A
3.	D		13.	D
4.	A		14.	B
5.	A		15.	B
6.	A		16.	C
7.	A		17.	B
8.	C		18.	B
9.	A		19.	C
10.	D		20.	B

21. A
22. B
23. C
24. B
25. C

SOLUTIONS TO PROBLEMS

1. $\frac{3}{32} + \frac{3}{16} + \frac{3}{8} + \frac{3}{4} = \frac{45}{32} = 1\frac{13}{32}$

2. Gross salary = ($11.52)(40) + ($17.28)(5) = $547.20

3. 2.620 ± .002 means from 2.618 to 2.622. The only selection in this range is 2.621.

4. ($60)($\frac{100}{50}$) + ($25)($\frac{100}{25}$)$220 if made in the bus shop. Savings = $275 - $220 = $55

5. 9/16" + 11/32" + 15/64" + 1 3/32" = 143/64 = 2 15/64" = 2.234"

6. Diameter = 14.5" ÷ π ≈ 4.62"

7. ($20)($\frac{100}{50}$) + ($10)($\frac{100}{25}$) = $80 if made in the bus shop. Savings = $990 - $80 = $10

8. [150+[(30(2 1/2)] − [(9)(5)] = [150+75] − 45 = 180, and 180/300 = 60%

9. (40)(60) ÷ 75 = 32

10. (1/4")(3/12) = 1/16" ≈ .062"

11. (20)(12) = 240", and 240" ÷ 9 1/2" ≈ 25.3 rounded down to 25 pieces of tubing

12. 14 3/8" − 7 5/8" − 5 1/4" − 1/16" = 1 3/8"

13. 12 7/16" + 14 5/16" + 9 3/16" + 9 1/8" + 6 1/4" + 5" ≈ 5 ft.

14. (2/3)(10') = 6 2/3' = 6'8"

15. 4000 − 240 = 3760 lbs. Then, 3760 ÷ 40 = 94 brake shoes

16. Take-home pay = ($37.32)(40) + ($55.98)(6) − .15[($37.32)(40) + ($55.98)(6)] - $54.00 - $27.00 = $1,473.738 ≈ $1,473.38

17. Subtracting the area for benches and equipment would leave an area of 240' by 140'. Now, deduct the 60' width. Final area = (240')(80') = 19,200 sq.ft.

18. In 2020, the value of the truck = $27,000 − (3)(.20)($27,000) = $10,800. The limit of the expenses for repairs = (.30)($10,800) = $3,240. After installing engine, $3,240 - $2,700 = $540 left for additional major repairs.

19. (20)($210)(.70)(.90)(.95) = $2,513.70

20. 7/16" + 11/16" + 5/32" + 7/8" = 69/32" ≈ 2.1563"

21. (150/750)(60) = 12 lbs.

22. 19.750" − 3.250" − 6.500" − 5.375" − .125" − .125" − 1.25" = 4.250" left over

23. (6)(10.8)(2) = 129.6 ≈ 130 miles

24. 33" − 32 3/4" = 1/4". Then, (1/4 ÷ 1/16)(20,000) = 80,000 miles

25. (5)(11.3)(2) = 113 miles, closest to 115 miles

TEST 2

DIRECTIONS: Each question or incomplete statement is followed by several suggested answers or completions. Select the one that BEST answers the question or completes the statement. *PRINT THE LETTER OF THE CORRECT ANSWER IN THE SPACE AT THE RIGHT.*

1. In looking over an alteration job on car bodies, you find that 96 pieces of 1" × 1" × 1'6" long square steel stock are needed to do this job. Steel weighs 480 lbs. per cu. ft. and costs $0.12 per lb.
   The total cost of this material is MOST NEARLY
   A. $40.00   B. $60.00   C. $80.00   D. $100.00

2. Assume that the breakdown cost of a particular motor job is as follows:
   Parts $160.00
   Labor   75.00
   Overhead   30.00
   The percentage of the total cost for labor is MOST NEARLY
   A. 20%   B. 25%   C. 28%   D. 32%

3. The engine hydraulic system and transmission on a certain type of tractor use the same type oil. This oil is delivered in 55 gallon drums.
   How many drums are needed to make all three changes on 10 of these tractors whose capacities are the following:
   Engine   58 quarts
   Transmission   70 quarts
   Hydraulic system   22 gallons
   A. 100   B. 50   C. 54   D. 10

4. A new shop layout requires the following:
   1,000 sq. ft. for tool room
   3,000 sq. ft. for parts room
   10,000 sq. ft. for service bays
   5,500 sq. ft. for isles
   The building should be AT LEAST _____ yards wide and 70 yards long.
   A. 10   B. 20   C. 25   D. 30

5. When filling a diesel engine cooling system, the mix required is 80% antifreeze and 20% water. You are required to fill seven systems containing 30 gallons each. The number of 5 gallon cans of antifreeze that are required is MOST NEARLY
   A. 210   B. 168   C. 34   D. 26

6. The floors of 2 cars are to be painted with a special test paint. Assume that the floor area in each car is 600 square feet. A gallon of this paint will cover 400 square feet.
   The number of gallons of this paint that you should pick up at the storeroom to paint the two car floors would be
   A. 6   B. 5   C. 4   D. 3

7. Assume that you are sent to the storeroom for 1,000 of 600-volt contact tips which are to be distributed equally to 5 foremen, but you find that the storeroom can only supply you with 825.
   If you distribute these 825 tips equally to the 5 foremen the number of tips that each foreman will receive is
   A. 165   B. 175   C. 190   D. 200

8. You are asked to fill six 5-gallon cans of oil from a full drum containing 52 gallons. When you have filled the six cans, the number of gallons of oil left in the drum will be MOST NEARLY
   A. 14   B. 16   C. 22   D. 30

9. A certain wire rope is made up of 6 strands, each strand containing 19 wires. The TOTAL number of wires in this wire rope is
   A. 25   B. 96   C. 114   D. 144

10. The hook should be the weakest part of any crane, hoist, or sling.
    According to this statement, if a particular hook has a rated capacity of 2½ tons, then the MAXIMUM load that should be lifted with this hook is _____ pounds.
    A. 150   B. 3,000   C. 5,000   D. 5,500

11. Assume that 2 car wheels weigh 635 pounds each and are attached to an axle weighing 1,260 pounds.
    The total weight of this assembly is MOST NEARLY _____ pounds.
    A. 1,270   B. 1,520   C. 1,895   D. 2,530

12. If an employee authorizes his employer to deduct 4% of his $1,200 weekly salary for a savings bond, the MINIMUM number of weekly deductions required to get enough money to buy a bond costing $144 is
    A. 3   B. 6   C. 8   D. 9

13. In weighing out a truckful of scrap metal, the scale reads 21,496 lbs.
    If the empty truck weighs 9,879 lbs., the amount of scrap metal, in pounds, is MOST NEARLY
    A. 10,507   B. 10,602   C. 11,617   D. 12,617

14. Four trays of material are placed on the body of a delivery truck for delivery to the inspection shop. Each tray is 4 feet wide and 4 feet long.
    If these trays are placed side by side on the floor of the delivery truck, together they will cover an area of the floor MOST NEARLY _____ square feet.
    A. 32   B. 48   C. 64   D. 72

15. Assume that you are operating a degreasing tank and its tray holds 5 gear cases. It takes 40 minutes to clean one tray of gear cases.
    At the end of 6 hours of operation (excluding lunch break and loading and unloading time), the number of gear case cleaned will be
    A. 30   B. 36   C. 45   D. 50

3 (#2)

16. If a serviceman's weekly gross salary is $160 and 20% is deducted for taxes, his take-home pay is
    A. $120   B. $128   C. $140   D. $144

Questions 17-18.

DIRECTIONS: Questions 17 and 18 are to be answered on the basis of the following paragraph.

The car maintenance department is considering the purchase of a certain car part from Manufacturer X for $140. An equivalent part can be purchased from Manufacturer Y for $100. The part made by Manufacturer X must be reconditioned every 3 years, using material costing $30 and requiring 6 hours of labor. The part made by Manufacturer Y must be reconditioned every 1½ years, using material costing $24 and requiring 5 hours of labor. The maintainer's rate of pay is $12 per hour.

17. The cost of operating with the part made by Manufacturer X (excluding the first cost) is MOST NEARLY _____ per year.
    A. $30   B. $32   C. $34   D. $42

18. The total cost of operating with the part made by Manufacturer Y over a period of 12 years, including the first cost of the part and assuming the part is scrapped at the end of 12 years, is MOST NEARLY
    A. $472   B. $572   C. $688   D. $772

19. The area of the steel plate shown in the sketch at the right is _____ sq. ft.
    A. 16
    B. 18
    C. 20
    D. 22

20. A car part made by a Manufacturer X has a purchase cost of $7,500 and a life of 5 years. It requires a yearly maintenance cost of $50. Manufacturer Y offers a similar part of this type for $4,800, with a life of 3 years and a yearly maintenance cost of $75.
    By purchasing the part offering a better overall value, the yearly savings per unit purchased would be
    A. $115   B. $125   C. $135   D. $140

21. A car part can be overhauled at the rate of 12 parts per hour. Each part requires new material costing $6 each.
    If the labor cost is $14 per hour, one part can be overhauled for a total cost (labor plus material) of MOST NEARLY
    A. $6.64   B. $7.16   C. $7.46   D. $8.20

4 (#2)

22. A car part costs $150 per 50 units when purchased in a finished condition from a vendor. The car part can be made in the shop at a total cost off $2.20 per unit, when made on a machine which can be purchased for $1,000.
The MINIMUM number of parts which must be made on this machine before the savings equal the cost of the machine is
   A. 850   B. 1,000   C. 1,250   D. 1,500

22.____

23. A pound of a certain type of metal washer contains 360 washers.
If ¼ of the material of each washer is removed by enlarging the center of each washer, the number of washers to the pound should then be MOST NEARLY
   A. 280   B. 300   C. 380   D. 480

23.____

24. A maintainer earns $32.52 per hour, and time and one-half for overtime. Ten percent of his total salary earned is deducted from his paycheck for social security and taxes. He also contributes $15.00 per week to a charitable organization. No other deductions are made.
If he works 2 hours over his basic 40 hours, his weekly take-home pay should be MOST NEARLY
   A. $1,398.36   B. $1,258.50   C. $1,243.50   D. $1,231.80

24.____

25. A car part costs $130 per 100 units if purchased from a vendor. The car part can be made on a machine which can be purchased for $1,000. Assume that this machine has a production life of 20,000 units with no salvage value, and that all shop costs amount to $80 per 100 units turned out in the shop.
The money that would be SAVED during the life of the machine would be
   A. $800   B. $8,000   C. 9,000   D. $18,000

25.____

KEY (CORRECT ANSWERS)

1. B
2. C
3. D
4. D
5. C

6. D
7. A
8. C
9. C
10. C

11. D
12. A
13. C
14. C
15. C

16. B
17. C
18. C
19. C
20. B

21. B
22. C
23. D
24. C
25. C

SOLUTIONS TO PROBLEMS

1. Total cost ≈ (96)(.01)(4)(.12) ≈ $55, which is closest to $60. Note that 1" × 1" × 1'6" ≈ (1/12')(1/12')(3/2') – 1.96 ≈ .01 cu. ft.

2. Labor = $75 ÷ $265 ≈ 28%

3. (10)(14.5+17.5+22) = 540. Then, 540 ÷ 55 ≈ 10 drums

4. Total sq. ft. = 19,500, which is 2166 2/3 sq. yds. Then, 2166 2/3 ÷ 70 ≈ 30.95 or 31

5. Amount of antifreeze = (.80)(7)(.30) = 168 gallons. Then, 168 ÷ 5 ≈ 34 cans

6. (600+600) ÷ 400 = 3 gallons

7. 825 ÷5 = 165 for each foreman

8. 52 – (6)(5) = 22 gallons left

9. (19)(6) = 114 wires

10. (2½)(2000) = 5000 pounds

11. (2)(635) + 1260 = 2530 pounds

12. ($1,200)(.04) = $48. Then, $144 ÷ $48 = 3 weekly deductions

13. 21,496 – 9,879 = 11,617 pounds

14. 4(4')(4') = 64 sq. ft.

15. 6 hrs. ÷ 2/3 hr. = 9 trays = 45 gear cases cleaned

16. Take-home pay = ($160)(.80) = $128

17. ($30)+(6)($12) = ($102 for 3 yrs. = $34 per year

18. 100 + 7(24) + 7(60) = 688

19. Separate the figure into regions as follows:
    I: 1'×2' = 2 sq.ft.
    II: 3'×4' = 12 sq.ft.
    III: (3'×4') ÷ 2' = 6 sq.ft.
    Total = 20 sq.ft.

    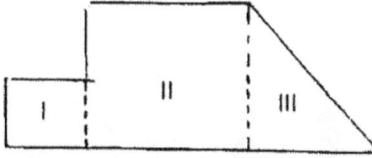

20. Manufacturer X: $7500 + ($50)(5) = $7750, so the cost per year is $7750 ÷ 5 = $1550
    Manufacturer Y: $4800 + (3)($75) = $5025, so the cost per year is $5025 ÷ 3 = $1675
    Using Manufacturer X, savings = $125 per year

6 (#2)

21. Cost of 12 parts = (12)($6) + $14 = $86. Then, the cost of one part = $86 ÷ 12 ≈ $7.16.2021

22. Savings per unit is $150/50 - $2.20 = $.80. Then, $1000 ÷ $.80 = 1250

23. 1 – ¼ = ¾. Then, 360 ÷ ¾ = 480

24. Take-home pay = [($32.52)(40)+($48.78)(2)][.90] - $15 ≈ $1,243.50

25. Amount if purchased from a vendor = $130(200) = $26,000. Using the machine, amount = $1000 + ($80)(200) = $17,000. Amount saved = $9000

TEST 3

DIRECTIONS: Each question or incomplete statement is followed by several suggested answers or completions. Select the one that BEST answers the question or completes the statement. *PRINT THE LETTER OF THE CORRECT ANSWER IN THE SPACE AT THE RIGHT.*

1. A Cat 983 Traxcavator can make a complete loading cycle from bank to truck and back to bank in 25 seconds.
   If the bucket contains 4 cu. yds of loose material, the MINIMUM amount of material that an operator should load in 4 hours is _____ cubic yards.
   A. 2,304   B. 2,100   C. 1,896   D. 576

   1._____

2. An excavation is 12' × 18' × 15' and is to be dug by a Cat 983 Traxcavator with 3 cubic yards of solid material excavated per pass.
   The MINIMUM number of passes required to dig the hole is _____ passes.
   A. 40   B. 46   C. 120   D. 126

   2._____

3. A Cat D8 tractor and 463 scraper can haul 22 cubic yards of cover material per trip.
   If it is required to cover an area 1,000 feet by 100 feet to a depth of 2 feet, the MINIMUM number of trips that will be required is MOST NEARLY
   A. 284   B. 337   C. 385   D. 421

   3._____

4. Gravel weighs 2,800 pounds per cubic yard.
   In order to carry 42,000 pounds of gravel, the capacity of a truck must be AT LEAST _____ cubic yards.
   A. 10   B. 12   C. 15   D. 18

   4._____

5. The average capacity of an Athey Wagon is 60 cubic yards. The Cat D8 tractor pulls 2 wagons.
   The MINIMUM number of trips to the fill that would be required to empty a barge loaded with 1,000 cubic yards of refuse is
   A. 9   B. 17   C. 30   D. 90

   5._____

6. When pulling 2 Athey trailers, the operator of a Cat D8 tractor can make a round trip from the crane to the fill and back in 15 minutes.
   Assuming that delays and breaks allow the man to work productively for 75% of the shift, the MAXIMUM number of trips that the operator can make in an 8-hour shift is
   A. 43   B. 32   C. 24   D. 16

   6._____

7. In plowing a street which is 24 feet wide, a motor grader can make an 8-ft. wide pass, with a 2-ft. overlap.
   If a roundtrip takes 4 minutes, the MINIMUM time needed to plow this street should be _____ minutes.
   A. 12   B. 16   C. 24   D. 32

   7._____

8. A scraper is loaded with 23 cubic yards of sand weighing 100 pounds per cubic foot.
   The weight of the load, in tons, is MOST NEARLY
   A. 20   B. 30   C. 40   D. 60

9. Assume a crankcase oil change of 6 quarts for every 150 service hours.
   How many 42 gallon drums of oil are required for 8,400 total service hours.
   A. 5   B. 2   C. 1   D. 1 1/3

10. Assume that a ruler is marked in 10ths of a foot instead of in inches.
    5 tenths on this ruler would be
    A. 4"   B. 5"   C. 6"   D. 7"

11. A truckload of 1½" stone from a 10 cubic yard truck will spread an area APPROXIMATELY _____ long, 6" deep, and _____ wide.
    A. 50'; 10'   B. 10';5'   C. 54';10'   D. 45'; 5'

12. A dump truck with a body 10 ft. long, 5 ft. wide, and 4 ft. deep has a volume of _____ cubic feet.
    A. 150   B. 200   C. 250   D. 300

13. A tractor is operated on a given landfill operation during the following time intervals in one day: from 8:15 A.M. to 11:45 A.M.; from 12:30 P.M. to 6:00 P.M.; from 6:45 P.M. to 11:30 P.M.
    The total net operating time, expressed in hours and minutes, is MOST NEARLY
    A. 13; 30   B. 13; 15   C. 13; 45   D. 12; 45

14. The area of ground contact (with standard track shoes) of a late model D8 Caterpillar Tractor is 4,296 sq. in.
    Expressed in square feet, this is MOST NEARLY
    A. 358   B. 29.8   C. 159.3   D. 21.37

15. A towing winch develops a bare drum line pull of 11.8 tons.
    This force represents, in pounds,
    A. 23,850   B. 28,300   C. 23,800   D. 23,600

16. The fuel tank gauge reads about ¾ of a full tank.
    If the tank capacity is 72.5 gallons, the amount of fuel in the tank is MOST NEARLY
    A. 53.2   B. 53.8   C. 54.5   D. 55.0

17. If a dump truck capable of carrying 40 2/3 cubic yards is ¾ loaded, it is carrying, in cubic yards,
    A. 28   B. 36½   C. 30½   D. 28 2/3

18. A load of sand filling a truck body 6 feet long, 5 feet wide, and 3 feet deep would contain _____ cubic feet.
    A. 14   B. 90   C. 33   D. 21

Questions 19-21.

DIRECTIONS: Questions 19 through 21 are to be answered on the basis of the diagrams of balanced levers shown below. P is the center of rotation, W is the weight on the lever, and F is the balancing force.

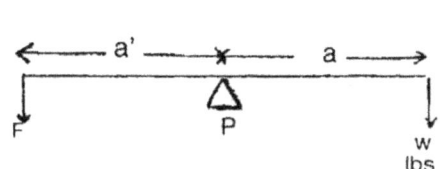
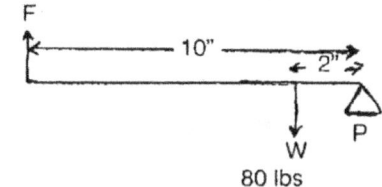

19. In Diagram 1, the force F required to balance the weight W lbs. on the lever shown is equal to _____ lbs.
    A. a/W   B. W/a   C. W   D. Wa

20. In Diagram 2, the force F required to balance the weight of 80 lbs. on the lever shown is _____ lbs.
    A. 4   B. 3   C. 16   D. 32

21. The mechanical advantage of the lever shown in Diagram 2 is
    A. 4   B. 5   C. 8   D. 12

22. The specific gravity of a liquid may be defined as the ratio of the weight of a given volume of the liquid to the weight of an equal volume of water. An empty bottle weighs 5 oz. When the bottle is filled with water, the total weight is 50 oz. When the bottle is filled with another liquid, the total weight is 95 oz. The specific gravity of the second liquid is MOST NEARLY
    A. .50   B. .58   C. 1.7   D. 2.0

23. If one inch is approximately equal to 2.54 centimeters, the number of inches in one meter is MOST NEARLY
    A. 14.2   B. 25.4   C. 39.4   D. 91.4

24. One-quarter divided by five-eighths is
    A. 5/32   B. 1/10   C. 2/5   D. 5/2

25. A man works on a certain job continuously, with no time off for lunch. If he works from 9:45 A.M. until 1:35 P.M. to finish the job, the total time which he spent on the job is MOST NEARLY _____ hours, _____ minutes.
    A. 3; 10   B. 3; 35   C. 3; 50   D. 4; 15

4 (#3)
KEY (CORRECT ANSWERS)

1.	A		11.	C
2.	A		12.	B
3.	B		13.	C
4.	C		14.	B
5.	A		15.	D
6.	C		16.	C
7.	B		17.	C
8.	B		18.	B
9.	B		19.	C
10.	C		20.	C

21. B
22. D
23. C
24. C
25. C

5 (#3)

SOLUTIONS TO PROBLEMS

1. 4 hrs. = (4)(60)(60) = 14,400 sec. Then, 14,400 ÷ 25 = 576. Thus, (576)(4 cu.yds.) = 2304

2. (12')(18')(15') = 3240 cu.ft. = 120 cu.yds. Then, 120 ÷ 3 = 40

3. (1000')(100')(2') = 200,000 cu.ft. ≈ 7407.4 cu.yds. Finally, 7407.4 ÷ 22 = 336.7, rounded up to 337 trips

4. 42,000 ÷ 2800 = 15 cu.yds.

5. (2)(60 cu.yds.) = 120 yds. Then, 1000 ÷ 120 = 8 1/3, which must be rounded up to 9 trips.

6. 8 hrs. ÷ 15 min. = 32. Then, (32)(.75) = 24 trips

7. 24' ÷ 8' = 3; however, with a 2 ft. overlap, only 6' gets plowed. So, (24÷6)(4 min) = 16 min.

8. 23 cu.yds = 621 cu.ft. Then, (621)(100) = 62,100 lbs. Finally, 62,100 ÷ 2000 ≈ 30 tons

9. 8400 ÷ 150 = 56. Then, (56)(6 qts.) = 336 qts. = 8 gallons. Finally, 84 ÷ 42 = 2 drums

10. 5 tenths = (5/10)(12") = 6"

11. (54')(1/2')(10') = 270 cu.ft. = 10 cu.yds.

12. Volume = (10')(5')(4') = 200 cu.ft.

13. 3 hrs. 30 min. + 5 hrs. 30 min. + 4 hrs. 45 min. = 12 hrs. 105 min. = 13 hrs. 45 min.

14. 4296 sq.in. = 4296 ÷ 144 ≈ 29.8 sq.ft.

15. 11.8 tons = (11.8)(2000) = 23,600 lbs.

16. (72.5)(.75) = 54.375, closest to 54.5 gallons

17. (40 2/3)(3/4) = 30½ cu.yds.

18. (6')(5')(3') = 90 cu.ft.

19. F = Wa/a = W lbs.

20. F = (80)(2) ÷ 10 = 16 lbs.

21. Mechanical advantage = 10/2 = 5

22. Specific gravity = $\frac{95-5}{50-5}$ = 2

23. 1 meter = 100 cm. ≈ (100) ÷(2.54) ≈ 39.4 in.

24. $1/4 \div 5/8 = \frac{1}{4} \cdot \frac{8}{5} = \frac{2}{5}$

25. 9:45 A.M. to 1:35 P.M. = 3 hrs. 50 min.

READING COMPREHENSION
UNDERSTANDING AND INTERPRETING WRITTEN MATERIAL
EXAMINATION SECTION
TEST 1

DIRECTIONS: Each question or incomplete statement is followed by several suggested answers or completions. Select the one that BEST answers the question or completes the statement. *PRINT THE LETTER OF THE CORRECT ANSWER IN THE SPACE AT THE RIGHT.*

Questions 1-2.

DIRECTIONS: Questions 1 and 2 are to be answered in accordance with the following paragraph.

    Steam cleaners get their name from the fact that steam is used to generate pressure and is also a by-product of heating the cleaning solution. Steam itself has little cleaning power. It will melt some soils, but it does no dissolve them, break them up, or destroy their clinging power. Rather surprisingly, good machines generate as little steam as possible. Modern surface chemistry depends on a chemical solution to dissolve dirt, destroy its clinging power, and hold it in suspension. Steam actually hinders such a solution, but heat helps its physical and chemical action. Cleaning is most efficient when a hot solution reaches the work in heavy volume.

1. In accordance with the above paragraph, for MOST efficient cleaning,   1.____
   A. a heavy volume of steam is needed
   B. hot steam is needed to break up the soils
   C. steam is used to dissolve the surface dirt
   D. a hot chemical solution should always be used

2. With reference to the above paragraph, the steam in a steam cleaner is used to   2.____
   A. generate pressure
   B. create b-product chemicals
   C. slow down the chemical action of the cleaning solution
   D. dissolve accumulations of dirt

Questions 3-5.

DIRECTIONS: Questions 3 through 5 are based on the information given in the following paragraphs. Use ONLY the information given in these paragraphs in answering these questions.

    METHOD A: Move voltmeter lead from BAT to GEN terminal of regulator. Retard generator speed until generator voltage is reduced to 2 volts on a 6-volt system or 4 volts on a 12-volt system. Move voltmeter lead back to BAT terminal of regulator. Bring generator back to specified speed and note voltage setting.

METHOD B: Connect a variable resistance into the field circuit. Turn out all resistance. Operate generator at specified speed. Slowly increase (turn in) resistance until generator voltage is reduced to 2 volts on a 6-volt system or 4 volts on a 12-volt system. Turn out all resistance again, and note voltage setting. Regulator cover must be in place. To adjust voltage setting, turn adjusting screw. Turn clockwise to increase setting and counterclockwise to decrease voltage setting.

3. According to the instructions given in the paragraphs, when taking readings,
   A. a variable resistance is to be connected into the generator armature circuit
   B. the generator voltage on a 12-volt system is reduced to 2 volts
   C. the cover is to be in place
   D. the voltmeter lead should be continuously connected to the BAT terminal

4. In following the instructions given in the paragraphs, the one of the following statements that is MOST NEARLY correct is:
   A. The adjusting screw must be turned clockwise to increase the voltage setting
   B. Method B makes use of a fixed resistor
   C. Method A makes use of a variable resistor
   D. The generator voltage is reduced by decreasing the resistance

5. The above instructions pertain MOST likely to a(n)
   A. voltage regulator   B. starting regulator
   C. amperage regulator   D. circuit breaker

Questions 6-7.

DIRECTIONS: Questions 6 and 7 are based upon the following paragraph. Use ONLY the information contained in this paragraph in answering these questions.

With the engine running at normal idling speed and the engine hood open, attach the vacuum gauge to the intake manifold. The vacuum gauge should read about 18 to 21 inches, and the pointer should be steady. A needle fluctuating between 10 and 15 inches may indicate a defective cylinder-head, gasket, or valve. An extremely low reading indicates a leak in the intake manifold or gaskets. Accelerate the engine with full throttle momentarily. Notice if the gauge indicator fails to drop to approximately 2 inches as the throttle is opened, and recoil to at least 24 inches as the throttle is closed. If so, this may be an indication of diluted oil, poor piston-ring sealing, or an abnormal restriction in the exhaust, carburetor, or air cleaner. The above reading apply to sea level. There will be approximately a 1inch drop for each 1,000 feet of altitude.

6. If a vacuum test is made on a properly operating engine at an altitude of 3,000 feet, the vacuum gauge should read MOST NEARLY
   A. 12"   B. 15"   C. 13"   D. 24"

7. If a vacuum test is made on an engine which has an abnormal restriction in the exhaust, this will be evidenced by
   A. a leak in the intake manifold
   B. the gauge indicator failing to drop to approximately 3 inches on opening the throttle
   C. the gauge fluctuating around 12 inches
   D. a steady high gauge reading

Questions 8-10.

DIRECTIONS: Questions 8 through 10 are to be answered in accordance with the information in the following paragraph.

The following is a set of instructions on engine shut-down procedure: When an engine equipped with an electric shut-down valve is used, the engine can be shut down completely by turning off the switch key on installations equipped with an electric shut-down valve, or by turning the manual shut-down valve lever. Turning off the switch key which controls the electric shut-down valve always stops the engine unless the override button on the shutdown valve has been locked in the open position. If the manual override on the electric shut-down valve is being used, turn the button full counterclockwise to stop the engine.
CAUTION: Never leave the switch key or the override button in the valve open or run position when the engine is not running. With overhead tanks, this would allow fuel to drain into the cylinder, causing hydraulic lock.

8. According to the above paragraph, it becomes apparent that if an engine does not stop when the electric shut-down valve switch key is shut off,
   A. an open manual switch is present
   B. the override button is locked in the closed position
   C. a closed manual switch is functioning
   D. the override button is locked in the open position

9. When using an engine equipped with an electric shut-down valve,
   A. no alternate method is available
   B. a manual method is not present
   C. a manual override can shut the engine down
   D. a manual override will not work

10. As a matter of caution, the switch key in the closed position or the override button in the stop position will
    A. assist in keeping fuel in the cylinders
    B. prevent fuel from flooding the cylinder cavities
    C. assist in producing hydraulic lock
    D. aid fuel dilution

Questions 11-12.

DIRECTIONS: Questions 11 and 12 are to be answered according to the information given in the following paragraph.

You have been instructed to expedite the fabrication of four special salt spreader trucks using chassis that are available in the shop. All four trucks must be delivered before the opening of business on December 1. Based on workload and available hours, the foreman of the body shop indicates that he could manufacture one complete salt spreader body in five weeks, with one additional week required for mounting and securing each body to the available chassis. No work could begin on the body until the engines and hydraulic component, which would have to be purchased, were available for use. The Purchasing Department has promised delivery of engines and hydraulic components three months after the order is placed. (Assume that all months have four weeks, and the same crew is doing the assembling and manufacturing.)

11. With reference to the above paragraph, assuming that the Purchasing Department placed the order at the beginning of the first week in February and ultimate delivery of the engines and components was delayed by six weeks, the date of completion of the first salt spreader truck would be CLOSEST to the end of the _____ week in _____. 11._____
    A. fourth; July
    B. second; August
    C. fourth; August
    D. first; September

12. With reference to the above paragraph, the LATEST date that the engines and associated hydraulic components could be requisitioned in order to meet the specified deadline would be CLOSEST to the beginning of the _____ week in _____. 12._____
    A. first; February
    B. first; March
    C. third; March
    D. first; April

Questions 13-20.

DIRECTIONS: Questions 13 through 20 are based on the paragraph on JACKS shown below. When answering these questions, refer to this paragraph.

JACKS

When using a jack, a workman should check the capacity plate or other markings on the jack to make sure the device is heavy enough to support the load. Where there is no plate, capacity should be determined and painted on the side of the jack. The workman should see that jacks are well lubricated, but only at points where lubrication is specified, and should inspect them for broken teeth or faulty holding fixtures. A jack should never be thrown or dropped upon the floor; such treatment may crack or distort the metal, thus causing the jack to break when a load is lifted. It is important that the floor or ground surface upon which the jack is placed be level and clean, and the safe limit of floor loading is not exceeded. If the surface is earth, the jack base should be set on heavy wood blocking, preferably hardwood, of sufficient size that the blocking will not turn over, shift, or sink. If the surface is not perfectly level, the jack may be set on blocking, which should be leveled by wedges securely placed so that they cannot be brushed or forced out of place. Extenders of wood or metal, intended to provide a higher rise where a jack cannot reach up to load or lift it high enough, should never be used. Instead, a larger jack should be obtained or higher blocking which is correspondingly wider and longer should be placed under the jack. All lifts should be vertical with the jack correctly centered for the lift. The base of the jack should be on a perfectly level surface, and the jack head, with its hardwood shim, should bear against a perfectly level meeting surface.

13. To make sure the jack is heavy enough to support a certain load, the workman should
    A. lubricate the jack
    B. shim the jack
    C. check the capacity plate
    D. use a long handle

14. A jack should be lubricated
    A. after using
    B. before painting
    C. only at specified points
    D. to prevent slipping

15. The workman should inspect a jack for
    A. manufacturer's name
    B. broken teeth
    C. paint peeling
    D. broken wedges

16. Metal parts on a jack may crack if
    A. the jack is thrown on the floor
    B. the load is leveled
    C. blocking is used
    D. the handle is too short

17. It would not be a safe practice for a workman to
    A. center the jack under the load
    B. set the jack on a level surface
    C. use hardwood for blocking
    D. use extenders to reach up to the load

18. Wedges may safely be used to
    A. replace a broken tooth
    B. prevent the overloading of a jack
    C. level the blocking under a jack
    D. straighten distorted metal

19. Blocking should be
    A. made of a soft wood
    B. placed between the jack base and the earth surface
    C. well lubricated
    D. used to repair a broken tooth

20. A hardwood shim should be used
    A. between the head and its meeting surface
    B. under the jack
    C. as a filler
    D. to level a surface

Questions 21-22.

DIRECTIONS: Questions 21 and 22 are to be answered ONLY on the basis of the information contained in the following paragraph.

Many experiments have been made on the effects of alcoholic beverages. These studies show that alcohol decreases alertness and efficiency. It decreases self-consciousness and, at the same time, increases confidence and feelings of ease and relaxation. It impairs attention and judgment. It destroys fear of consequences. Usual cautions are thrown to the winds. Habit systems become disorganized. The driver who uses alcohol tends to disregard his usual safety practices. He may not even be aware that he is disregarding them. His reaction time slows down; normally quick reactions are not possible for him. To make matters worse, he may not realize he is slower. His eye muscles may be so affected that his vision is not normal. He cannot correctly judge the speed of his car or of any other car. He cannot correctly estimate distances being covered by each. He becomes a highway menace.

21. The paragraph states that the drinking of alcohol makes a driver   21.____
    A. *more* alert   B. *less* confident
    C. *more* efficient   D. *less* attentive

22. From the above paragraph, it is reasonable to assume that a driver may   22.____
    overcome the bad effects of drinking alcohol by
    A. being more cautious
    B. relying on his good driving habits to a greater extent than normally
    C. watching the road more carefully
    D. waiting for the alcohol to wear off before drinking

Questions 23-25.

DIRECTIONS: Each question consists of a statement. You are to indicate whether the statement is TRUE (T) or FALSE (F). PRINT THE LETTER OF THE CORRECT ANSWER IN THE SPACE AT THE RIGHT.

When in use, the storage battery becomes hot, and water evaporate from the cells of the battery, so clean water preferably distilled, must be added at frequent intervals. This action keeps the level of the battery liquid above the top of the battery plates.

23. All water loss from a storage battery occurs when the battery is in use.   23.____

24. The water added to a storage battery does not have to be distilled.   24.____

25. Water in the storage battery must be kept level with the top of the battery   25.____
    plates.

KEY (CORRECT ANSWERS)

1.	D	11.	A
2.	A	12.	B
3.	C	13.	C
4.	A	14.	C
5.	A	15.	B
6.	B	16.	A
7.	B	17.	D
8.	D	18.	C
9.	C	19.	B
10.	B	20.	A

21. D
22. F
23. F
24. T
25. F

TEST 2

DIRECTIONS: Each question or incomplete statement is followed by several suggested answers or completions. Select the one that BEST answers the question or completes the statement. *PRINT THE LETTER OF THE CORRECT ANSWER IN THE SPACE AT THE RIGHT.*

Questions 1-2.

DIRECTIONS: Questions 1 and 2 are based on the following paragraph

    Because electric drills run at high speed, the cutting edges of a twist drill are heated quickly. If the metal is thick, the drill point must be withdrawn from the hole frequently to cool it and clear out chips. Forcing the drill continuously into a deep hole will heat it, thereby spoiling its temper and cutting edges. A portable electric drill has the advantage that it can be taken to the work and used to drill holes in material too large to handle in a drill press.

1. According to the above paragraph, overheating of a twist drill will
    A. slow down the work   B. cause excessive drill breakage
    C. dull the drill   D. spoil the accuracy of the work

1.____

2. According to the above paragraph, one method of preventing overheating of a twist drill is to
    A. use cooling oil
    B. drill a smaller pilot hole first
    C. use a drill press
    D. remove the drill from the work frequently

2.____

Questions 3-5.

DIRECTIONS: Questions 3 through 5, inclusive, are to be answered in accordance with the paragraph below.

    A steam heating system with steam having a pressure of less than 10 pounds is called a low-pressure system. The majority of steam-heating systems are of this type. The steam may be provided by low-pressure boilers installed *expressly* for the purpose, or it may be generated in boiler at a higher pressure and reduced in pressure before admitted to the heating mains. In other instances, it may be possible to use exhaust steam which has been made to run engines and other machines and which still contains enough heat to be utilized in the heating system. The first case represents the system of heating used in the ordinary residence or other small building; the other two represent the systems of heating employed in industrial buildings where a power plant is installed for general power purposes.

3. According to the above paragraph, whether or not a steam heating system is considered a low pressure system is determined by the pressure
    A. generated by the boiler
    B. in the heating main
    C. at the inlet side of the reducing valve
    D. of the exhaust

3.____

4. According to the above paragraph, steam used for heating is sometimes obtained from steam
   A. generated principally to operate machinery
   B. exhausted from larger boilers
   C. generated at low pressure and brought up to high pressure before being used
   D. generated by engines other than boilers

5. As used in the above paragraph, the word *expressly* means
   A. rapidly   B. specifically   C. usually   D. mainly

Questions 6-7.

DIRECTIONS: Questions 6 and 7 are to be answered in accordance with the following paragraph.

When one is making the selection of grinding wheel specifications, the first variable factor to consider is the wheel speed, which influences the grade and the bond of the wheel. It is recommended that the grade should be determined in this way: the higher the wheel speed with relation to work speed, the softer the wheel should be. When, for any reason, the wheel speed is reduced, then it may be expected that the wheel will wear faster, but this can be overcome by choosing a wheel of a harder grade, assuming that the grade was correct for the initial speed.

6. It can be said that the MOST important piece of information in the above paragraph is:
   A. The higher the relative wheel speed, the softer should be the wheel
   B. Wheel speed is a variable factor
   C. At low speeds wheels wear rapidly
   D. When a wheel slows down, it should be replaced by a harder grade

7. According to the above paragraph, no indication is made that
   A. there are other factor too be considered beside speed
   B. hard wheels at low speed wear faster than soft wheels at high speed
   C. the lower the speed, the harder should be the grade
   D. the selection of the bond of the wheel is affected by speed

Questions 8-9.

DIRECTIONS: Questions 8 and 9 are to be answered ONLY according to the information in the following paragraph.

Metal spraying is used for many purposes. Worn bearings on shafts and spindles can be readily restored to original dimensions with any desired metal or alloy. Low-carbon steel shafts may be supplied with high-carbon steel journal surfaces, which can then be ground to size after spraying. By using babbitt wire, bearings can be lined or babbitted while rotating. Pump shafts and impellers can be coated with any desired metal to overcome wear and corrosion. Valve seats may be re-surfaced. Defective castings can be repaired by filling in blow-holes and checks. The application of metal spraying to the field of corrosion resistance is growing, although the major application in this field is in the use of sprayed zinc. Tin, lead, and aluminum have been used considerably. The process is used for structural and tank applications in the field as well as in the shop.

8. According to the above paragraph, worn bearing surfaces on shafts are metal-sprayed in order to
   A. prevent corrosion of the shaft
   B. fit them into larger-sized impellers
   C. return them to their original sizes
   D. replace worn babbitt metal

8._____

9. According to the above paragraph, rotating bearings can be metal-sprayed using
   A. babbitt wire
   B. high-carbon steel
   C. low-carbon steel
   D. any desired metal

9._____

Questions 10-11.

DIRECTIONS: Questions 10 and 11 are to be answered ONLY according to the information in the following paragraph.

The wheels used for internal grinding should general be softer than those used for other grinding operations because the contact area between the wheel and work is comparatively large. A soft wheel that will cut with little pressure should be used to prevent springing the spindle. The grade of the wheel depends upon the character of the work and the stiffness of the machine; and where a large variety of work is being ground, it may not be practicable to have an assortment of wheels adapted to all conditions. By adjusting the speed, however, a wheel not exactly suited to the work in hand can often be used. If the wheel wears too rapidly, it should be run faster; and if it tends to glaze, the speed should be diminished.

10. On the basis of the above passage only, it may BEST be said that
    A. the type and grade of wheel are independent of the sturdiness of the machine
    B. by increasing the wheel speed, parts can easily be internally ground
    C. wheels used for outside grinding usually have a smaller contact area between the wheel and work
    D. to carry on hand an assortment of wheels for all conceivable internal grinding jobs is economical

10._____

11. On the basis of the above passage only, it may BEST be said that
    A in general, if a wheel wears too rapidly, the speed should be decreased
    B. by decreasing the wheel speed, a wheel not quite appropriate for the job may sometimes be used
    C. where a large variety of work is being ground, the grade of wheel depends on the diameter of the wheel
    D. if a wheel tends to glaze, it should run faster

11._____

Questions 12-15.

DIRECTIONS: Questions 12 through 15, inclusive, are to be answered ONLY in accordance with the following paragraph.

Cylindrical surfaces are the most common form of finished surface found on machine parts, although flat surfaces are also very common; hence, many metal-cutting *processes* are for the purpose of producing either cylindrical or flat surfaces. The machines used for cylindrical or flat shapes may be, and often are, utilized also for forming the various irregular or special shapes required on many machine parts. Because of the prevalence of cylindrical and flat surfaces, the student of manufacturing practice should learn first about the machines and methods employed to produce these surfaces. The cylindrical surfaces may be internal as in holes and cylinders. Any one part may, of course, have cylindrical sections of different diameters and lengths and include flat end or shoulders; and frequently there is a threaded part or possibly some finished surface that is not circular in cross-section. The prevalence of cylindrical surfaces on machine parts explains why lathes are found in all machine shops. It is important to understand the various uses of the lathe because many of the operations are the same fundamentally as those performed on other types of machine tools.

12. According to the above paragraph, the MOST common form of finished surfaces found on machine parts is
    A. cylindrical   B. elliptical   C. flat   D square

13. According to the above paragraph, any one part of cylindrical surface may have
    A. chases   B. shoulders   C. keyways   D. splines

14. According to the above paragraph, lathes are found in all machine shops because cylindrical surfaces on machine parts are
    A. scarce   B. internal   C. common   D. external

15. As used in the above paragraph, the work *processes* means
    A. operations   B. purposes   C. devices   D. tools

Questions 16-17.

DIRECTIONS: Questions 16 and 17 are to be answered ONLY in accordance with the following paragraph.

The principle of interchangeability requires manufacture to such specification that component parts of a device may be selected at random and assembled to fit and operate satisfactorily. Interchangeable manufacture, therefore, requires that parts be made to definite limits of error and to fit gages instead of mating parts. Interchangeability does not necessarily involve a high degree of precision; stove lids, for example, are interchangeable but are not particularly accurate, and carriage bolts and nuts are not precision products but are completely interchangeable. Interchangeability may be employed in unit production as well as mass production systems of manufacture.

16. According to the above paragraph, in order for parts to be interchangeable, they must be
    A. precision-machined
    B. selectively-assembled
    C. mass-produced
    D. made to fit gages

17. According to the above paragraph, carriage bolts are interchangeable because they are
    A. precision-made
    B. sized to specific tolerances
    C. individually matched products
    D. produced in small units

Questions 18-22.

DIRECTIONS: Questions 18 through 22 are to be answered in accordance with the following passage.

TITANIC AIR COMPRESSOR

Valves: The compressors are equipped with Titanic plate valves which are automatic in operation. Valves are so constructed that an entire valve assembly can readily be removed from the head. The valves provide large port area with short lift and are accurately guided to insure positive seating.

Starting Unloader: Each compressor (or air end) is equipped with a centrifugal governor which is bolted directly to the compressor crankshaft. The governor actuates cylinder relief valves so as to relieve pressure from the cylinders during starting and stopping. The motor is never required to start the compressor under load.

Air Strainer: Each cylinder air inlet connection is fitted with a suitable combination air strainer and muffler.

Pistons: Pistons are lightweight castings, ribbed internally to secure strength, and are accurately turned and ground. Each piston is fitted with four (4) rings, two of which are oil control rings. Piston pins are hardened and tempered steel of the full floating type. Bronze bushings are used between piston pin and piston.

Connecting Rods: Connecting rods are of solid bronze designed for maximum strength, rigidity, and wear. Crank pins are fitted with renewable steel bushings. Connecting rods are of the one-piece type, there being no bolts, nuts, or cotter pins which can come loose. With this type of construction, wear is reduced to a negligible amount, and adjustment of wrist pin and crank pin bearings is unnecessary.

Main Bearings: Main bearings are of the ball type and are securely held in position by spacers. This type of bearing entirely eliminates the necessity of frequent adjustment or attention. The crankshaft is always in perfect alignment.

Crankshaft: The crankshaft is a one-piece heat-treated forging of best quality open-hearth steel, of rugged design, and of sufficient size to transmit the motor power and any additional stresses which may occur in service. Each crankshaft is counter-balanced (dynamically balanced) to reduce vibration to a minimum, and is accurately machined to properly receive the ball bearing races, crank pin bushing, flexible coupling, and centrifugal governor. Suitable provision is made to insure proper lubrication of all crankshaft bearings and bushings with the minimum amount of attention.

Coupling: Compressor and motor shafts are connected through a Morse Chain Company all-metal enclosed flexible coupling. This coupling consists of two sprockets, one mounted on, and keyed to, each shaft; the sprockets are wrapped by a single Morse Chain, the entire assembly being enclosed in a split aluminum grease packed cover.

18. The crank pin of the connecting rod is fitted with a renewable bushing made of
    A. solid bronze
    B. steel
    C. slight-weight casting
    D. ball bearings

19. When the connecting rod is of the one-piece type,
    A. the wrist pins require frequent adjustment
    B. the crank pins require frequent adjustment
    C. the cotter pins frequently will come loose
    D. wear is reduced to a negligible amount

20. The centrifugal governor is bolted DIRECTLY to the
    A. compressor crankshaft
    B. main bearing
    C. piston pin
    D. muffler

21. The number of oil control rings required for each piston is
    A. one
    B. two
    C. three
    D. four

22. The compressor and motor shafts are connected through a flexible coupling. These couplings are _____ to the shafts.
    A. keyed
    B. brazed
    C. soldered
    D. press fit

Questions 23-25.

DIRECTIONS: Questions 23 through 25, inclusive, are to be answered in accordance with the following paragraph.

Wherever a soil pipe has to be provided for in a partition, special care must be taken that the hubs do not project beyond the finish face of the plaster. Before framing a building, it is desirable to ascertain where the stacks are and to provide for them. Building regulations require the stacks to be of 4-inch cast-iron even in small dwellings. With a 4-inch stack, the hub is 6 1/8 inches in diameter; and, therefore, 2 by 6 studs must be used. Special care should be taken that no plaster comes in contact with a soil pipe for *subsequent* settlement may cause cracking.

23. As used in the above paragraph, *subsequent* means MOST NEARLY
    A. heavy
    B. sudden
    C. later
    D. soon

24. According to the above paragraph, 4" cast-iron soil pipes are used because
    A. they will not project beyond the face of the plaster
    B. it is easier to plaster over 4" pipe
    C. they can be located easier
    D. they are required by law

25. According to the above paragraph, the reason plaster should NOT be in direct contact with soil pipe is because
    A. the plaster would be damaged by moisture
    B. rust will bleed through the plaster
    C. of the possibility of cracks due to settlement
    D. it is harder to plaster over 4" pipe

KEY (CORRECT ANSWERS)

1.	C	11.	B
2.	D	12.	A
3.	B	13.	B
4.	A	14.	C
5.	B	15.	A
6.	A	16.	D
7.	B	17.	B
8.	C	18.	B
9.	A	19.	D
10.	C	20.	A

21. B
22. A
23. C
24. D
25. C

DIESEL ENGINES
TROUBLE SHOOTING

CONTENTS

		Page
I.	THE TROUBLESHOOTER	1
II.	TROUBLESHOOTING DIESEL ENGINES	2
III.	ENGINE FAILS TO START	2
IV.	AIR STARTING SYSTEM MALFUNCTIONS	3
V.	ELECTRIC START MALFUNCTIONS	5
VI.	MALFUNCTIONING OF THE INJECTION SYSTEM	8
VII.	IRREGULAR ENGINE OPERATION	9
VIII.	SYMPTOMS OF ENGINE TROUBLE	20

DIESEL ENGINES
TROUBLESHOOTING

Anyone who has had experience analyzing troubles in gasoline engines, such as automobile engines, will find similarities between the procedures he has used and those described in this chapter. The mechanical similarity between gasoline and diesel engines dictates that many of their problems will be shared. The principal differences are the result of the diesel engine's greater size, fuel injection, use of superchargers, and application to a marine environment.

In this chapter we shall be concerned with troubles encountered in starting an engine and with troubles encountered after an engine is started. The troubles listed are chiefly of the kind that can be corrected without major overhaul or repair, and troubles that can be identified by erratic operation of the engine, by warnings given by the instruments, or by inspection of the engine parts and systems.

Keep in mind that the troubles we listed are general and may, or may not, apply to a particular diesel engine. When working with a specific engine, check the manufacturer's technical manual.

I. THE TROUBLESHOOTER

Complete failure of a power plant at a crucial moment may imperil all personnel. Even comparatively minor engine trouble, if not recognized and corrected as soon as possible, may develop into a major breakdown. Therefore, it is essential that every operator of an internal-combustion engine train himself to be a successful troubleshooter.

It may happen that an engine will continue to operate even when a serious casualty is imminent. However, if troubles are impending, there will probably be symptoms present, and the success of a troubleshooter depends partially upon his ability to recognize these symptoms when they occur. The good operator uses most of his senses to detect trouble symptoms. He may see, hear, smell, or feel the warning of trouble to come. Of course, common sense is also a requisite. Another factor upon which the success of a troubleshooter depends is his ability to locate the trouble after once deciding something is wrong with the equipment. Then he must be able to determine as rapidly as possible what corrective action must be taken. In learning to recognize and locate engine troubles, experience is the best teacher.

Instruments play an important part in the detection of engine troubles. The engine operator should read the instruments and record their indications regularly. If the recorded indications vary radically from those specified by engine operating instructions, it is a warning that the engine is not operating properly and that some type of corrective action must be taken. Familiarity with the specifications given in engine operating instructions is essential, especially those pertaining to temperatures, pressures and speeds. When instrument indications vary considerably from the specified values, the operator should know the probable effect on the engine. When variations occur in instrument indications, before taking any corrective action the operator should be sure that such variations are not the fault of the instrument. Instruments should be checked immediately when they are suspected of being inaccurate.

Periodic inspections are also essential in detecting engine troubles. Failure of visible parts, presence of smoke, or leakage of oil, fuel, or water can be discovered by such inspections. Cleanliness is probably one of the greatest aids in the detection of leakage.

When an engine is secured because of trouble, the procedure for repairing the casualty follows an established pattern, if the trouble has been diagnosed. If the location of the trouble is not known, it must be found. To inspect every part of an engine whenever a trouble occurs would be an almost endless task. The cause of a trouble can be found much more quickly if a systematic and logical method of inspection is followed. Generally speaking, a well-trained troubleshooter can isolate a trouble by identifying it with one of the engine systems. Once the trouble has been associated with a particular system, the next step is to trace out the system until you find the cause of the trouble. Troubles generally originate in only one system, but remember that troubles in one system may cause damage to another system or to component engine parts. When a casualty involves more than one system of the engine, trace each system separately and make corrections as necessary. It is obvious that you must know the construction, function, and operation of the various systems as well as the parts of each system for a specific engine before you can satisfactorily locate and remedy troubles.

Even though there are many troubles which may affect the operation of a diesel engine, satisfactory performance depends primarily on the presence of sufficiently high compression pressure and the injection of the right amount of fuel at the proper time. Proper compression depends basically on the pistons, piston rings, and valve gear, while the right amount of fuel obviously depends on the fuel injectors and actuating mechanism. Such troubles as lack of engine power, unusual or erratic operation, and excessive vibration may be caused by either insufficient compression or faulty injector action.

II. TROUBLESHOOTING DIESEL ENGINES

Many of the troubles encountered by an engine operator can be avoided if the prescribed instructions for starting and operating an engine are followed. The lists of troubles which follow cannot be considered complete, and all of these troubles do not necessarily apply to all diesel engines because of differences in design. Specific information on troubleshooting for all the diesel engines used would require more space than is available here.

Even though a successful troubleshooter generally associates a trouble with a particular system or assembly, the troubles we discuss will be according to when they might be encountered, either before or after the engine starts. The troubles are indicative of the system to which they apply. Therefore, further identification is unnecessary.

III. ENGINE FAILS TO START

In general, the troubles which prevent an engine's starting may be grouped under the following headings: (1) the engine can neither be cranked nor barred over, (2) the engine cannot be cranked, but it can be barred over, and (3) the engine can be cranked, but it still fails to start. Figure 1 illustrates various conditions which commonly cause difficulties in cranking, jacking over, or starting the engine.

Engine Cannot Be Cranked Nor Barred Over

Most prestarting instructions for large engines specify that the crankshaft of an engine should be turned one or more revolutions before starting power is applied. If the crankshaft cannot be turned over, check the turning gear to be sure that it is properly engaged. If the turning gear is properly engaged and the crankshaft still fails to turn over, check to see whether the cylinder test (relief) valves or indicator valves are closed and are holding water or oil in the cylinder. When the turning gear operates properly, and the cylinder test valves are open, but the engine nevertheless cannot be cranked or barred over, the source of the trouble will probably be of a much more serious nature. A piston or other part may be seized or a bearing may be fitting too tightly. Sometimes the difficulty cannot be remedied except by removing a part or an assembly.

Some engines have ports through which pistons can be inspected. If inspection reveals that the piston is defective, the assembly must be removed. Figure 2 illus-

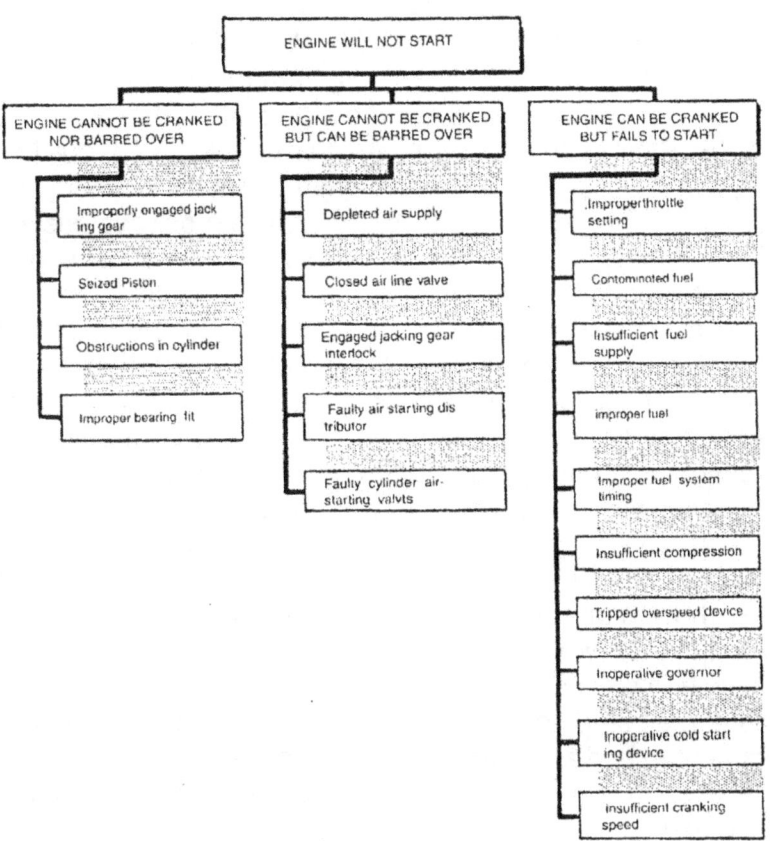

Figure 1.—Troubles which may prevent a diesel engine's starting.

trates testing for stuck piston rings through the scavenging-air distributor manifold port.

If the condition of an engine without cylinder ports indicates that a piston inspection is required, the whole assembly must be taken out of the cylinder.

Engine bearings have to be carefully fitted or installed according to the manufacturer's instructions. When an engine cannot be jacked over because of an improperly fitted bearing, someone probably failed to follow instructions when the unit was being reassembled.

Engine Cannot Be Cranked But Can Be Barred Over

Most of the troubles that prevent the cranking of an engine, but not serious enough to prevent barring over, can be traced to the starting system although other factors may prevent an engine's cranking. Only troubles related to starting systems are identified in this chapter.

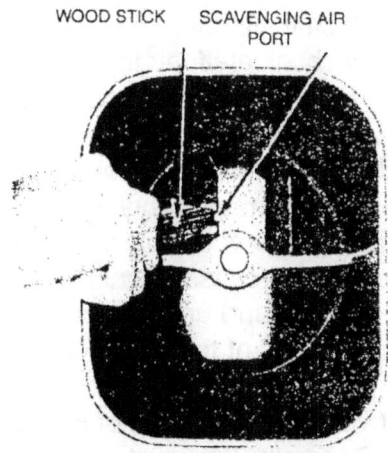

Figure 2.—Checking the condition of the piston rings.

If an engine fails to crank when starting power is applied, first check the turning or jacking gear to be sure that it is disengaged. If this gear is not the source of trouble, then the trouble is probably with the starting system.

IV. AIR STARTING SYSTEM MALFUNCTIONS

Although the design of different air starting systems varies, the function remains the same. In general, such systems must have a source of air such as the compressor or the air system; a storage tank; air flask(s); an air timing mechanism; and a valve in the engine cylinder to admit the air during starting and to seal the cylinder while the engine is running.

DEFECT IN TIMING MECHANISM.- All air starting systems have a unit designed to admit starting air to the proper cylinder at the proper time. The type of unit as well as its name—timer, distributor, air starting pilot valve, air starting distributor, and air distributor—may vary from one system to another. The types of air timing mechanisms which may be encountered are the direct mechanical lift, the rotary distributor, and the plunger type distributor valve. The timing mechanism of an air starting system is relatively trouble free except as noted in the following situations.

Direct Mechanical Lift.-The operation of the direct mechanical-lift air timing mechanism involves the use of cams, push rods, and rocker arms, and the mechanism is subject to parts' failures similar to those occurring in corresponding major engine parts. Therefore, the causes of trouble in the actuating gear and the necessary maintenance procedures will be found under information covering similar parts of the major engine systems.

Most troubles are a result of improper adjustment. Generally, this involves the lift of the starting air cam or the timing of the air starting valve. The starting air cam must lift the air starting valve sufficiently to give a proper clearance between the cam and cam valve follower when the engine is running. If proper clearance does not exist between these two parts, hot gases will flow between the valve and the valve seat, causing excessive heating of the parts. Since the starting air cam regulates the opening of the air starting valve, those with adjustable cam lobes should be checked frequently to ensure that the adjusting screws are tight.

The proper values for lift, tappet clearance, and time of valve opening for a direct mechanical lift timing mechanism should be obtained from the manufacturer's technical manual for the particular engine. Make adjustments only as specified.

Rotary Distributor.-The rotary distributor timing mechanism requires a minimum of maintenance, but there may be times when the unit will become inoperative and will have to be disassembled and inspected. Generally, the difficulty is caused by a scored rotor, a broken spring, or improper timing.

Since foreign particles in the air can cause scoring of the rotor, which results in excessive air leakage, the air supply must be kept as clean as possible. Another cause of scoring is lack of lubrication. If the rotor in a hand-oiled system becomes scored because of insufficient lubrication, the equipment could be at fault, or lubrication instructions may not have been followed. In either a hand-oiled or a pressure-lubricated system, check the piping and the passages to see that they are open. When scoring is not too serious, the rotor and body should be lapped together. A thin coat of Prussian blue can be used to determine whether the rotor contacts the distributor body.

A broken spring may be the cause of an inoperative timing mechanism if a coil spring is used to maintain the rotor seal. If the spring is broken, replacing the spring is the only way to ensure an effective seal.

An improperly timed rotary distributor will prevent an engine's cranking. Timing should be checked against information given in the instructions for the specific engine.

Plunger Type Distributor Valve.-In a plunger type distributor valve timing mechanism, the valve requires little attention; however, it may stick occasionally and prevent proper functioning of the air starting system. On some engine installations, the pilot air valve of the distributor may not open, while on other installations this valve may not close. The trouble may be caused by dirt and gum deposits, broken return springs, or the lack of lubrication. Deposits and lack of lubrication will cause the unit valve plungers to bind and stick in the guides, while a broken valve return spring prevents the plunger's following the cam profile. A distributor valve that sticks should be disassembled and thoroughly cleaned; any broken springs must be replaced.

FAULTY AIR STARTING VALVES.-Air starting valves admit starting air into the engine cylinder and then seal the cylinder while the engine is running. These valves may be of the pressure-actuated or of the mechanical lift type.

Pressure-Actuated Valves.-In a pressure-actuated valve, the principal' trouble encountered is sticking. The valve may stick open for a number of reasons. A gummy or resinous deposit may cause the upper and lower pistons to stick to the cylinders. (This deposit is formed by the oil and condensate which may be carried into the actuating cylinders and lower cylinders. Oil is necessary in the cylinders to provide lubrication and to act as a seal; however, moisture should be eliminated.) The formation of this resinous deposit can be prevented by draining the system storage tanks and water traps as specified in operating instruction. The deposit on the lower piston may be greater than that in the actuating cylinder because of the heat and combustion gases which add to the formation if the valve remains open. When the upper piston is the source of trouble, sticking can usually be relieved, without removing the valve, by using light oil or diesel fuel and working the valve up and down. When this method is used to relieve a sticking valve, be sure that the valve surfaces are not burned or deformed. If this method does not relieve the sticking condition, the valve will have to be removed, disassembled, and cleaned.

Pressure-actuated starting valves sometimes fail to operate because of broken or weak valve return springs. Replacement is generally the only solution to this condition; however, some valves are constructed with a means of adjusting spring tension. In such valves increasing the spring tension may eliminate the trouble.

Occasionally the actuating pressure of a valve will not release, and the valve will stick open or be sluggish in closing. The cause is usually clogged or restricted air passages. Combustion gases will enter the air passageways, burning the valve surfaces; these burned surfaces usually have to be reconditioned before they will maintain a tight seal. Keeping the air passages open will eliminate extra maintenance work on the valve surfaces.

Mechanical Lift Valves. The mechanical-lift type air starting valve is subject to leakage which, in general, is caused by the valve's sticking open. Any air starting valve that sticks or leaks creates a condition which makes an engine hard to start. If the leakage in the air starting valve is excessive, the resulting loss in pressure may be sufficient to prevent starting.

Leakage in this type valve can be caused by an over-tightened packing nut. Over-tightening the packing nut is sometimes employed to stop minor leaks around the valve stem when starting pressure is applied, but it may prevent seating of the air valve. As in the pressure-actuated valve, return spring tension may be insufficient to return the valve to the valve seat after admitting the air charge. If this occurs, gases from the cylinder will leak into the valve while the engine is running.

Obstructions such as particles of carbon between the valve and valve seat will hold the valve open, permitting combustion gases to pass. A valve stem bent by careless handling during installation also may prevent a valve's closing properly.

If a valve hangs open for any of these reasons, hot combustion gases will leak past the valve and valve seat. The gases burn the valve and seat and may result in a leak between these two surfaces even though the original causes of the stocking are eliminated.

A leaking valve should be completely disassembled and inspected. It is subject to a resinous deposit similar to that found in a pressure-actuated air valve. A specified cleaning compound should be used for the removal of the deposit. Be sure the valve stem is not bent. Check' the valve and valve seat surfaces carefully. Scoring or discoloration should be eliminated by lapping with a fine lapping compound. Jewelers' rouge or talcum powder with fuel oil may be used for lapping.

From the preceding discussion, you can readily see that the air starting system may be the source of many troubles that will prevent an engine's cranking even though it can be barred over. A few of the troubles can be avoided if prestarting and starting instructions are followed. One such instruction, sometimes overlooked, is that of opening the valve in the air line. Obviously, with this valve closed the engine will not crank. Recheck the instructions for such an oversight as a closed valve, an empty air storage receiver, or an engaged jacking gear before starting any disassembly.

V. ELECTRIC START MALFUNTIONS

Electric starting system malfunctions fall into the following categories:

1. Nothing happens when the starter switch is closed.
2. Starter motor runs but does not engage the engine.
3. Starter motor engages but cannot turn the engine.

The first situation is the result of an electrical system failure. The failure could be an open circuit caused by broken connections or burned out components. Circuit continuity should be tested to ensure that the relay closes and that the battery provides sufficient voltage and current to the starter circuit. If the circuit is complete, there may be resistance through faulty battery connections. Considerable current is needed to operate the solenoid and starter motor.

If the starter runs free of engagement, it will produce a distinctive hum or whine. The lack of engagement is usually caused by dirt or corrosion which prevents proper operation of the solenoid or Bendix gears.

If the starter motor engages the flywheel ring gear but is either not able to turn the engine or cannot turn it quickly enough to obtain starting speed, the cause may be lack of battery power, or more likely, a mechanical problem. If the engine can be barred over, there is excessive friction in the meshing of the starter pinion and the ring gear. Either the teeth are deformed, or the starter pinion is out of alignment. Either case would have been preceded by noise the last time the starter was used. A major repair may be necessary.

Engine Cranks But Fails To Start

Even when the starting equipment is in an operating condition, an engine may fail to start. A majority of the possible troubles which prevent an engine's starting are associated with fuel and the fuel system. However, parts or assemblies which are defective or inoperative may be the source of some trouble. Failure to follow instructions may be the cause of an engine failing to start. The corrective action is obvious for such items as leaving the fuel throttle in the OFF position and leaving the cylinder indicator valves open. If an engine fails to start, follow prescribed starting instructions and recheck the procedure.

FOREIGN MATTER IN THE FUEL OIL SYSTEM.-In the operation of an internal-combustion engine, cleanliness is of paramount importance. This is especially true in the handling and care of diesel fuel oil. Impurities are the prime source of fuel pump and injection system troubles. Sediment and water cause wear, gumming, corrosion, and rust in a fuel system. Even though fuel oil is generally delivered clean from the refinery, handling and transferring increase the chances of fuel oil's becoming contaminated.

Corrosion frequently leads to replacement or at least to repair of the part. Steps should be taken continually to prevent the accumulation of water in a fuel system, not only to eliminate the cause of corrosion but also to ensure proper combustion in the cylinders. All fuel should be centrifuged, and the fuel filter cases should be drained periodically to prevent excessive collection of water.

Water in fuel is injurious to the entire fuel system and will cause irreparable damage in a short time. It not only corrodes the fuel injection pump, where close clearances must be maintained, but also corrodes and erodes the injection nozzles. The slightest corrosion can cause a fuel injection pump to bind and seize and, if not corrected, will lead to excessive leakage. Water will cause the orifices of injection nozzles to erode until they will not spray the fuel properly, thus preventing proper atomization. When this occurs, incomplete combustion and engine knocks result.

Air in the fuel system is another possible trouble which may prevent an engine's starting. Even if starting is possible, air in the fuel system will cause the engine to miss and knock, and perhaps to stall.

When an engine fails to operate, stalls, misfires, or knocks, there may be air in the high-pressure pumps and lines. In many systems, the expansion and compression of such air may take place without the injection valves' opening. If this occurs, the pump is AIRBOUND. You can determine whether air exists in a fuel system by bleeding a small amount of fuel from the top of the fuel filter; if the fuel appears quite cloudy, there are probably small bubbles of air in the fuel.

INSUFFICIENT FUEL SUPPLY.-An insufficient fuel supply may result from any one of a number of defective or inoperative parts in the system. Such items as a closed inlet valve in the fuel piping or an empty supply tank are more apt to be the fault of the operator than of the equipment. But an empty tank may be caused by leakage, either in the lines or in the tank.

Leakage.-Leakage in the low-pressure lines of a fuel system can usually be traced to cracks in the piping; usually these cracks occur on threaded pipe joints at the root of the threads. Such breakage is caused by the inability of the nipples and pipe joints to withstand shock, vibration, and strains resulting from the relative motion between smaller pipes and the equipment to which they are attached.

Metal fatigue can also be a cause of breakage; each system should have a systematic inspection of the installation of fittings and piping to determine whether all parts are satisfactorily supported and sufficiently strong. In some instances, nipples may be connected to relatively heavy parts, such as valves and strainers, which are free to vibrate. Since vibration contributes materially to the fatigue of nipples, rigid bracing should be installed. When practicable, bracing should be secured to the unit itself, instead of to the hull or other equipment.

Leakage in the high-pressure lines of a fuel system also results from breakage. The breakage usually occurs on either of the two end fittings of a line and is caused by lack of proper supports or by excessive nozzle opening pressure. Supports are usually supplied with an engine and should not be discarded. Excessive opening pressure of a nozzle—generally due to improper spring adjustment or to clogged nozzle orifices—may rupture the high-pressure fuel lines. A faulty nozzle generally requires removal, inspection, and repair plus the use of a nozzle tester.

Leakage from fuel lines may be due also to improper replacements or repairs. When a replacement is necessary, always use a line of the same length and diameter as the one removed. Varying the length and diameter of a high-pressure fuel line will change the injection characteristics of the injection nozzle.

In an emergency, high-pressure fuel lines can usually be satisfactorily repaired by silver soldering a new fitting to the line. After making a silver solder repair, test the line for leaks and be certain no restrictions exist.

Most leakage trouble occurs in the fuel lines, but leaks may occasionally develop in the fuel tank. These leaks must be eliminated immediately, because of potential fire hazard.

The principal causes of fuel tank leakage are improper welds and metal fatigue. Metal fatigue is usually the result of inadequate support at the source of trouble; excessive stresses develop in the tank, and cracks result.

Clogged Fuel Filters.-Another factor that can limit the fuel supply to such an extent that an engine will not start is the clogged fuel filters. As soon as it is known that clogging exists, the filter elements should be replaced. Definite rules for such replacement cannot be established for all engines. Instructions generally state that elements will not be used longer than a specified time, and there are reasons that an element may not function properly even for the specified interval.

Filter elements may become clogged because of dirty fuel, too small filter capacity, failure to drain the filter sump, and failure to use the primary strainer. Usually, clogging is indicated by such symptoms as stoppage of fuel flow, increase in pressure drop across the filter, increase in pressure upstream of the filter, or excessive accumulation of dirt on the element (observed when the filter is removed for inspection). Symptoms of clogged filters vary in different installations, and each installation should be studied for external symptoms, such as abnormal instrument indications and engine operation. If external indications are not apparent, visual inspection of the element will be necessary, especially if it is known or suspected that dirty fuel is being used.

Fuel filter capacity should at least equal fuel supply pump capacity. A filter with a small capacity clogs more rapidly than a larger one, because the space available for dirt accumulation is more limited. There are two standardized sizes of fuel filter elements-large and small. The small element is the same diameter as the large but is only one-half as long. This construction permits substitution of two small elements for one large element.

The interval of time between element changes can be increased by making use of the drain cocks on a filter sump; removal of dirt through the drain cock will make room for more dirt to collect.

If new filter elements are not available for replacement and the engine must be operated, you can wash some types of totally clogged elements and get limited additional service. This procedure is for emergencies only. An engine must never be operated unless all the fuel is filtered, therefore a "washed filter" is better than none at all.

Fuel must never flow from the supply tanks to the nozzles without passing through all stages of filtration. Strainers, as the primary stage in the fuel filtration system, must be kept in good condition if sufficient fuel is to flow in the system. Most strainers are equipped with a blade mechanism which is designed to be turned by hand. If the scraper element cannot be turned readily by hand, the strainer should be disassembled and cleaned. This minor preventive maintenance will prevent breakage of the scraping mechanism.

Transfer Pumps.-If the supply of fuel oil to the system is to be maintained in an even and uninterrupted flow, the fuel transfer pumps must be functioning properly. These pumps may become inoperative or defective to the point that they fail to discharge sufficient fuel for engine starting. Generally, when a pump fails to operate, some parts have to be replaced or reconditioned. For some types of pump, it is customary to replace the entire unit. However, for worn packing or seals, satisfactory repairs may be made. If plunger-type pumps fail to operate because the valves have become dirty, submerge and clean the pump in a bath of diesel oil.

Repairs of fuel transfer pumps should be made in accordance with maintenance manuals supplied by the individual pump manufacturers.

VI. MALFUNCTIONING OF THE INJECTION SYSTEM.

The fuel injection system is the most intricate of the systems in a diesel engine, and the troubles which may occur depend on the system in use. Since an injection system functions to deliver fuel to the cylinder at a high pressure, at the proper time, in the proper quantities, and properly atomized, it is evident that special care and precautions must be taken in making adjustments and repairs.

High-Pressure Pump.-If a high-pressure pump in a fuel injection system becomes inoperative, an engine may fail to start. Information on the troubles which make a pump inoperative, and the information necessary for overcoming such troubles, is more than can be given in the space available here.

Timing.-Regardless of the installation or the type of fuel injection system used, maximum energy obtainable from fuel cannot be gained if the timing of the injection system is incorrect. Early or late injection timing may prevent an engine's starting. If the engine does start, it will not perform satisfactorily. Operation will be uneven and vibration will be greater than usual.

If fuel enters a cylinder too early, detonation generally results, causing the gas pressure to rise too rapidly before the piston reaches top dead center. This in turn causes a loss of power and high combustion pressures. Low exhaust temperatures may be an indication that fuel injection is too early.

When fuel is injected too late in the engine cycle, overheating, lowered firing pressure, smoky exhaust, high exhaust temperatures, or loss of power may occur.

Correction of an improperly timed injection system should be accomplished by following the instructions given in the appropriate manufacturer's technical manual.

INSUFFICIENT COMPSION.-Proper compression pressures are essential if a diesel engine is to operate satisfactorily. Insufficient compression may be the reason that an engine fails to start. If low pressure is suspected as the reason, compression should be checked with the appropriate instrument. If the test indicates pressures below standard, disassembly is required for complete inspection and correction.

INOPERATIVE ENGINE GOVERNOR.-There are many troubles which may render a governor inoperative, but those encountered in starting an engine are generally caused by bound control linkage or, if the governor is hydraulic, by low oil level. Whether the-governor is mechanical or hydraulic, binding of linkage is generally due to distorted, misaligned, defective, or dirty parts. If binding is suspected, linkage and governor parts should be moved and checked by hand. Any undue stiffness or sluggishness in the movement of the linkage should be eliminated.

Low oil level in hydraulic governors may be due to leakage of oil from the governor, or to failure to maintain the proper oil level. Leakage of oil from a governor can generally be traced to a faulty oil seal on the drive shaft or power piston rod, or to a poor gasket seal between parts of the governor case.

The condition of oil seals should be checked if oil must be added too frequently to governors with independent oil supplies. Dependent on the point of leakage, oil seal leakage may or may not be visible on external surfaces. There will be no external sign if leakage occurs through the seal around the drive shaft, while leakage through the seal around the power piston will be visible.

Oil seals must be kept clean and pliable; therefore, the seals must be properly stored so that they do not become dry and brittle, or dirty. The repair of leaky oil seals requires a replacement. Some of the leakage troubles can be prevented if proper installation and storage instructions for oil seals are followed.

INOPERATIVE OVERSPEED SAFETY DEVICES.-Overspeed safety devices are designed to shut off fuel or air in the event engine speed becomes excessive. It is imperative that these devices be maintained in operable condition at all times. Inoperative overspeed devices may cause an engine not to start. They may be inoperative because of improper adjustment, faulty linkage, a broken spring, or the overspeed device may have been accidentally tripped during the attempt to start the engine. The overspeed device must always be put in an operative condition before the engine is operated.

If the overspeed device fails to operate when the engine overspeeds, the engine may be secured by manually cutting off the fuel oil or the air supply to the engine. Most engines are equipped with special devices or valves to cut off the air or fuel in an emergency.

INSUFFICIENT CRANKING SPEED.- If the engine cranks slowly, the necessary compression temperature cannot be reached. Low starting air pressure may be the source of such trouble.

Slow cranking speed may also be the result of an increase in the viscosity of the lubricating oil. This trouble is encountered during periods when the air temperature is lower than usual. The oil specified for use during normal operation and temperature is not generally suitable for cold climate operation.

VII. IRREGULAR ENGINE OPERATION

The engine operator must constantly be alert to detect any symptoms which might indicate the existence of trouble. Forewarning is often given in the form of sudden or abnormal changes in the supply, the temperature, or the pressure of the lubricating oil or of the cooling water. Color and temperature of exhaust afford warning of abnormal conditions and should be checked frequently. Fuel, oil, and water leaks are an indication of possible troubles. Keep the engine clean to make such leaks easier to spot.

An operator soon becomes accustomed to the "normal" sounds and vibrations of a properly operating engine. An abnormal or unexpected change in the pitch or tone of an engine's noise, or a change in the magnitude or frequency of a vibration, warns the alert operator that all is not well. The occurrence of a new sound such as a knock, a drop in the fuel injection pressure, or a misfiring cylinder are other trouble warnings for which an operator should be constantly alert during engine operation.

The following discussion on possible troubles, their causes, and the corrective action necessary, is general rather than specific. The information is based on instructions for some of the engines used, and it is typical of most, though not all, models of diesel engines for use. A few troubles listed may apply to only one model. For specific information on any particular engine, consult the manufacturer's technical manual.

Engine Stalls Frequently Or Stops Suddenly

Several of the troubles which may cause an engine to stall or stop were discussed earlier under starting troubles. Such troubles as air in the fuel system, clogged fuel filters, unsatisfactory operation of fuel injection equipment, and incorrect governor action not only cause starting failures or stalling but also may cause other troubles as well. For example, clogged fuel oil filters and strainers may lead to loss of power, to misfires or erratic firing, or to low fuel oil pressure. Unfortunately, a single engine trouble does not always manifest itself as a single difficulty but may be the cause of several major difficulties.

Factors which may cause an engine to stall include the following: misfiring, low cooling water temperature, improper application of load, improper timing, obstruction in the combustion space or in the exhaust system, insufficient intake air, piston seizure, and defective auxiliary drive mechanisms.

MISFIRING.-When an engine misfires or fires erratically, or when one cylinder misfires regularly, the possible troubles can usually be associated with the fuel or fuel system, worn parts, or the air cleaner or silencer. In determining what causes a cylinder to misfire, you should follow prescribed procedures given in the appropriate technical manual. Procedures will vary among engines because of differences in the design of parts and equipment.

Many of the troubles resulting from fuel contamination require overhaul and repair. However, a cylinder may misfire regularly in some systems because of the fuel pump cut-out mechanism. Some fuel pumps are equipped with this type of mechanism so that fuel supply can be cut off from a cylinder to measure compression pressures. You should check first for an engaged cut-out mechanism (if installed) when a cylinder is misfiring and disengage it during normal engine operation.

Loss Of Compression.-A cylinder may misfire due to loss of compression which may be caused by a leaking cylinder head gasket, by leaking or sticking cylinder valves, by worn pistons, liners, or rings, or by a cracked cylinder head or block. If loss of compression pressure causes an engine to misfire, a check of the compression pressure of each cylinder should be made. Some indicators are designed to measure compression as well as firing pressure while the engine is running at full speed. Others are designed to check only the compression pressures with the engine running at a relatively slow speed. Figure 3 illustrates the application of some different types of pressure indicators.

After an indicator is installed, operate the engine at the specified rpm and record the cylinder compression pressure. Follow this procedure on each cylinder in turn. The pressure in any one cylinder should not be lower than the specified psi, nor should the pressure for any one cylinder be excessively lower than the pressures in the other cylinders. The maximum pressure variation permitted between cylinders is given on engine data sheets or in the manufacturer's technical manual. A compression leak is indicated when the pressure in one cylinder is considerably lower than that in the other cylinders.

A test indicating a compression leak means some disassembly, inspection, and repair. The valve seats and cylinder head gaskets must be checked for leaks and the valve stems must be inspected for sticking. A cylinder head or block may be cracked. If these parts are not the source of trouble, compression is probably leaking past

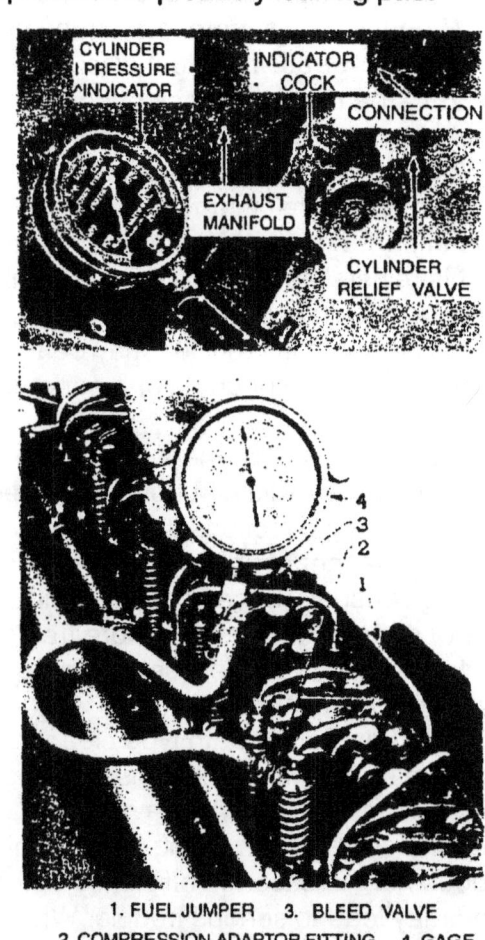

Figure 3.—Engine cylinder pressure indicator applications.

the piston because of insufficient sealing of the piston rings.

Clogged Air Cleaners And Silencers.- Sometimes the reason for an engine's firing erratically or misfiring is clogged air cleaners and silencers. Air cleaners must be cleaned at specified intervals, as recommended in the engine manufacturer's technical manuals. A clogged cleaner reduces the intake air, thereby affecting the operation of the engine. Clogged air cleaners may cause not only misfiring or erratic firing but also such difficulties as hard starting, loss of power, engine smoke, and overheating.

When a volatile solvent is used for cleaning an air cleaner element, it is of extreme importance that the cleaner be dry before it is reinstalled on the engine. Volatile solvents are excellent cleaning agents but, if permitted to remain in the filter, may be the cause of engine overspeeding or a serious explosion.

Oil bath type air cleaners and filters are the source of very little trouble if serviced properly. Cleaning directions are generally given on the cleaner housing. The frequency of cleaning is usually based on a specified number of operating hours, but more frequent cleanings may be necessary where unfavorable conditions exist.

When filling an oil bath type cleaner, follow the manufacturer's filling instructions. Most air cleaners of this type have a FULL mark on the oil reservoir. Filling beyond this mark does not increase the efficiency of the unit and may lead to serious trouble. When the oil bath is too full, the intake air may draw oil into the cylinders. This excess oil-air mixture, over which there is no control, may cause an engine to "run away," resulting in serious damage.

LOW COOLING WATER TEMPERATURE.-If an engine is to operate properly, the cooling water temperature must be maintained within specified temperature limits. When cooling water temperature becomes lower than recommended for a diesel engine, ignition lag is increased, causing detonation, which results in "rough" operation and may cause an engine to stall.

The thermostatic valves that control cooling water temperature operate with a minimum of trouble. Cooling water temperatures above or below the value specified in the technical manual sometimes indicate that the thermostat is inoperative. However, high or low cooling water temperature does not always indicate thermostat trouble. The engine load may be insufficient to maintain proper cooling water temperatures, or the temperature gage may be inaccurate or inoperative. Check these items before removing a thermostatic control unit.

When a thermostat is suspected of faulty operation, it must be removed from the engine and tested.

A thermostat may be checked as follows:

1. A container which does not block or distort vision is needed. Fill the container, preferably a glass beaker, with water.

2. Heat the water to the temperature at which the thermostat is supposed to start opening. This temperature is usually specified in the appropriate technical manual. Use an accurate thermometer to keep a check on the water temperature. A hot plate or a burner may be used as a source of heat. Stir the water frequently to ensure uniform distribution of the heat.

3. Suspend the thermostat in such a manner that operation of the bellows will not be restricted. A wire or string will serve as a satisfactory means of suspension.

4. Immerse the thermostat and observe its action. Check the thermometer readings carefully to see whether the thermostat begins to open at the recommended temperature. (The thermostat and thermometer must NOT touch the container.)

5. Increase the temperature of the water until the specified FULL OPEN temperature is reached. The immersed thermostatic valve should be fully open at this temperature.

The thermostat should be replaced if, when it is tested, there is no movement, or if there is a divergence of more than a specified number of degrees between the temperature at which the thermostat begins to open, or opens fully, and the actuating temperatures specified in the manufacturer's technical manual.

The Fulton-Sylphon automatic temperature regulator is relatively trouble-free. The unit controls temperatures by positioning a valve to bypass some water around the cooler. This system provides for a full flow of the water although only a portion may be cooled. In other words, the full volume of cooling water is circulated at the proper velocity, which eliminates the possibility of the formation of steam pockets in the system.

Generally, when the automatic temperature regulator fails to maintain cooling water at the proper temperature, improper adjustment is indicated. However, the element of the valve may be leaking or some part of the valve may be defective. Failure to follow the proper adjustment procedure is the only cause for improper adjustment of an automatic temperature regulator. Check and follow the proper procedure in the manufacturer's technical manual issued for the specific equipment.

The adjustment consists of changing the tension of the spring (which opposes the action of the thermostatic bellows) with a special tool which is used to turn the adjusting stem knob or wheel. Increasing the spring tension raises the temperature range of the regulator, and decreasing it lowers the temperature range.

When a new valve of this type is placed in service, a number of steps must be taken to ensure that the valve stem length is proper and that all scale pointers make accurate indications. All adjustments should be made in accordance with the valve manufacturer's technical manual.

OBSTRUCTION IN THE COMBUSTION SPACE.-Such items as broken valve heads and valve stem locks, or keepers, which come loose because of a broken valve spring, may cause an engine to come to an abrupt stop. If an engine continues to run when such obstructions are in the combustion chamber, the piston, liner, head, and injection nozzle will be severly damaged.

OBSTRUCTION IN THE EXHAUST SYSTEM.-This type of trouble is seldom encountered if proper installation and maintenance procedures are followed. When a part of an engine exhaust system is restricted, an increase in the exhaust back pressure will result. This may cause high exhaust temperatures, loss of power, or even stalling. An obstruction which causes excessive back pressure in an exhaust system is generally associated with the silencer or muffler.

The manifolds of an exhaust system are relatively trouble-free if related equipment is designed and installed properly. Improper design or installation may result in water's backing up into the exhaust manifold. In some installations, silencer design may be the cause of water's flowing into the engine. The source of water which may enter an engine must be found and eliminated. This may require replacing some parts of the exhaust system with components of an improved design, or may require relocating such items as the silencer and piping.

Inspect exhaust manifolds for water or symptoms of water. Accumulation of salt or scale in the manifold usually indicates that water has been entering from the silencer. Turbochargers on some engines have been known to seize because of salt water's entering the exhaust gas turbine from the silencer. Entry of water into an engine may be detected also by the presence of corrosion or of salt deposits on the engine exhaust valves. If inspection reveals signs of water in an engine or in the exhaust manifold, steps should be taken immediately to correct the trouble. Check the unit for proper installation. Wet-type silencers must be installed with the proper sizes of piping. If the inlet water piping is too large, an excess of water may be injected into the silencer. If a silencer has no continuous drain and the engine is at a lower level than the exhaust outlet, water may back up into the engine.

Dry-type silencers may become clogged with an excessive accumulation of oil or soot. When this occurs, exhaust back pressure increases, causing troubles such as high exhaust temperatures, loss of power, or possibly stalling. A dry-type silencer clogged with oil or soot is also subject to fire. Clogging can usually be detected by fire, soot, or sparks which may come from the exhaust stack. An excessive accumulation of oil or soot in a dry-type silencer may be due to a number of factors, such as failure to drain the silencer, poor condition of the engine, or improper engine operating conditions.

Silencers should be cleaned of oil and soot accumulations at necessary intervals. Even though recommended cleaning periods may be specified, conditions of operation may require more frequent inspections and cleaning. For example, an accumulation of soot and oil is more likely to occur during periods of prolonged idling than when the engine is operating under a normal load. Idling periods should be held to a minimum.

INSUFFICIENT INTAKE AIR.-Insufficient intake air, which may cause an engine to stall or stop, may be due to blower failure or to a clogged air silencer or air filter. Even though all other engine parts function perfectly, efficient engine operation is impossible if the air intake system fails to supply a sufficient quantity of air for complete combustion of the fuel.

Troubles that may prevent a centrifugal blower's performing its function generally involve damage to the rotor shaft, thrust bearings, turbine blading, nozzle ring, or blower impeller. Damage to the rotor shaft and thrust bearings usually occurs as a result of insufficient lubrication, an unbalanced rotor, or operation with excessive exhaust temperature.

Centrifugal blower lubrication difficulties may be caused by failure of the oil pump to prime, low lube oil level, clogged oil passages or oil filter, or a defect in the relief

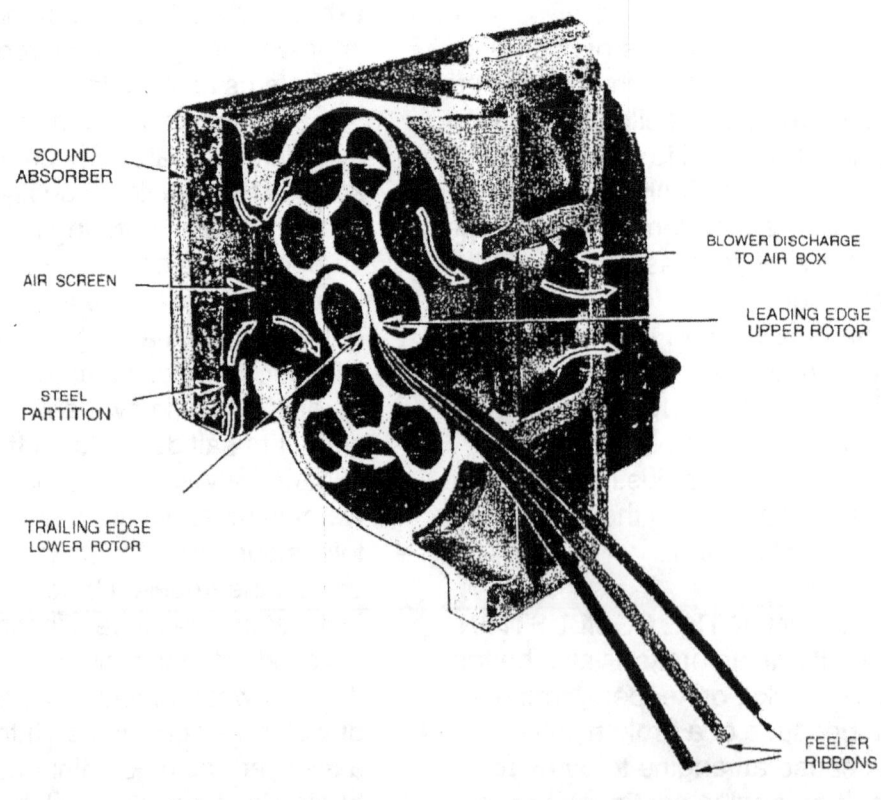

Figure 4.—Checking clearances of positive-displacement blower lobes.

valve which is designed to maintain proper lube oil pressure.

If an unbalanced rotor is the cause of shaft or bearing trouble, there will be excessive vibration. Unbalance may be caused by a damaged turbine wheel blading, or by a damaged blower impeller.

Operating a blower when the exhaust temperature is above the specified maximum safe temperature generally causes severe damage to turbocharger bearings and other parts. Every effort should be made to find and eliminate causes of excessive exhaust temperature before the turbocharger is damaged.

Turbine blading damage in a centrifugal-type blower may be caused by operating with an excessive exhaust temperature, operating at excessive speeds, bearing failures, failure to drain the turbine casing, the entrance of foreign bodies, or turbine blades which break loose.

Damage to an impeller of a centrifugal blower may result from thrust or shaft bearing failure, entrance of foreign bodies, or loosening of the impeller on the shaft.

Since blowers are high-speed units and operate with a very small clearance between parts, minor damage to a part might result in extensive blower damage and failure.

Although there is considerable difference in principle and construction of the positive-displacement blower (Roots) and the axial-flow positive-displacement blower (Hamilton-Whitfield), the problems of operation and maintenance are similar.

Some of the troubles encountered in a positive-displacement type blower are similar to those already mentioned in our discussion of the centrifugal-type blowers. However, the source of some troubles may be different because of construction differences.

Positive-displacement type blowers are equipped with a set of gears to drive and synchronize the rotation of the rotors. Many of these blowers are driven by a serrated shaft. Regardless of construction differences, the basic problem in both types of blowers is to maintain the necessary small clearances. If these clearances are not maintained, the rotors and the case will be damaged, and the blower will fail to perform its function.

Worn gears are one source of trouble in positive-displacement type blowers. A certain amount of gear wear is expected, but damage resulting from excessively worn gears indicates, improper maintenance procedures. During inspections, the values of backlash should be recorded in the material history. This record can be used to establish the rate of increase in wear, to estimate the life of the gears, and to determine when it will be necessary to replace the gears.

Scored rotor lobes and casing may cause blower failure. Scoring of blower parts may be caused by worn gears, improper timing, bearing failure, improper end clearance, or by foreign matter. Any of these troubles may be serious enough to cause contact of the rotors and extensive damage to the blower.

Timing of blower rotors not only involves gear backlash but also the clearances between leading and trailing edges of the rotor lobes and between rotor lobes and casing. Clearance between these parts can be measured with thickness gages, as illustrated in figure 4. If clearances are incorrect, check the backlash of the drive gear first. If the backlash is excessive, the gears must be replaced. Then the rotors must be retimed according to the method outlined in the appropriate manufacturer's technical manual.

Failure of serrated blower shafts may be the result of failure to inspect the parts or of improper replacement of parts. When inspecting serrated shafts, be sure that they fit snugly and that wear is not excessive. When serrations of either the shaft or hub have failed for any reason, both parts must be replaced.

PISTON SEIZURE.—Piston seizure may be the cause of an engine's stopping suddenly. The piston becomes galled and scuffed. When this occurs, the piston may

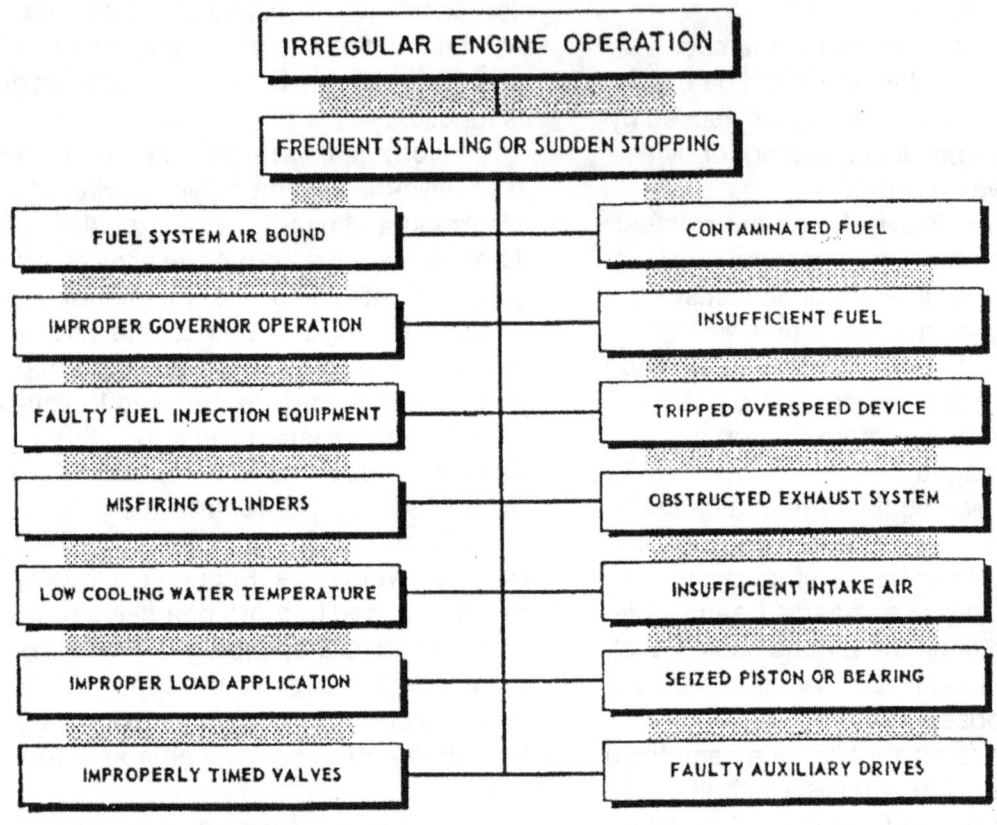

Figure 5.—Possible troubles which may cause an engine to stall frequently or to stop suddenly.

possibly break or extensive damage may be done to other major engine parts. The principal causes of piston seizure are insufficient clearance, excessive temperatures, or inadequate lubrication.

DEFECTIVE AUXILIARY DRIVE MECHANISMS.-Defects in auxiliary drive mechanisms may cause an engine to stop suddenly. Since most troubles in gear trains or chain drives require some disassembly, we shall limit our discussion to only the causes of such troubles.

Gear failure is the principal trouble encountered in gear trains. Engine failure and extensive damage can occur because of a broken or chipped gear. If you hear a metallic clicking noise in the vicinity of a gear housing, it is almost a certain indication that a gear tooth has broken.

Gears are most likely to fail because of improper lubrication, corrosion, misalignment, torsional vibration, excessive backlash, wiped bearings and bushings, metal obstructions, or improper manufacturing procedures.

Gear shafts, bushings and bearings, and gear teeth must be checked during periodic inspections for scoring, wear, and pitting. All oil passages, jets, and sprays should be cleaned to ensure proper oil flow. All gear-locking devices must fit tightly to prevent longitudinal gear movement.

Chains are used in some engines for camshaft and auxiliary drives; in others, they are used to drive certain auxiliary rotating parts. Troubles encountered in chain drives usually result from wear or breakage. Troubles of this nature may be caused by improper tension, lack of lubrication, sheared cotter pins, or misalignment.

Figure 5 is a summary of the possible troubles which may cause an engine to stall

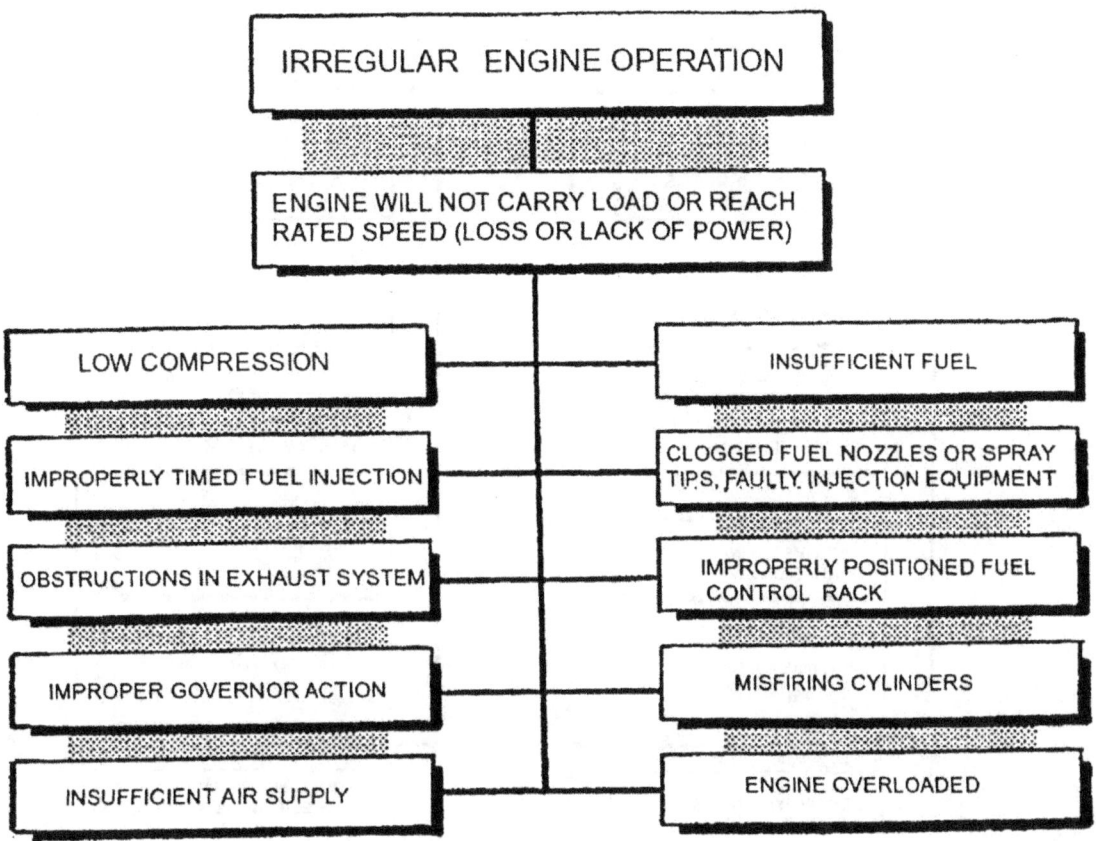

Figure 6.—Possible causes of insufficient power in an engine.

facturer's technical manual and the special technical manuals for the particular equipment. These special manuals are available for the most widely used models of hydraulic governors and overspeed trips, and they contain specific details on testing, adjusting, and repairing.

Engine Hunts or Will Not Secure

Some troubles which may cause an engine to hunt are similar to those which may cause an engine to resist securing efforts. Generally, these two forms of irregular engine operation are caused by troubles originating in the fuel system and speed control system.

SPEED CONTROL SYSTEM.—The speed control system of an internal-combustion engine includes those parts designed to maintain the engine speed at some exact value, or between desired limits, regardless of changes in load on the engine. Governors are provided to regulate fuel injection so that the speed of the engine can be controlled as the load is applied. The governor also acts to prevent overspeeding as in rough seas when the load might be suddenly reduced when the propellers leave the water.

If certain parts of the fuel system or governor fail to function properly, the engine may hunt-that is, vary at a constant throttle settingor it may be difficult to stop the engine.

FUEL CONTROL RACKS.-Fuel control racks that have become sticky or jammed may cause governing difficulties. If the control rack of a fuel system is not functioning properly, the engine speed may decrease as the load is removed or the engine may hunt continuously, or it may hunt only when the load is changed. A sticky or jammed control rack may prevent an engine's responding to changes in throttle setting and may even prevent securing. Any such condition could manube serious in an

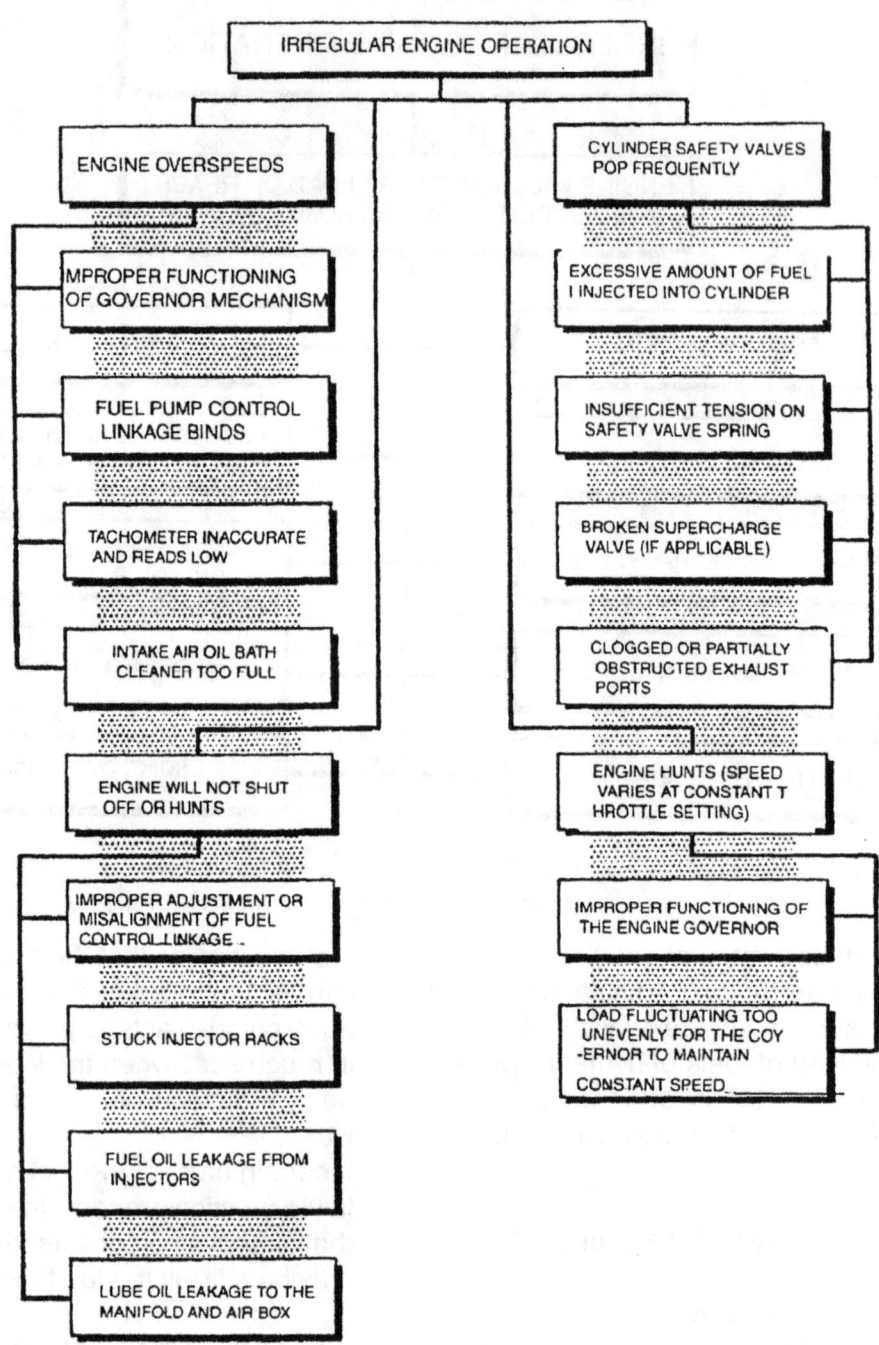

Figure 7.—Additional causes of irregular engine operation.

frequently or stop suddenly. Some doubt may exist as to the difference between stalling and stopping. In reality, there is none unless we associate certain troubles with each. In general, troubles which cause FREQUENT STALLING are those which can be eliminated with minor adjustments or maintenance. If such troubles are not eliminated, it is quite possible that the engine can be started, only to stall again. Failure to eliminate some of the troubles which cause frequent stalling may lead to troubles with cause SUDDEN STOPPING.

Engine Will Not Carry Load

Many of the troubles which can lead to loss of power in an engine may also cause the engine to stop and stall suddenly, or may even prevent its starting. Compare the list of some of the troubles that may cause a power loss in the engine in figure 6 with those in figures 1 and 5. Such items as insufficient air, insufficient fuel, and faulty operation of the governor appear on all three charts. Many of the troubles listed are closely related, and the elimination of one may eliminate others.

The operator of an internal-combustion engine may be confronted with additional major difficulties, such as those indicated in figure 7. Here, again, you can see that many of these possible troubles are similar Jo those already discussed in connection with starting failures and with engine stalling and stopping. The discussion which follows covers only those troubles not previously considered.

Engine Overspeeds

When an engine overspeeds, the trouble can usually be associated with either the governor mechanism or the fuel control linkage, as previously discussed. When information on a specific fuel system or speed emergency situation. Your job is to make every effort possible to prevent the occurrence of such conditions.

You can check for a sticky rack by securing the engine, disconnecting the linkage to the governor, and then attempting to move the rack by hand. There should be no apparent resistance to the motion of the rack if the return springs and linkage are disconnected. A stuck control rack may be caused by the plunger's sticking in the pump barrel; dirt in the rack mechanism; damage to the rack, sleeve, or gear; or improper assembly of the injector pump.

The cause of sticking or jamming must be determined and damaged parts must be replaced. If sticking is due to dirt, a thorough cleaning of all parts will probably correct the trouble. Errors in assembly can be avoided by carefully studying the assembly drawings and instructions.

LEAKAGE OF FUEL OIL.-Leakage of fuel oil from the injectors may cause an engine to continue to operate when you attempt to shut it down. Regardless of the type of fuel system, the results of internal leakage from injection equipment are, in general, somewhat the same. Injector leakage will cause unsatisfactory engine operation because of the excessive amount of fuel entering the cylinder. Leakage may also cause detonation, crankcase dilution, smoky exhaust, loss of power, and excessive carbon formation on spray tips of nozzles and other surfaces of the combustion chamber.

ACCUMULATION OF LUBE OIL.- Another trouble which may prevent stopping an engine is accumulation of lube oil in the intake air passagesmanifold or air box. Such an accumulation creates an extremely dangerous condition. Excess oil can be detected by removing inspection plates on covers and examining the air box and manifold. If oil is discovered, it should be removed and the necessary corrective maintenance should be performed. If oil is drawn suddenly in large quantities from the manifold or air box into the cylinder of the engine and bums, the engine may run away. The engine governor has no control over the sudden increase of speed that occurs.

An air box or air manifold explosion is also a possibility if excess oil is allowed to accumulate. Some engine manufacturers have provided safety devices to reduce the hazards of such explosions.

Excess oil in the air box or manifold of an engine also increases the tendency toward carbon formation on liner ports, cylinder valves, and other parts of the combustion chamber.

The causes of excessive lube oil accumulation in the air box or manifold will vary depending on the specific engine. Generally, the accumulation is due to an obstruction in either the air box or separator drains.

In an effort to reduce the possibility of crankcase explosions and runaways, some engine manufacturers have designed a means to ventilate the crankcase. In some engines, ventilation is accomplished by a passage between the crankcase and the intake side of the blower. In other engines, an oil separator or air maze is provided in the passage between the crankcase and blower intake.

In either type of installation, stoppage of the drains will cause an excessive accumulation of oil. It is essential that drain passages be kept open by being properly cleaned whenever necessary.

Oil may enter the air box or manifold from sources other than crankcase vapors.

Table 1.-Symptoms of engine trouble

	INSTRUMENT INDICATIONS			SMOKE	CONTAMINATION OF LUBE
	PRESSURE	TEMPERATURE	SPEED		OIL, FUEL, OR WATER
POUNDING (MECHANICAL)	LOW LUBE OIL PRESSURE	LOW LUBE OIL TEMPERATURE	IDLING SPEED NOT NORMAL	BLACK EXHAUST SMOKE	FUEL OIL IN THE LUBE OIL
	HIGH LUBE OIL PRESSURE	HIGH LUBE OIL TEMPERATURE	MAXIMUM SPEED NOT NORMAL	BLUISH-WHITE EXHAUST SMOKE	WATER IN THE LUBE OIL
KNOCKING (DETONATION)	LOW FUEL OIL PRESSURE (IN LOW-PRESSURE FUEL SUPPLY SYSTEM)	LOW COOLING WATER TEMPERATURE (FRESH)		SMOKE ARISING FROM CRANKCASE	OIL OR GREASE IN THE WATER WATER IN THE FUEL OIL
					AIR OR GAS IN THE WATER
CLICKING (METALLIC)	LOW COOLING WATER PRESSURE (FRESH)	HIGH COOLING WATER TEMPERATURE (FRESH)		SMOKE ARISING FROM CYLINDER HEAD	METAL PARTICLES IN LUBE OIL
	LOW COOLING WATER PRESSURE (SALT)	LOW CYLINDER EXHAUST TEMPERATURE		SMOKE FROM ENGINE AUXILIARY EQUIPMENT (BLOWERS, PUMPS. ETC.)	
RATTLING	HIGH COOLING WATER PRESSURE (SALT)	HIGH EXHAUST TEMPERATURE IN ONE CYLINDER			
	LOW COMPRESSION PRESSURE				
	LOW FIRING PRESSURE				
	HIGH FIRING PRESSURE				
	LOW SCAVENGING AIR RECEIVER PRESSURE (SUPERCHARGE ENGINE)				
	HIGH EXHAUST BACK PRESSURE				

A defective blower oil seal, a carryover from an oil type air cleaner, or defective oil piping may be the source of trouble.

Another possible source may be an excessively high oil level in the crankcase. Under this condition, an oil fog is created in some engines by moving the parts. An oil fog may be caused also by excessive clearance in the connecting rod and main journal bearings. In some types of crankcase ventilating systems, the oil fog will be drawn into the blower. When this occurs, an abnormal amount of oil may accumulate in the air box. Removal of the oil will not remove the trouble. The cause of the accumulation must be determined and the necessary repair must be accomplished.

If a blower oil seal is defective, replacement is the only satisfactory method of correction. When installing new seals, be sure the shafts are not scored and the bearings are in satisfactory condition. Special precautions must be taken during installation to avoid damaging oil seals. Damage to an oil seal during installation is usually not discovered until the blower has been reinstalled and the engine has been put into operation. Be sure an oil seal gets the necessary lubrication. The oil not only lubricates the seal, reducing friction, but also carries away any heat that is generated. New oil seals are generally soaked in clean, light lube oil before assembly.

Cylinder Safety Valves Pop Frequently

On some engines, a cylinder relief (safety valve) is provided for each cylinder. The function of the valve is to open when the cylinder pressures exceed a safe operating limit. The valve opens or closes a passage leading from the combustion chamber to the outside of the cylinder. The valve face is held against the valve seat by spring pressure. Tension on the spring is varied with an adjusting nut, which is locked when the desired setting is attained. The desired setting varies with the type of engine and may be found by referring to the manufacturer's technical manual.

Cylinder relief valves should be set at the specified lifting pressure. Continual lifting (popping) of the valves indicates excessive cylinder pressure of malfunction of the valves, either of which should be corrected immediately. Repeated lifting of a relief valve indicates that the engine is being overloaded, the load is being applied improperly, or the engine is too cold. Also, repeated lifting may indicate that the valve spring has become weakened, ignition or fuel injection is occurring too early, the injector is sticking and leaking, too much fuel is being supplied, or, in air injection engines, that the spray valve air pressure is too high. When frequent popping occurs, the engine must be stopped to determine and remedy the cause of the trouble. In an emergency, the fuel supply may be cut off in the affected cylinder. Relief valves must never be locked closed, except in an emergency. When emergency measures are taken, the valves must be repaired or replaced, as necessary, as soon as possible.

When excessive fuel is the cause of frequent safety valve lifting, the trouble may be due to the improper functioning of a high-pressure injection pump, a leaky nozzle or spray valve, or a loose fuel cam (if adjustable); or, in some systems such as the common rail, the fuel pressure may be too high.

A safety valve that is not operating properly should be removed, disassembled, cleaned and inspected. Check the valve and valve seat for pitting and excessive wear and the valve spring for possible defective conditions. When a safety valve is removed for any reason, the spring tension must be reset. This procedure varies to some extent, dependent on the valve construction.

Except in emergencies, it is advisable to shut an engine down when troubles cause safety valve popping.

Clogged or partially obstructed exhaust ports may also cause the cylinder safety valve to lift. This condition will be of infrequent occurrence if proper planned maintenance procedures are followed. If it does occur, the resulting increase in cylinder pressure may be sufficient to cause safety valve popping. Clogged exhaust ports will also cause overheating of the engine, high exhaust temperatures, and sluggish engine operation.

Clogging of cylinder ports can be avoided by removing carbon deposits at prescribed intervals. Some engine manufacturers make special tools for port cleaning. Round wire brushes of the proper size are satisfactory for this work. Care must be taken in cleaning cylinder ports to prevent carbon's entering the cylinderthe engine should be barred to such a position that the piston blocks the port.

VIII. SYMPTOMS OF ENGINE TROUBLE

In learning to recognize the symptoms that may help you locate the causes of engine trouble, you will find that experience is the best teacher. Even though written instructions are essential for efficient troubleshooting, the information usually given serves only as a guide. It is very difficult to describe the sensation that you should feel when checking the temperature of a bearing by hand; the specific color of exhaust smoke when pistons and rings are worn excessively; and, for some engines, the sound that you will hear if the crankshaft counterweights come loose. You must actually work with the equipment in order to associate a particular symptom with a particular trouble. Written information, however, can save you a great deal of time and eliminate much unnecessary work. Written instructions will make detection of troubles much easier in practical situations. Symptoms which indicate that a trouble exists may be in the form of an unusual noise or instrument indication, smoke, or excessive consumption or contamination of the lube oil, fuel, or water. Table 1 is a general listing of various trouble symptoms which the operator of an engine may encounter.

NOISES

The unusual noises which may indicate that a trouble exists or is impending may be classified as pounding, knocking, clicking, and rattling. Each type of noise must be associated with certain engine parts or systems which might be the source of trouble.

Pounding is a mechanical knock or hammering (not to be confused with a fuel knock). It may be caused by a loose, excessively worn, or broken engine part. Generally, troubles of this nature will require major repair.

Detonation (knocking) is caused by the presence of fuel or lubricating oil in the air charge of the cylinders during the compression stroke. Excessive pressures accompany detonation. If detonation is occurring in one or more cylinders, an engine should be stopped immediately to prevent possible damage.

Clicking noises are generally associated with an improperly functioning valve mechanism or timing gear. If the cylinder or valve mechanism is the source of metallic clicking, the trouble may be due to a loose valve stem and guide, insufficient or excessive valve tappet clearances, a loose cam follower or guide, broken valve springs, or a valve that is stuck open. A clicking in the timing gear usually indicates that there are some damaged or broken gear teeth.

Rattling noises are generally due to vibration of loose engine parts. However, an improperly functioning vibration damper, a failed antifriction bearing, or a gear-type pump operating without prime are also possible sources of trouble when rattling noises occur.

When you hear a noise, first make sure that it is a trouble symptom. Each diesel engine has a characteristic noise at any specific speed and load. The noise will change with a change in speed or load. As an operator you must become familiar with the normal sounds of an engine. Abnormal sounds must be investigated promptly. Knocks which indicate a trouble may be detected and located by special instruments or by the use of a "sounding bar" such as a solid iron screwdriver or bar.

INSTRUMENT INDICATIONS

An engine operator probably relies on the instruments to warn him of impending troubles more than on all the other trouble symptoms combined. Regardless of the type instrument being used, the indications are of no value if inaccuracies exist. Be sure an instrument is accurate and operating properly. All instruments must be tested at specified intervals, or whenever they are suspected of being inaccurate.

SMOKE

The presence of smoke can be quite useful as an aid in locating some types of trouble, especially if used in conjunction with other trouble symptoms. The color of exhaust smoke also can be used as a guide in troubleshooting.

The color of engine exhaust is a good, general indication of engine performance. The exhaust of an efficiently operating engine has little or no color. A dark, smoky exhaust indicates incomplete combustion; and the darker the color, the greater the amount of unburned fuel in the exhaust. Incomplete combustion may be due to a number of troubles. Some manufacturers associate a particular type of trouble with the color of the exhaust. The more serious troubles are generally identified with either black or bluish-white exhaust colors.

EXCESSIVE CONSUMPTION OF LUBE OIL, FUEL, OR WATER

An operator should be aware of engine trouble whenever excessive consumption of any of the essential liquids occurs. The possible troubles signified by excessive consumption will depend on the system in question; leakage, however, is one trouble which may be common to all. Before starting any disassembly, check for leaks in the system in which excessive consumption occurs.

FUNDAMENTALS OF AUTOMOTIVE POWER TRAINS AND CHASSIS

CONTENTS

		Page
I.	POWER TRAIN COMPONENTS	1
II.	BRAKE SYSTEMS	12
III.	SUSPENSION SYSTEMS	19
IV.	FRAME	22

BASIC FUNDAMENTALS OF AUTOMOTIVE POWER TRAINS AND CHASSIS

The mechanism that transmits the power of a vehicle's engine to the wheels and accessory equipment is called the power train. In a simple situation, a set of gears or a chain and sprocket could perform this task, but automotive vehicles are not designed for simple operating conditions. They are designed to have pulling power as well as to move at high speeds, to travel in reverse as well as forward, and to operate on rough terrain as well as on smooth roads. To meet these varying demands, a number of units have been added including clutches, transmissions, propeller shafts, universal joints, differentials, and live axles.

The chassis is the assembly of mechanisms that make up the major operating part of the vehicle. It usually includes everything except the vehicle body. This assembly includes the engine, the frame which supports the engine and the power train, the steering and braking systems, and the suspension system.

This chapter provides information on the various components, or subassemblies, that make up the automotive power train and chassis. In effect, it establishes the relationship between these various parts and shows how they work together in the automotive vehicle. To maintain and service these components, or subassemblies, you must know where to find them on a vehicle. You must also understand their purpose and how they operate. This chapter contains a general discussion of these subject; the operation and maintenance manuals which accompany each piece of equipment will give you more detailed information.

I. POWER TRAIN COMPONENTS

The common elements of the power train system assembled in a typical vehicle are shown in the following figure. The main components of the power train are described as follows:

CLUTCH.
By means of the clutch, the operator can disconnect the engine from the remainder of the power train. This is essential when starting the engine, thus allowing the vehicle to stand motionless while the engine is running. It also allows gradual engagement of the engine to the power train and gear ratio changing to meet varying road conditions.

TRANSMISSION.
An internal combustion engine cannot develop appreciable torque at low speeds; it develops maximum torque only at one speed, and the crankshaft of an engine must always rotate in the same direction. Because of these limitations, a transmission is necessary in automotive vehicles. The transmission provides the mechanical advantage that enables the engine to propel the vehicle under adverse conditions of the load. It also provides the operator with a selection of vehicle speeds while the engine is held at speeds within the effective torque range, and it allows disengaging and reversing the flow of power from the engine to the wheels.

PROPELLER SHAFT.
A propeller shaft is used to transfer the power from the transmission located near the front of the vehicle to the differential near the rear.

UNIVERSAL JOINTS.

It is necessary to provide flexibility in the power train if springs are to be used on the vehicle. As the load is increased or decreased, and as the vehicle travels over uneven surfaces, the vertical distance between the transmission output shaft and the axle will change. This flexibility is provided by the use of universal joints which permit transfer of torque at an angle.

SLIP JOINTS.

As the load is changed, and as the vehicle travels over uneven ground, the distance from the axle to the transmission varies. Slip joints allow for this variation.

DIFFERENTIAL.

A differential is required to compensate for the difference in distance the rear wheels travel when the vehicle rounds a turn. The differential permits application of power to the rear wheels while allowing each wheel to turn at a different speed when the vehicle is rounding a curve.

AXLES.

An axle is a shaft supporting a vehicle on which the wheels turn. A *live axle* is one that supports part of the weight of a vehicle and also drives the wheels connected to it. A *dead axle* is one that carries part of the weight of a vehicle, but does not drive the wheels. The usual front axle of a vehicle is a dead axle and the rear axle is a live axle. In four-wheel drive vehicles, both front and rear axles are live axles, and in six-wheel drive vehicles, all three axles are live axles.

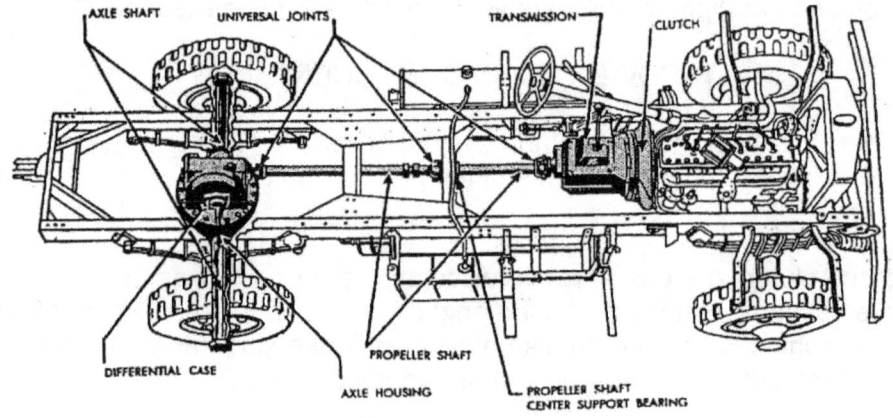

TYPICAL POWER TRAIN

THE CLUTCH

A clutch in an automotive vehicle is the mechanism in the power train that connects the engine crankshaft to, or disconnects it from, the transmission and thus the remainder of the power train. Since the internal combustion engine does not develop a high starting torque, it must be disconnected from the power train and allowed to operate without load until it develops enough torque to overcome the inertia of the vehicle when starting from rest. The application of the engine power to the load must be gradual to prove smooth engagement and to lessen the shock on the driving parts. After engagement, the clutch must transmit all the engine power to the transmission without slipping. Further, it is desirable to disconnect the engine from the power train during the time the gears in the transmission are being shifted from one gear ratio to another.

Clutches are located in the power train between the engine and the transmission assembly.

Clutches transmit power from the clutch driving plate to the driven member by friction. In the disk clutch, the driving plate or member, which is secured to the engine flywheel, is gradually brought into contact with the driven member (disk), which is attached to the transmission input shaft. The contact is made and held by strong spring pressure controlled by the operator with the clutch pedal. With only light spring pressure, there is little friction between the two members and the clutch is permitted to slip. As the spring pressure increases, friction also increases, and less slippage occurs. When the operator removes his foot from the clutch pedal and full spring pressure is applied, the speed of the driving plate and driven disk is the same, and all slipping stops. There is then a direct connection between the flywheel and transmission input shaft.

Malfunction Detection. Several types of clutch troubles that may be encountered during vehicle operation are: slipping, chattering or grabbing when engaging, spinning or dragging when engaged, and clutch noises. As an operator, you would explain the malfunction on the Operator's Trouble Report and turn the report into the maintenance shop for corrective action.

Clutch Lubrication. Although some clutches do not require lubrication, there are other types of clutches that require it at periodic intervals. The clutch-pedal control shaft and clutch linkage are among some of the lubricating points that would be greased at normal regular servicing intervals in accordance with the manufacturer's lubrication manual.

MANUAL TRANSMISSIONS

The transmission is part of the power train. It is located in the rear of the engine between the clutch housing and the propeller shaft. The transmission transfers engine power from the clutch shaft to the propeller shaft, and allows the operator a means of varying the gear ratio between the engine and the rear wheels.

Dual ratio, or two-speed, rear axles are sometimes used on trucks. They contain two different gear ratios which can be selected at will by the driver, usually by a manual-control lever. A dual-ratio rear axle serves the same purpose as the auxiliary transmission, and like the latter, it doubles the number of gear ratios available for driving the vehicle under the various loads and road conditions.

Operator's Maintenance. It is the operator's responsibility to check with the manufacturer's instruction manual for instruction on the proper type and amount of recommended lubricant to be used in the transmission case. You must maintain the lubricant at the proper level. The normal level of lubricant to be placed in a transmission is usually at the bottom of the filler plug opening. By maintaining the proper level, gear teeth are protected, foaming is reduced, and thus the transmission will continue to perform properly.

Malfunction Detection. Several types of transmission troubles that may be encountered in vehicle operation are: hard shifting into gears, transmission slips out of *first* or *reverse*, transmission slips out of *second*, transmission slips out of high, no power through transmission, transmission noisy in gear, gear clash in shifting, and oil leaks. As an operator, you would explain the malfunction on the Operator's Trouble Report enabling the mechanic to check out the possible cause of trouble reported.

AUTOMATIC TRANSMISSION

The transmissions described previously are manual transmissions; that is, they require a clutch and a lever for shifting gears. The automatic transmission is used in almost all types of automotive and construction equipment. Automatic transmissions are composed of a fluid coupling or hydraulic torque converter and a system of planetary gears controlled automatically.

Fluid Couplings.
Fluid couplings are widely used with automatic transmissions. By slipping at idling speeds and by holding to increase power as engine speed increases, fluid couplings act as a sort of automatic clutch. There is no mechanical connection between the engine and transmission, but power is transmitted through the use of oil.

The principle of fluid drive can best be illustrated through the use of a pair of electric fans facing each other. If one fan is operated with power, the air blast from this fan will cause the other fan to rotate.

There is considerable power loss through slippage at low speeds, but at intermediate or high driving speeds the power loss is very small. It ranges from 1 percent at 25 miles per hour to one-quarter percent at 60 miles per hour.

Torque Converters.
A torque converter is a special form of fluid coupling. It is one of the most common types of automatic transmissions and is widely used in the latest models of automotive and construction equipment.

The torque converter consists of three basic elements: the pump (driving member), the turbine (driven member), and the stator (reaction member). All of these members have curved vanes. The stator is placed between the load and the power source to act as a fulcrum and is secured to the torque converter housing. The pump throws out oil in the same direction in which the pump is turning. As the oil strikes the turbine blade, it forces the turbine to rotate, and the oil is directed toward the center of the turbine. Then the oil leaves the turbine and moves in a direction opposite to that of the pump. As the oil strikes the stator, it is redirected to flow in the same direction as the pump, thereby adding its force to that of the pump. Torque is multiplied by the velocity and direction given to the oil by the pump, plus the velocity and direction of the oil entering the pump from the stator.

Planetary Gears.
Automatic transmissions use a system of planetary gears to enable the torque from the torque converter or fluid coupling to be used as efficiently as possible.

Planetary units are the heart of the modern automatic transmission. An understanding of the power flow through the planetary units is essential to an understanding of the operation of the automatic transmission.

Four basic parts make up the planetary gear system. These basic parts are the sun gear, the ring (or internal) gear, the planet pinions, and the planet carrier.

The sun gear is so named because it is the center of the system. The term *planet* is used to describe these pinions and gears because they rotate around the sun gear. The ring gear, or internal gear, is so called because of its shape and because it has internal teeth.

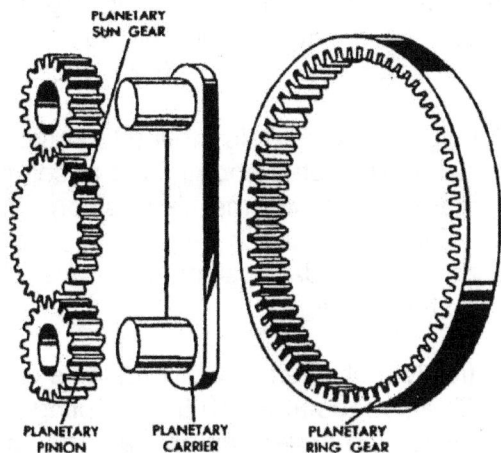

There are several advantages inherent in the planetary gear system. One of the advantage is the compactness of the system. Another advantage is that there is more tooth contact to carry the load, in that each gear of the planetary system is usually in contact with at least two other gears of the system. The gears are always in mesh. There can be no tooth damage due to tooth clash or partial engagement. The big advantage is the one which makes it so popular: namely, the ease of shifting gears. Planetary gear sets in automatic transmissions are shifted without any skill on the part of the driver.

There are various ways in which power may be transmitted through the planetary gear set. shaft from the engine may be connected to drive the sun gear, it may be connected to drive the planet carrier, or it may be connected to drive the ring gear. The propeller shaft also may be connected to any of these members. However, only power can be transmitted in the planetary gear system when (1) the engine is delivering power to one of the three member, (2) the propeller shaft is connected to one of the other members, and (3) the remaining member is held against rotation. All three conditions must be satisfied for power to be transmitted in the system. Automatic transmissions provide the means for holding a member through hydraulic servos or spring pressure.

Operation. Most automatic transmissions are basically the same. They combine a fluid torque converter with a planetary gear set, and control the shifting of the planetary gears with an automatic hydraulic control system.

To start the engine, the selector lever must be in the Neutral or Park position. It is good practice to apply the service brakes before starting the engine and keep them applied after the engine is running. In the automatic transmission, the fluid torque converter is attached to the engine crankshaft and serves as the engine flywheel. This means that whenever the engine runs, engine power flows into the converter and drives the converter output (turbine) shaft. There is no neutral in the torque converter. Neutral is provider in the planetary gear set by the release of bands and clutches.

With the engine running, you can *feel* the transmission go into gear and into neutral as the selector level is moved from Park or Neutral to Drive, Low, or Reverse. If the engine is running at fast (cold) idle, the vehicle will start to move as soon as the transmission goes into gear, unless the parking or service brakes are applied. If the engine is idling at normal (hot) idle, the vehicle will not move. You can, however, *feel* the transmission go into gear. Part of this *feel* is the audible decrease in engine rpm. The engine is now running under a load. The torque converter and the planetary gear set are actually transmitting engine torque to the driveshaft. The torque applied, however, is not sufficient to move the vehicle.

For all normal forward driving, the selector is moved to Drive. As the throttle is advanced from the idle position, the vehicle will start off smoothly and accelerate steadily. The transmission is designed to operate at a steady-throttle position. Most drivers depress the accelerator pedal to definite position and hold it there steadily until the desired speed is attained. Depending on the accelerator pedal position, the transmission will upshaft automatically to intermediate and then to high.

The transmission automatically multiplies and/or transmits engine torque to the driveshaft as driving conditions demand. The speeds at which the coupling point and the gear shifts occur are controlled partially by the driver. The driver has only a partial control in the Drive position, because the transmission in the Drive position will shift the planetary gear set into the higher gear to prevent engine overspeeding regardless of throttle position.

The transmission can multiply engine torque as much as 5.4 times. The torque converter can multiply engine torque as much as 2.2 times. The planetary gear set in low gear multiplies the torque converter output torque 2.46 times. The maximum engine torque multiplication in the transmission is 2.2 x 2.46 or 5.41 times. This means that the transmission can receive an engine output torque of 100 ft-lbs and deliver 541 ft-lbs torque to the driveshaft. Of course, frictional losses have to be subtracted from the 541 ft-lbs.

The driver can force downshaft the transmission from high to intermediate at speed up to about 65 mph. A detent on the downshift linkage warns the driver when the carburetor is wide open. Accelerator pedal depression through the detent will bring in the downshift.

With the throttle closed, the transmission will downshift automatically as the vehicle speed drops to about 10 mph. With the throttle open at any position up to the detent, the downshifts will come in automatically at speeds about 10 mph and in proportion to throttle opening. This prevents engine lugging on steep hill climbing.

When the selector lever is moved to L (low) with the transmission in high, the transmission will downshift to intermediate or to low depending on the road speed. At speeds below about 25 mph, the downshift will be from high to low.

With the selector in Low position, the transmission cannot upshift. On some vehicles the Low position is called Hill Control, since low gear provides maximum engine braking. When maximum engine braking is desired, the transmission must not upshift, because an upshift will reduce engine braking effort. When the selector is moved to Reverse, the hydraulic control system shifts the planetary gear set to reverse. When the selector lever is moved to Park, a spring force is applied against a pawl to engage the parking pawl with a parking gear on the output shaft. When the pawl is engaged, the transmission output shaft (and, therefore, the rear wheels) is mechanically locked to the transmission main case.

In summary:
1. An automatic transmission has the torque converter to act as an automatic clutch. This automatic clutch permits the vehicle to stand still at engine idle, but automatically

goes to work at a full-throttle start so that the transmission can take maximum engine torque, multiply it more than four times and deliver it to the driveshaft.
2. It is practically impossible to *kill* the engine under any driving condition.
3. At a start, engine speed is fast and vehicle speed is slow. With a steady throttle, engine speed remains fairly constant while vehicle speed increases to 65 mph. You found that the torque converter and planetary gear set *know* when engine torque should be multiplied, how much to multiply it, and when to transmit it to the driveshaft.
4. The ratio changes (shifts) occur at full-engine torque within a fraction of a second and without extreme harshness.

Operator's Maintenance. Periodic service by the operator includes checking the transmission oil level when the engine is idling and at normal operating temperature, the vehicle is level, and the transmission control lever is in Park. Remove dipstick and note oil level. If it is low, and sufficient transmission fluid (the oil used in all automatic transmission is special and is composed of mineral oil and additives). In the transmission, it is used as a combination power-transmission medium, hydraulic control fluid, heat transfer medium, bearing surface lubricant, and gear lubricant. In all cases, the manufacturer's recommendations should be followed when servicing and filling the transmission with transmission fluid.

Caution: Do not overfill the transmission because overfilling will cause foaming and shifting troubles.

Malfunction Detection. Several types of automatic transmission troubles that may be encountered during vehicle operation are: No drive in any selected position; engine speed accelerates on standstill starts but vehicle acceleration lags; engine speed accelerates during upshifts; transmission will not upshift; upshift harsh; closed throttle (coast) downshift harsh; will not downshift; vehicle creeps excessively in drive; vehicle creeps in neutral; no drive in reverse, improper shift points; unusual transmission noise; and oil leaks. As an operator, you must explain the malfunction on the Operator's Trouble Report and turn the report into the maintenance shop for corrective action.

AUXILIARY TRANSMISSIONS

Auxiliary transmissions are mechanisms mounted in the rear of the regular transmission to provide an increased number of gear ratios. The types most commonly used, normally have only a low and a high (direct) range, incorporated into a transfer assembly. The low range provides an extremely low gear ratio on hard pull. At all other times, the high range is used, and the power passes through the main shaft. Gears are shifted by a separate gearshift lever in the driver's cab.

Transfer Cases. Transfer cases are placed in the power trains of vehicles driven by all wheels. Their purpose is to provide the necessary offsets for additional propeller shaft connections to drive the wheels.

Transfer cases in heavier vehicles have two speed positions and a declutching device for disconnecting the front driving wheels. Two speed transfer cases serve also as auxiliary transmissions.

Some transfer cases are quite complicated. When they have speed changing gear, declutching device, and attachment for three or more propeller shafts, they are even larger than the main transmission.

Some transfer cases contain an overrunning sprag unit (or units) on the front output shaft. (A sprag unit is a form of overrunning clutch; power can be transmitted through it in one direction but not in the other.) On these transfer cases, the transfer is designed to drive the front axle slightly slower than the rear axle. During normal operation, when both front and rear wheels turn at the same speed, only the rear wheels drive the vehicle. However, if the rear wheels should lose traction and begin to slip, they tend to turn faster than the front wheels. As this happens, the sprag unit automatically engages so that the front wheels also drive the vehicle. The sprag unit simply provides an automatic means of engaging the front wheels in drive whenever additional tractive effort is required. There are two types of sprag-unit-equipped transfers: a single-sprag-unit transfer and a double-sprag unit transfer. Essentially, both types work in the same manner.

Power Takeoffs. Power takeoffs are attachments in the power train used for obtaining power to drive auxiliary accessories. They are attached to the transmission, auxiliary transmission, or transfer case.

Malfunction detection and operator maintenance for auxiliary transmissions are similar to those for the manual transmission.

PROPELLER SHAFT ASSEMBLY

The propeller shaft assembly consists of a propeller shaft, a slip joint, and one or more universal joints. This assembly provides a flexible connection through which power is transmitted from the transmission to the live axles.

The propeller shaft may be solid or tubular. A solid shaft is somewhat stronger than the hollow or tubular shaft of the same diameter, but the hollow shaft is stronger than a solid shaft of the same weight. Hollow shafts are used in the open.

A slip joint is provided at one end of the propeller shaft to take care of end play. The driving axle, being attached to the springs, is free to move up and down while the transmission is attached to the frame and cannot move. Any upward or downward movement of the axle, as the spring are flexed, shortens or lengthens the distance between the axle assembly and the transmission. To compensate for this changing distance, the slip joint is provided at one end of the propeller shaft.

The usual type of slip joint consists of a splined stub shaft, welded to the propeller shaft, which fits into a splined sleeve in the universal joint.

A universal joint is a connection between two shafts that permits one to drive the other at an angle. Passenger vehicles and trucks usually have universal joints at both ends of the propeller shaft.

Universal joints normally do not require any maintenance other than lubrication. Some universal joints (U-joints) have grease fittings and should be lubricated when the vehicle has a preventive maintenance inspection. Others may require disassembly and lubrication periodically. When lubricating U-joints that have grease fittings, use a low pressure grease gun to avoid damaging seals.

FINAL DRIVES

A final drive is that part of the power train that transmits the power delivered through the propeller shaft to the drive wheels or to sprockets, in the case of tracklaying equipment. Because it is encased in the rear axle housing, the final drive is usually referred to as a part of the rear axle assembly. It consists of two gears called the ring gear and pinion. These are beveled gears, and they may be spur, spiral, or hypoid.

The function of the final drive is to change by 90 degrees the direction of the power transmitted through the propeller shaft to the driving axles. It also provides a fixed reduction between the speed of the propeller shaft and the axle shafts and wheels. In passenger car this reduction varies from about 3 to 1 to 5 to 1. In trucks, it can vary from to 1 to as much as 11 to 1.

The gear ratio of a final drive having bevel gears is found by dividing the number of teeth on the driven or ring gear by the number of teeth on the pinion. In a worm gear final drive, the gear ratio is found by counting the number of revolutions of the worm gear required for one revolution of the driven gear.

Most final drives are of the gear type. Hypoid gears are used in passenger cars and light trucks to eliminate the rear seat propeller shaft tunnel or to permit a lower body design. They permit the bevel driven pinion to be placed below the center of the ring gear, thereby lowering the propeller shaft. Worm gears allow a large speed reduction and are used to a limited extent on larger trucks. Spiral bevel gears are similar to hypoid gears. They are used in both passenger cars and trucks to replace spur gear that are considered too noisy.

DIFFERENTIALS

Associated with the final drive and contained in the rear axle housing is the differential. The purpose of the differential is easy to understand when you compare a vehicle to a company of men marching in mass formation. When the company makes a turn, the men in the inside file must take short steps, almost marking time, while men in the outside file must take long steps and walk a greater distance to make the turn. When a motor vehicle turns a corner, the wheels on the outside of the turn must rotate faster and travel a greater distance than the wheels on the inside. This causes no difficulty for front wheels of the usual passenger car because each wheel rotates independently. However, in order to drive the rear wheels at different speeds, the differential is needed. It connects the individual axle shaft for each wheel to the bevel drive gear. Therefore, each shaft can turn at a different speed and still be driven.

To overcome the situation where one spinning wheel might be undesirable, some trucks are provided with a *differential lock*. This is a simple dog clutch, controlled manually or automatically which locks one axle shaft to the differential case and bevel drive gear. Although this device forms a rigid connection between the two axle shafts and makes both wheels rotate at the same speed, it is used, very little. Too often the driver forgets to disengage the lock after using it. There are, however, automatic devices for doing almost the same thing. One of these, which is rather extensively used today, is the high-traction differential. This does not work, however, when one wheel loses traction completely. In this respect, it is inferior to the differential lock.

With the no-spin differential, one wheel cannot spin because of loss of tractive effort and thereby deprive the other wheel of driving effort. For example, one wheel is on ice and the other wheel is on dry pavement. The wheel on ice is assumed to have no traction. However, the wheel on dry pavement will pull to the limit of its tractional resistance at the pavement. The wheel on ice cannot spin because wheel speed is governed by the speed of the wheel applying tractive effort.

AXLES

A live axle is one that supports part of the weight of a vehicle and also drives the wheels connected to it. A dead axle is one that carries part of the weight of a vehicle but does not drive the wheels.

In 4-wheel drive vehicles, both front and rear axles are live axles, and in 6-wheel drive vehicles, all three axles are live axles. The third axle, part of a *bogie drive* is joined to the rearmost axle by a trunnion axle. The axle trunnion is attached rigidly to the frame. Its purpose is to help in distributing the load on the rear of the vehicle to the two live axles which it connects.

There are four types of live axles used in automotive and construction equipment. They are: plain, semifloating, three-quarter floating, and full floating.

The plain live axle, or nonfloating rear axle, is seldom used in construction equipment today. The axle shafts in this assembly are called nonfloating because they are supported directly in bearings located in the center and ends of the axle housing. In addition to turning the wheels, these shafts carry the entire load of the vehicle on their outer ends. Plain axles also support the weight of the differential case.

The semifloating axle that is used on most passenger cars and light trucks has its differential case independently supported. The differential carrier relieves the axle shafts from the weight of the differential assembly and the stresses caused by its operation. For this reason, the inner ends of the axle shafts are said to be floated. The wheels are keyed or bolted to outer ends of axle shafts and the outer bearings are between the shafts and the housing. The axle shafts, therefore, must take the stresses caused by turning or skidding of the wheels. The axle shaft in a semifloating live axle can be removed after the wheel and brake drum have been removed.

The axle shafts in a three-quarter floating axle may be removed with the wheels, which are keyed to the tapered outer ends of the shafts. The inner ends of the shafts are carried as in semifloating axle. The axle housing, instead of the shafts, carries the weight of the vehicle because the wheels are supported by bearings on the outer ends of the housing. However, axle shafts must take the stresses caused by the turning, or skidding, of the wheels. Three-quarter floating axles are used in some trucks but in very few passenger cars.

The full floating axle is used in most heavy trucks. These axle shafts may be removed and replaced without removing the wheels or disturbing the differential. Each wheel is carried on the end of the axle tube on two ball bearings or roller bearings and the axle shafts are bolted to the wheel hub. The wheels are driven through a flange on the ends of the axle shaft which is bolted to the outside of the wheel hub. The bolted connection between axle and wheel does not make this assembly a true full floating axle, but nevertheless, it is called a floating axle. A true full floating axle transmits only turning effort, or torque.

MAINTENANCE

There are very few adjustments that must be made to the power train during normal operations. As an operator, your primary duties will be limited to lubrication of the power train. You can reduce repairs by proper lubrication and periodic inspection of these power train units.

Proper lubrication depends upon the use of the right kind of lubricants which must be put in the right places in the amounts specified by the lubrication charts. The charts provided with the vehicle will show what units in the power train will require lubrication, and where they are located.

In checking the level of the lubricant in gear cases, keep these two important points in mind:

First, always carefully wipe the dirt away from around the inspection plug and then use the proper size wrench to remove the inspection plugs. A wrench too large will round the corners and prevent proper tightening of the plug. For the same reason, never use a pipe wrench or a pair of pliers for removing plugs.

Secondly, be sure the level of the lubricant is right—usually just below or on a level with the bottom of the inspection hole. Before checking the level, allow the vehicle to stand for a while on a level surface so the gear oil can cool and find its own level. Gear oil heated and churned by revolving gears expands and forms bubbles. Although too little gear oil in the gear boxes is responsible for many failures of the power train, do not add too much gear lubricant. Too much oil causes extra maintenance.

Excessive oil or grease can find its way past the oil seals or gear cases. It may be forced out of a transmission into the clutch housing and result in a slipping clutch; or it may get by the rear wheel bearings from the differential housing to cause brakes to slip or grab. Always clean differential and live axle housing vents to prevent leaking seals.

Universal joints and slip joints at the ends of propeller shafts are to be lubricated if fittings are provided. Some of these joints are packed with grease when assembled, others have grease fittings. Do not remove these plugs until you consult the manual or your chief for instructions.

Some passenger cars and trucks have a leather boot or shoe covering the universal and slip joints. The boot prevents grease from being thrown from the joints and it also keeps dirt from mixing with the grease. A mixture of dirt and grease forms an abrasive that will wear parts in a hurry. Never use so much grease on these joints that the grease will be forced out of the boot. The extra grease will be lost and the added weight of the grease will tend to throw the propeller shaft out of balance.

When you are to give a vehicle a thorough inspection, inspect the power train for loose gear housings and joints. Look for bent propeller shafts that are responsible for vibrations, and examine the gear housing and joints for missing crews and bolts. Check to see that the U-bolts fastening the springs to the rear axle housing are tight. A loose spring hanger can throw the rear axle assembly out of line, and place additional strain on the propeller shaft and final drive. When making these inspections, always check the steel lugs for tightness.

After tightening the gear housing, loose connections, and joints, road test the vehicle to see if the various units in the power train are working properly. Shift the gears into all operating speeds and listen for noisy sounds. Report all improper operation of the power train units on the Operator's Trouble Report enabling the mechanic to check out possible causes.

DRIVING WHEELS

Wheels attached to live axles are the driving wheels. The number of wheels and number of driving wheels is sometimes used to identify equipment. Wheels attached to the outside of the driving wheels make up dual wheels. Dual wheels give additional traction to the driving wheels and distribute the weight of the vehicle over a greater area of road surface. They are considered as single wheels in describing vehicles. For example, a 4x2 (four by two) could be a passenger car or a truck having four wheels with two of them driving. A 4x4 indicates a vehicle having four wheels with all four driving. In some cases, these vehicles will have dual wheels in the rear. You would describe such a vehicle as a 4x4 with dual wheels.

A 6x4 truck, although having dual wheels in the rear, is identified by six wheels, four of them driving. Actually, the truck has ten wheels but the wheel attached to each driving wheel could be removed without changing the identity of the truck. If the front wheels of this truck were driven by a live axle, it would be called a 6x6.

II. BRAKE SYSTEMS

Good brakes are an absolute necessity for the safe operation of a motor vehicle. The modern day vehicle is capable of moving at extremely high speeds, and this results in an ever increasing demand for more efficient braking systems. Braking systems must not only be able to stop the vehicle, but must stop it in as short a distance as possible.

Friction is the resistance to relative motion between two surfaces in contact with each other. Thus, when a stationary surface is forced into contact with a moving surface, the resistance to relative motion or the rubbing action between the two surfaces will slow down the moving surface. In nearly all brake systems, the brake drums provide the moving surface and the brake shoes provide the stationary surface. The friction between the brake drums and the brake shoes slows the drum, wheel, and the friction between the tires and the road surface slows the vehicle, eventually bringing it to a complete stop.

INDIVIDUAL BRAKES

On modern equipment individual service brakes are provided for each wheel and are operated by a foot pedal. The equipment also has an emergency or parking brake. The parking brake is operated by a separate pedal or a hand lever.

Individual brakes are classified into three types: external contracting brake, internal expanding brake, and disk brake.

External Contracting Brakes. External contracting brakes are sometimes used for parking brakes on motor vehicles and for controlling the speed of auxiliary equipment drive shafts.

In operation, the brake band (or shoe) of an external contracting brake is tightened around the rotating drum by moving the brake lever. The brake hand is made of comparatively thin, flexible steel, shaped to fit the drum, with a frictional lining riveted to the inner surface. This flexible brake band cannot withstand the high pressure required to produce the friction that will stop a heavily loaded or fast moving vehicle, but works well as a parking brake.

In an external contracting brake, the brake band is anchored opposite the point where the pressure is applied. In addition to supporting the band, the anchor proves a means for adjusting brake lining clearance. Other adjusting screws and bolts are provided at the ends of the band.

Internal Expanding Brakes. Internal expanding brakes are used almost exclusively as wheel brakes. This type of brake permits a more compact and economical construction. The brake shoe and brake operating mechanism are supported on a backing plate or brake shield which is attached to the vehicle axle. The brake drum, attached to the rotating wheel, acts as a cover for the shoe and operating mechanism and furnishes a frictional surface for the brake shoe.

In operation, the brake shoe of an internal expanding brake is forced outward against the drum to produce the braking action. One end of the shoe is hinged to the backing plate by an anchor pin, while the other end is unattached and can be moved in its support by the operating mechanism. When force from the operating mechanism is applied to the unattached end of the shoe, the shoe expands and brakes the wheel. A retracting spring returns the shoe to the original position when braking action is no longer required.

The brake-operating linkage alone does not provide sufficient mechanical advantage for positive braking. Some means of supplementing the physical application of the braking system has to be used to increase pressure on the brake shoes. A self-energizing action is very helpful in accomplishing this, once setting of the shoes is started by physical effort. While there are variations of this action, it is always obtained by the shoes themselves, which tend to revolve with the revolving drum.

When the brake shoe is anchored (see figure below) and the drum revolves in the direction shown, the shoe will tend to revolve with the drum when it is forced against the drum. As a result, the shoe will exert considerable pressure against the anchor pin. Since the pin is fixed to the brake shield, this pressure will tend to wedge the shoe tightly in between the pin and the drum as shown. As the initial braking pressure is increased on the cam, the wedging action increases and the shoe is forced still more tightly against the drum to increase the friction. This self-energizing results in more braking action than could be obtained with the actuating pressure alone. Brakes making use of this principle to increase pressures on the braking surfaces are known as self-energizing (or servo) brakes.

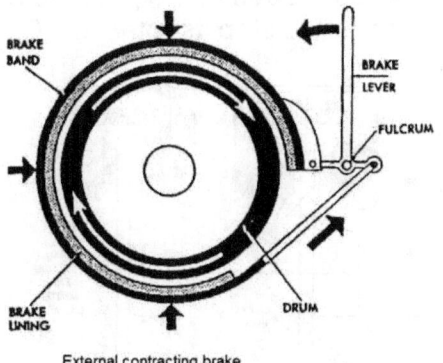

External contracting brake

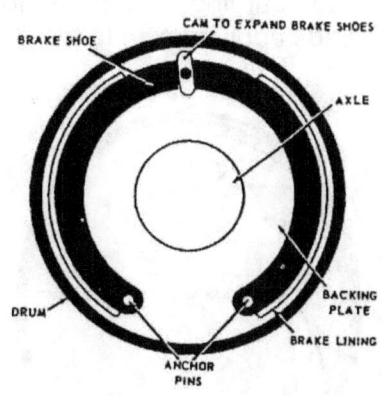

Internal expanding brake

It is most important that the operator control the total braking action at all times; therefore, the self-energizing action should increase only upon application of additional "actuating" pressure at the brake pedal. The amount of self-energizing action available depends mainly on location of the anchor pin. As the pin is moved toward the center of the drum, wedging action increases until a point is reached where the shoe will automatically lock. The pin must be located outside this point so that the operator can control the braking.

When two shoes are anchored on the bottom of the backing plate, self-energizing action is effective on only one shoe. The other shoe tends to revolve away from its pivot, which reduces its braking action. When the wheel is revolving in the opposite direction, the self-energizing action is produced on the opposite shoe.

Two shoes are usually mounted so that self-energizing action is effective on both. This is accomplished by pivoting the shoes to each other and leaving the pivot free of the backing plate. The only physical effort required is for operating the first, or primary, shoe. Both shoes then apply additional pressure to the braking surfaces with no increase in the pressure on the operating linkage. The anchor pins are fitted into slots in the free ends of the brake shoes. This method of anchoring allows the movement of the shoes necessary to expand against the drum when the shoes are forced against the drum, and the self-energizing action of the primary shoe is transmitted through the pivot to the secondary shoe. Both shoes will tend to revolve with the drum and will be wedged against the drum by the one anchor pin. The other anchor pin will cause a similar action when the wheel is revolving in the opposite direction.

The operating mechanism for wheel brakes differs with the brake systems, and so do the brake shoe adjusting devices. The brake drums and brake shoes, however, are similar in all wheel brakes.

Most modern automotive brakes have a self-adjusting feature that automatically adjust the brakes when they need it as a result of brake lining wear.

Disk Brakes. The disk brake has a metal disk instead of a drum, and a pair of flat pads instead of curved brake shoes. The figure below shows a sectional view of a typical disk brake assembly. The two flat pads are located on the two sides of the disk. The assembly in which the flat pads are held is called the caliper assembly. In operation, the pads are forced against the two sides of the disk by the movement of pistons in the caliper assembly. The pistons are actuated by hydraulic pressure from the master cylinder. The effect is to clamp the rotating disk between the stationary pads as illustrated below. This is the same action you get when you pick up a piece of paper; our fingers and thumb clamp on both sides of the paper to hold it. In the same way, the pads apply friction to the disk and attempt to stop its rotation. This provides the braking action.

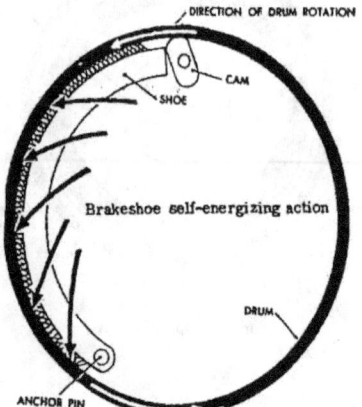

Brakeshoe self-energizing action

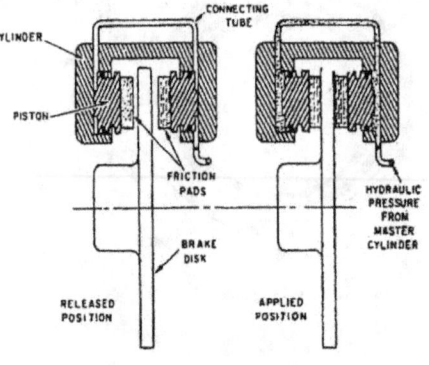

Sectional view of disk brake in released and applied position.

MECHANICAL HANDBRAKES

In most automotive vehicles, the handbrake has its own hookup. Either external contracting brake bands are located on the drive shaft or some type of mechanical linkage operates the rear wheel brakes.

HYDRAULIC BRAKE SYSTEMS

A hydraulic brake system is primarily a liquid connection or coupling between the brake pedal and the individual brake shoes and drums. The system consists of one master cylinder connected by pipes and flexible tubing to the wheel cylinders. The wheel cylinders control the movement of the brake shoes at each wheel.

The brake fluid in hydraulic systems is composed of alcohol and caster oil or glycerin. This liquid neither freezes nor boils at temperatures encountered in year-round operations. When the brake pedal in a hydraulic brake system is depressed, the hydraulic fluid forces the pistons in the wheel cylinder against the brake shoes. The shoes expand against the brake drum and stop the vehicle. Hydraulic brakes are self-equalizing brakes. If the actuating pistons were all the same size, each brake in the hydraulic system would receive an identical hydraulic force when the brakes are applied because a force exerted at any point upon a closed liquid is distributed equally through the liquid in all directions. Some brake systems have larger wheel cylinders in the front than in the rear. This is because, when stopping, more of the vehicle's weight is felt in front and, therefore, more front wheel braking effort is required.

The mechanical advantage of any brake system is the relation between the pressure applied by the operator on the brake pedal to the pressure exerted on the braking surfaces.

The master cylinder has two functions. It is a reservoir for the brake fluid, and it contains the piston and the valves which change mechanical force to hydraulic pressure when the brake pedal is depressed. The pressure on the brake pedal moves the piston within the master cylinder, forcing the brake fluid from the master cylinder through tubing and flexible hose to the wheel cylinders. As pressure on the pedal is increased, greater hydraulic pressure is built up within the brake cylinders, and thus greater force is put forth against the ends of the brake shoes. When pressure on the pedal is released, the springs on the brake shoes return the wheel cylinder pistons to their released positions. This action forces the brake fluid back through the flexible hose and tubing to the master cylinder.

Most older model cars are equipped with the single system master cylinder. This system is, however, being replaced with dual system master cylinders.

The operation of a dual system master cylinder is basically the same as a single master cylinder. The dual system master cylinder, however, has two pistons, two separate fluid reservoirs, and two output ports. Thus, the dual system master cylinder has two separate hydraulic pressure systems. One of the hydraulic systems normally is connected to the front brakes, and the other system is the rear brakes. If either the front or rear hydraulic system fails, the other system remains operational.

The master cylinder, like other parts in the brake system, is subject to wear, leaks, and deposits or corrosion on the cylinder wall and piston. Master cylinder reservoir fluid level should be checked periodically and clean brake fluid added, as needed, to maintain fluid level approximately ½" from the top of the reservoir.

The brake lines transmit fluid and pressure from the master cylinder to the wheel cylinders, which in turn change the hydraulic pressure into mechanical force. The wheel cylinders are mounted on the brake backing plate. Inside each cylinder are two pistons that move in opposite directions by hydraulic pressure, which pushes the brake shoes against the brake drum. The brake shoes are made of iron, steel, or cast aluminum. They support the brake lining and transmit force to the lining, which is attached to the face of the shoe and make contact with the inner surface of the brake drums. During contact with one another the lining and the drum create the frictional surface that gives the braking effect.

AIRBRAKE SYSTEMS

Air, like all gases, is easily compressed. Compressed air exerts pressure and this pressure will be equal in all directions. Air under pressure can be conveniently stored and carried through lines or tubes. Considerable force is available for braking since operating air pressure may be as high as 100 psi. All brakes on a vehicle, and on a trailer (when one is used), are operated together by means of a brake valve.

The compressor is driven from the engine crankshaft or one of the auxiliary shafts. The three common methods of driving the compressor from the engine are gear, belt, and chain.

The compressor may be lubricated from the engine crankcase or be self-lubricated. Cooling may be either by air or liquid from the engine.

The purpose of the compressor governor is to automatically maintain the air pressure in the reservoir between the maximum pressure desired (100-105 psi) and the minimum pressure required for safe operation (80-85 psi) by starting and stopping compression.

The two steel tanks which are components of most air brake systems are called reservoirs. These tanks are used to cool, store, and remove moisture from the air and give a smooth flow of air to the brake system.

A safety valve consists of an adjustable spring-loaded ball check valve in a body. It is used to protect the system against excessive pressures and is usually mounted on a reservoir. The safety valve is normally set at 150 psi but can be varied to suit the vehicle requirements.

A pressure gauge is attached to any line which registers reservoir pressure and is mounted to the dashboard of the vehicle.

The brake valve is the operator's control of the air brake system. When the brake valve is engaged, air from the reservoir flows through the valve to the brakes. The three types of brake valves used in the air brake systems are pedal, treadle, and hand. When you press the pedal of an airbrake system, air under pressure in a reservoir is released to the brake lines by an air valve. This air goes to the brake chambers located close to the wheel brakes, which contain flexible diaphragms. The force of the air admitted to these chambers cause the diaphragms to operate the brake shoes through a mechanical linkage.

An air pressure gage will let you know if you have proper air pressure within the reservoir (60 lbs. pressure is minimum). This gage is usually found on the instrument panel of a truck or bus. If the pressure fails to build up or exceeds the maximum limits after building up, secure the truck until the fault is corrected.

Independent control of trailer brakes is valuable under adverse conditions when it is sometimes desirable to apply the brakes on the trailer without applying the brakes on the truck or tractor. The independent trailer control valve, conveniently located in the cab, provides the operator with perfect control of his trailing load at all times.

VACUUM BRAKES

In the vacuum brake system, depressing the brake pedal opens a valve between the power cylinder, which contains a piston, and the intake manifold to which the power cylinder is connected. To apply the brakes, air is exhausted from the cylinder ahead of the piston, while atmospheric pressure acts on the rear side of the piston to exert a powerful pull on the rod attached to the piston.

When the brake valve is closed, the chamber ahead of the piston is shut off from the intake manifold and is open to the atmosphere. The pressure is then the same on both sides of the piston; therefore, no pull is exerted upon the pull rod. The brake shoe return springs then release the brakes and return the piston to its original position in the power cylinder.

Hydrovac is a trade name for a one-unit vacuum power braking system. It combines into one assembly a hydraulic control valve, a vacuum power cylinder and a hydraulic slave cylinder. This assembly is connected to both the master cylinder and the wheel brakes, eliminating the need for mechanical connections with the brake pedal.

When you press the brake pedal, fluid is forced from the master cylinder through the check valve to the slave cylinder and on to the wheel cylinders. The foot pedal pressure, acting through the master cylinder, acts also against the slave cylinder piston, assisting the vacuum pistons and push rods to press upon the brake shoes.

OPERATOR MAINTENANCE

Periodic brake service by the operator includes the use of proper brake fluid; checking brake fluid level; inflating tires properly; checking for loose connections or parts; checking for leaks in the system; draining air reservoirs daily; and checking the self-contained lubricating oil system of air compressors daily.

MALFUNCTION DETECTION

The types of brake trouble that may be encountered in vehicle operation are: brake pedal goes to the floorboard with no resistance; one brake drags; all brakes drag; vehicle pulls to one side when braking; soft or spongy pedal; excessive pedal effort required; noisy brakes; air in the system; loss of brake fluid; brakes heat up during driving and fail to release; leaky brake cylinder; grabbing brake action; and brake pedal can be depressed without slowing the vehicle. As an operator, you must explain the malfunction on the Operator's Trouble Report and turn it into the maintenance shop for necessary correction.

STEERING MECHANISMS

All steering mechanisms have the same basic parts. The steering linkage ties the front wheels together and connects them to the steering gear case at the lower end of the steering column, which in turn connects the gear case to the steering wheel.

The arms and rods of the steering linkage have ball or ball and socket ends to provide a swivel connection between them. These jointed ends are provided with grease fittings, dust seals or boots, and many of them have end-play adjustment devices. These joints and devices must be adjusted and lubricated regularly.

The tie-rod is usually located behind the axle and keeps the front wheels in proper alignment. To provide for easier steering and maximum leverage, the tie-rod may be separated into two lengths and connected to the steering gear near the center of the vehicle.

The drag link between the steering arm and the pitman arm may be long or short, depending on the installation.

The pitman arm, splined to the shaft extending from the steering gear case, moves in an arc, its position depending on which way the steering wheel is turned. It is approximately vertical when the front wheels are straight ahead. Therefore, the length of the drag link is determined by the distance between the steering arm and the vertical position of the pitman arm. Unlike the tie-rods, the length of the drag link is not adjustable.

The steering gear case contains the gears that control the movement of the pitman arm and steering linkage.

POWER STEERING

Power steering has been used for a number of years on heavy-duty applications, but it is only in recent years that power steering has been applied to any extent on automotive vehicles. The principle of power steering is very simple. A booster arrangement is provided which is set in operation when the steering wheel is turned. The booster then takes over and does most of the work of steering. Power steering has used compressed air, electrical mechanisms, and hydraulic pressure. Hydraulic pressure is used on the vast majority of power-steering mechanisms today.

In the hydraulic power-steering system, a continuously operating pump provides hydraulic pressure. As the steering wheel is turned, valves are operated to admit this hydraulic pressure to a cylinder. Then, the pressure causes a piston to move—and the piston does most of the steering work.

There are actually two general types of power-steering systems. In one, the integral type, the power operating assembly is located in the steering gear case. In the other, the linkage type, the power operating assembly is part of the steering linkage.

In the linkage-type power-steering system, the power cylinder or booster cylinder is not part of the steering gear. Instead, the power cylinder is connected into the steering linkage. In addition, the valve assembly is included in the steering linkage, either as a separate assembly or united with the power cylinder.

WHEEL ALIGNMENT

Steering control depends greatly upon the position of the wheels in relation to the rest of the vehicle and the surface over which it travels. Any changes from the specified setting of the wheels affect steering and the riding control of the vehicle. Therefore, the proper wheel alignment is important for vehicle control.

Steering geometry is the term manufacturers use to describe steering and front wheel alignment. Steering geometry includes pivot inclination, wheel caster, wheel chamber, toe-in and toe-out. These terms refer to angles in the front wheel alignment which may change because of driving over rough terrain, striking stationary objects, and accident damage.

OPERATOR MAINTENANCE

Doing maintenance servicing by the operator, the service that the steering linkage normally requires is periodic lubrication of the connecting joints between the links which contain bushings.

When vehicles are equipped with manually operated steering, check the steering gear housing for sufficient lubrication and add recommended manufacturer's gear lubricant, if necessary. For vehicles equipped with power steering, check belt tension which can cause low oil pressure and hard steering. Check fluid level. If the fluid level is low, add fluid to bring it up to the recommended level. Use only special power steering fluid recommended. If the level is low, the possibility exists that there is a leak. Check all hose and power-steering connections for signs of leaks. Leakage may occur at various points in the power-steering unit if the seals are defective. Report conditions to the maintenance shop for replacement of any defective seal, or it may only be necessary to tighten the connections to eliminate leaks.

MALFUNCTION DETECTION

The types of steering trouble that may be encountered in vehicle operation are: excessive play in the steering system; hard steering; vehicle wanders; vehicle pulls to one side when braking; front wheel shimmy at low speeds; front-wheel tramps (high speed shimmy); steering kickback; tires squeal on turns; improper tire wear; and noises. As an operator, you would explain the malfunction on the Operator's Trouble Report and turn it into the maintenance shop for corrective actions.

III. SUSPENSION SYSTEM

A suspension system is a system of anchoring and suspending the wheels or tracks from the frame by means of springs. The suspension system is an important feature of military vehicles; it supports the weight and allows them to be driven under varying loads and speed conditions over bumpy roads and rough terrain without great risk of damage.

The usual components of a suspension system are the springs and shock absorbers. Some suspension systems also have torsion bars.

SPRINGS

Springs support the frame and the body of the vehicle, as well as the load the vehicle carries. They allow the wheels to withstand the shocks of uneven road surfaces and provide a flexible connection between the wheels and the body. The best spring is the one which absorbs road shock rapidly and returns to its normal position slowly. Such a spring, however, is very rare, if not an impossibility. Extremely flexible, or soft springs, allow too much movement of the vehicle superstructure, while still, hard springs do not allow enough movement.

The springs do no support the weight of the wheels, rims, tires, and axles. These parts make up the unsprung weight of the vehicle. The unsprung weight decreases the action of the springs and is, therefore, kept to a minimum to permit the springs to do the job of supporting the vehicle frame and load.

The three types of spring suspension usually found in vehicles are: the longitudinal, the lengthwise mounting, which is the most common; the independent, which is generally used in front suspensions; and transverse, which is the crosswise mounting.

The multiple leaf spring consists of a number of steel strips or leaves of different lengths, fastened together by a bolt through the center. Each end of the largest or master leaf is rolled in an eye which serves as a means of attaching the spring to the spring hanger and spring shackle. Leaf rebound clips surround the leaves at two or more intervals along the spring to keep them from separating on the rebound after the spring has been depressed. The clips allow the spring leaves to slide but prevent them from separating and throwing the entire rebound stress on the master leaf. Thus, the spring acts as a flexible beam. Leaf springs may be suspended lengthwise (parallel to the frame), or cross-wise.

When installed lengthwise, both ends of the spring are attached to the frame and the center is clamped to the axle or spring seat. In some trucks and cars the rear springs are clamped under the axle, instead of over it to lower the center of gravity. A low center of gravity will help prevent a heavily loaded truck from upsetting.

Springs installed crosswise have the ends attached to the axle, and the frame rests on the center of the spring. Torque arms or radius rods are required with this type of spring suspension to absorb the driving thrust of the wheels. The driving thrust and brake action of wheels tend to twist the springs from the spring hangers and shackles connecting them to the frame or axles.

Spring hangers are fittings to which the spring ends are attached. A bolt or pin passes through the bushing in the spring eye and is secured to the spring hanger on the frame. The bushing and shackle bolt or pin, therefore, provide the bearing surface which supports the load on the spring.

The spring bushings may be made of bronze or rubber. They may be pressed or screwed into the spring eye, depending on the design. The steel bolts or pins that pass through the bushing are also either plain or threaded. Threaded bushings and shackle bolts offer a greater bearing surface and are replaced more easily when they become worn.

When a leaf spring is compressed, it must straighten out or break. Therefore, spring shackles are required at one or both ends of the spring. Spring shackles provide a swinging support and allow the spring to straighten out when compressed. One shackle is used in either the front or rear support of springs installed lengthwise. Two shackles are used in supporting springs installed crosswise.

You will see many types of spring shackles. The link shackle and U-shackle are the most common. Link shackles are used in heavy vehicles, and the U-type is more common for use on passenger cars and light trucks.

You will find link shackles used to support a transverse spring on the dead front axle of some wheeled tractors. Most wheeled tractors do not even have springs, and all load cushioning is obtained through large, low pressure tires.

Track-type tractors are equipped with one large leaf spring supported without spring shackles. It is fastened to the engine support and rests on the frames supporting the tracks and rollers. Brackets on the track frames keep the spring from shifting. The main purpose of the spring is to relieve the running gear of stresses during operation.

Some vehicles are equipped with leaf springs at the rear wheels only; others are so equipped both front and rear.

Coil springs are most generally used on independent suspension systems. They provide a very smooth riding quality. Their use has normally been limited to passenger vehicles. Recently, however, they have been used to a limited extent on trucks. The spring seat and hanger, shaped to fit the coil ends, hold the spring in place. Spacers made of rubberized fabric are placed at each end of the coil to prevent squeaking. The rubber bumper, mounted in the spring supporting member, prevents metal to metal contact when the spring is compressed. Most vehicles are equipped with coil springs at the two front wheels, while some other have them at both front and rear.

SHOCK ABSORBERS
Springs alone are never satisfactory in a light vehicle suspension system. A stiff spring gives a hard ride because it does not flex and rebound when the vehicle passes over a bump. On the other hand, too flexible a spring rebounds too much, and the vehicle rides roughly. To smooth the riding qualities of the vehicle, shock absorbers are used. They prevent excessive jolting of the vehicle by balancing spring stiffness and flexibility. They allow the springs to return to rest slowly after having been compressed. Although single-acting shock absorbers check only spring rebound, double-acting shock absorbers check spring compression as well as spring rebound, permitting the use of the more flexible springs.

FRONT AXLE SUSPENSION
Most passenger car front wheels are individually supported with independent suspension systems. The ones you are likely to encounter are the coil spring and the torsion bar suspension systems. These are used with independent front axles and shock absorbers.

REAR AXLE SUSPENSION
Driving wheels are mounted on a live driving axle that is suspended by springs attached to the axle housing. Leaf springs are generally used for suspending live axles. Coil springs are used on a number of passenger cars with torque tube drive.

OPERATOR MAINTENANCE
Under normal operation, and given proper maintenance, suspension systems would not need adjustments or replacement for many miles. The spring assemblies of the suspension system should be checked regularly to ensure that shackles are tight and that bushings within the shackles are not worn excessively or frozen tight. Occasionally, spraying lubricating oil on the spring leaves helps to prevent squeaking at the ends of the spring leaves. Following the lubrication chart furnished for a particular vehicle, check and lubricate the front suspension system including linkage, kingpin, and ball joints. During your checks you may find shock absorber bushings worn; if so, it is best to have the bushings replaced, or in some instances a complete replacement of the shock absorbers is needed.

MALFUNCTION DETECTION
Some types of suspension troubles that may be encountered in vehicle operation are: hard steering, vehicle wander, vehicular pulls to one side during normal driving, front-wheel shimmy, front-wheel tramp (high speed shimmy), steering kickback, hard or rough ride, sway on

turns, spring breakage, sagging springs, and noises. As an operator, you would explain the malfunction on the Operator's Trouble Report and turn the trouble report into the maintenance shop for corrective action.

IV. FRAME

The chassis is the assembly of mechanisms that make up the major operating part of the vehicle. It is usually assumed to include everything except the vehicle body. The individual operating assemblies are mounted on the frame, which must be strong enough to support the weight of the vehicle and its rated load without distortion. The frame must be rigid enough to keep the units of the vehicle in proper alignment and to protect them against the stresses and strains of road and surface shocks.

The frame is generally constructed of cold-rolled open-hearth steel, but sometimes of alloy steel to lighten the weight of the vehicle. The side members or rails are the heaviest parts of the frame. The cross members are fixed to the side members rigidly enough to prevent weaving and twisting of the frame. Angular pieces of metal called gusset plates are riveted or welded at the point where members are joined for added strength.

The number, size, and arrangement of cross members depend on the type of vehicle for which the frame is designed. Usually, a front cross member supports the radiator and front end of the engine as well as stiffens the frame. The rear cross members furnish support for the fuel tanks and rear trunk on passenger cars, and the two-bar connections for trucks. Additional cross members are added to the frame to support the rear of the engine and power train and to secure the rigidity required.

The cross members of most small vehicles are designed in either X or K form. The front cross members are wider and of heavier construction than the back members because they support the engine and the front wheels. The side members are shaped to accommodate the body and support its weight. They narrow toward the front of the vehicle to permit a shorter turning radius for the wheels and widen under the main part of the body where the body is secured to the frame. Trucks and trailers usually have frames with straight side members to accommodate several designs of bodies and to give the vehicle added strength to withstand heavier loads. Heavy duty trucks and trailers have I-beam frames.

Brackets and hangers which are bolted or riveted to the frame to support the shock absorbers, fenders, running boards, and springs are usually made of case or pressed steel.

BASIC FUNDAMENTALS OF TRACTORS AND ATTACHMENTS

CONTENTS

		Page
I.	Use of Tractors and Attachments	1
II.	Capabilities, Gross Limits, and Utilization of Tractors and Attachments	9
III.	Operation of Tractors and Attachments	9
IV.	Operator's Maintenance	27
V.	Tractor Tires	32
VI.	Changing Front-End Tractor Attachment	32
VII.	Changing Rear-Mounted Tractor Attachment	33
VIII.	Safety	35

BASIC FUNDAMENTALS OF TRACTORS AND ATTACHMENTS

A tractor may be used simply as a PRIME MOVER to tow or push another piece of construction equipment (a scraper, for example). Or, it may be used, equipped with one of several types of ATTACHMENTS (such as a dozer blade or a winch), as a self-contained piece of construction equipment. In selecting a tractor, you must consider the job for which it will be used, such as bulldozing, pulling a scraper, or ripping. Other factors to consider are the length of haul and the terrain to be worked. Tractors are indispensable in practically all road and airfield construction operations.

Many different makes, models, and sizes of tractors are used in industry and commerce. You will find, however, that most of the tractors are either the crawler type or the rubber-tired type.

General information on starting, operating, and maintaining crawler and rubber-tired tractors and their attachments is given in this chapter. Also included is information on the capabilities, gross limits, optimum working distances, and utilization of tractors; recognition of hand signals used during tractor operations; procedures to follow when changing tires and attachments; and safety precautions to be observed when changing tires and when operating, or working near, tractors.

I. USE OF TRACTORS AND ATTACHMENTS

Tractors and attachments used by industry are designed primarily to ensure the performance of earthwork functions under varied conditions. Design specifications and performance characteristics of tractors and attachments developed for industry use indicate their capabilities and limitations under adverse conditions. You must recognize these capabilities and limitations to make the most efficient use of tractors and attachments which they may operate.

CRAWLER-TYPE TRACTOR

The crawler type tractor is perhaps the most basic and versatile machine in the construction field. (See fig. 1.) It is used where maximum power is required at relatively low speeds and operates particularly well on loam or gravel. You will find the crawler tractor especially suited for sidehill excavations. It is preferred to the rubber-tired tractor for this purpose because of the lower center of machine gravity, better traction, and stability. The crawler tractor can be used as a power unit for winches, hoists, and side booms.

Crawler tractors are usually rated by size and power. The pull developed at the drawbar is expressed in pounds or as drawbar horsepower. At a low gear, the drawbar pull is greater; as the speed increases, the drawbar pull decreases. Although the specifications for crawler tractors may vary among the different manufacturers, the maximum speeds are seldom in excess of 7 mph.

The crawler type tractor is used primarily where it is advantageous to sacrifice high travel speed to obtain high drawbar pounds pull and traction. The crawler tractor attains much of its all-type-terrain versatility from its low ground bearing pressure at the track, which varies from about 6 to 9 pounds per square inch, depending on the particular model. Crawler tractors have a distinct "flotation" advantage over rubber-tired tractors which have a bearing pressure of about 25 to 35 pounds per square inch. Crawler tractors can operate in muck or water as deep as the height of the tracks. Operation in deeper water is possible, for short periods of time, if the tractor is properly waterproofed. For long moves, crawler tractors should be transported on heavy trailers. They may be moved under their own power at slow rates of speed but this shortens their operational life.

TRACTORS AND ATTACHMENTS

Figure 1.— Typical crawler tractor with dozer blade.

RUBBER-TIRED TRACTOR

Rubber-tired tractors are the result of efforts of the construction industry to obtain units with higher travel speed than are possible with crawler tractors. Many rubber-tired tractors presently available have maximum speeds in excess of 30 mph.

Rubber-tired tractors are capable of providing many of the same functions as crawler tractors, and are used in conjunction with crawler tractors on many projects. The high travel speeds possible with rubber-tired tractors give them an advantage on jobs requiring travel over considerable distances. However, the high speeds are obtained at the expense of pulling effort.

Rubber-tired tractors are used where hauls are long enough to develop high average haul and return speed, or where tracks would be harmful to surfaces under construction. These tractors operate well on loam, gravel, smooth rock, or paved surfaces. Recent improvements in design give rubber-tired tractors almost the same traction capability, under normal conditions, as the crawler type, but full drawbar pull cannot be attained in sand or mud because of tire slippage. Slippage on some rubber-tired tractors is largely overcome by using weight transfer devices, which transfer some of the load weight to the drive wheels of the tractor. In dire emergency and under the direct authorization of the leading petty officer, deflating the tires slightly will reduce slippage to a certain extent. The high speed of rubber-tired tractors makes them particularly desirable as prime

Figure 2.— M.R.S. model I-110 tractor with dozer blade.

Figure 3.—A typical straight dozer blade.

movers for scrapers and dump trailers on comparatively long hauls on good haul roads. They are also excellent prime movers for heavy equipment trailers or trailer-mounted equipment, such as crushing and screening plants. Some rubber-tired tractors are well adapted for use with dozer blades.

Rubber-tired tractors are designed for greater speed and mobility than crawler tractors, while providing almost as much power. Experience has found that rubber-tired tractors used in earthmoving operations can move materials more economically than either crawler tractors with scrapers or truck and shovel. This is particularly true where speed is the primary consideration on long hauls. Beside towing earthmoving scrapers, the rubber-tired tractor can, through the use of various mounted attachments, perform the same work as the crawler tractor in pioneer phases of construction. However, the rubber-tired tractor's capability to perform this type of work is limited by its traction and comparatively high bearing pressure. The use of the wide base, low pressure, and large diameter tires has improved but not eliminated these shortcomings.

TRACTOR BLADES

The most common type of tractor attachment is the DOZER BLADE, a heavy rectangular steel blade which is mounted on the front of the tractor and used for pushing earth either straight ahead (DRIFTING) or to one side (SIDE CASTING).

A tractor which is equipped with a dozer blade is called a DOZER or BULLDOZER. If the blade is one which can be used only at an angle of 90 degrees to the center axis of the tractor, the attachment is called a STRAIGHT DOZER BLADE. If the blade is one which can be ANGLED approximately 30 degrees to either side from its current 90 degree preposition, the attachment is called an ANGLEDOZER BLADE. A typical straight dozer blade is shown in figure 9-3, and an angledozer blade is shown in figure 9-4. The straight dozer blade is used mainly

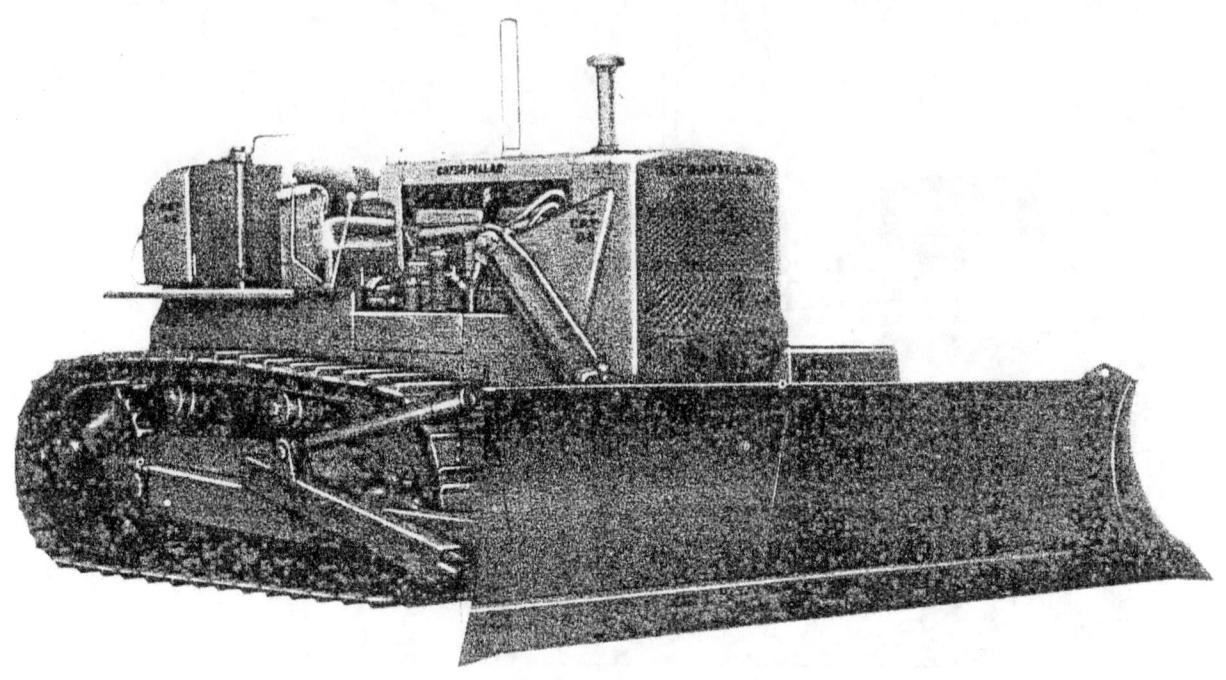

Figure 4.— A typical angledozer blade.

for straight drifting, but can be used for side casting by making a series of pivoting passes with the tractor. The angledozer blade is used mainly for side casting.

Another tractor blade attachment which is used less frequently than those discussed above is the U-blade (fig. 5.) The U-blade has the sides advanced farther than the center. This makes it possible to transport a larger load by reducing side spill. The U-blade functions well in rough pioneering on sidehills and is ideal for stockpiling coal, sand, rock, and gravel.

RIPPER

Another type of tractor attachment is the ripper (fig. 6), which provides a powerful tool for breaking up material too compact to be broken by dozers, graders, and the like. The ripper is also used to uproot boulders and stumps; to loosen shale, sandstone, and asphalt pavement; and to rip up concrete slabs. After ripping these materials, easier and more efficient removal can be accomplished by supporting equipment.

A dozer blade may have ripper teeth hinged to the back of it in such a way that they float on the ground when the blade is moving forward, and dig in when the blade is moving backward.

WINCHES

Winches are mounted on tractor-dozer units (track and wheeled) or trucks. On a tractor-dozer unit, the winch is mounted in the rear and is directly geared to the rear power takeoff on the tractor, as illustrated in figure 7. This arrangement permits development of a line pull that is 50 to 100 percent greater than tractor pull. Tractor-mounted winches are used for uprooting trees and stumps, hoisting and skidding felled trees, and freeing mired equipment.

Some limitations encountered when using winches may be due to the limited pulling capacity and size of the tractor. The terrain may also affect maneuverability of the tractor.

SCRAPERS

Scrappers which are nonmotorized may be towed either by rubber-tired or crawler-type tractors. An example of a scraper towed by a crawler-type tractor is shown in figure 9-8. A scraper towed by a wheel-type tractor is shown in figure 9.

The crawler-type tractor is normally used for towing when large loads must be moved at

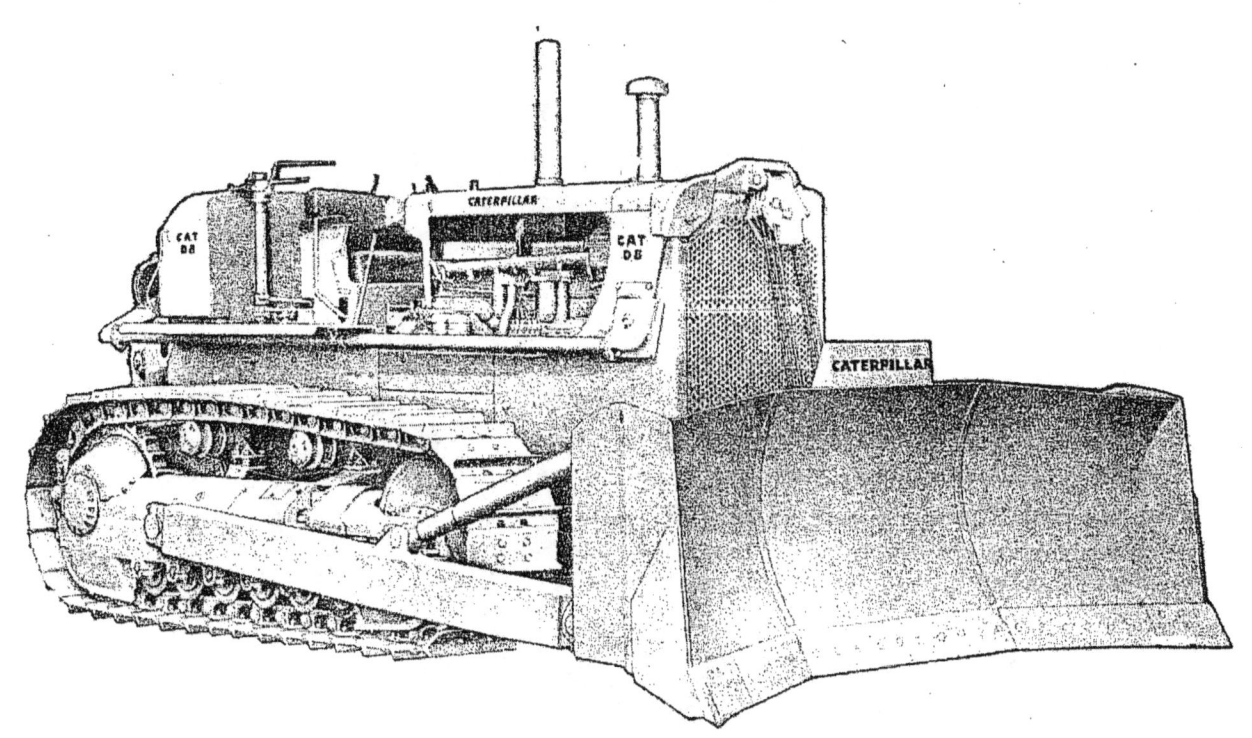

Figure 5.— A typical U-blade.

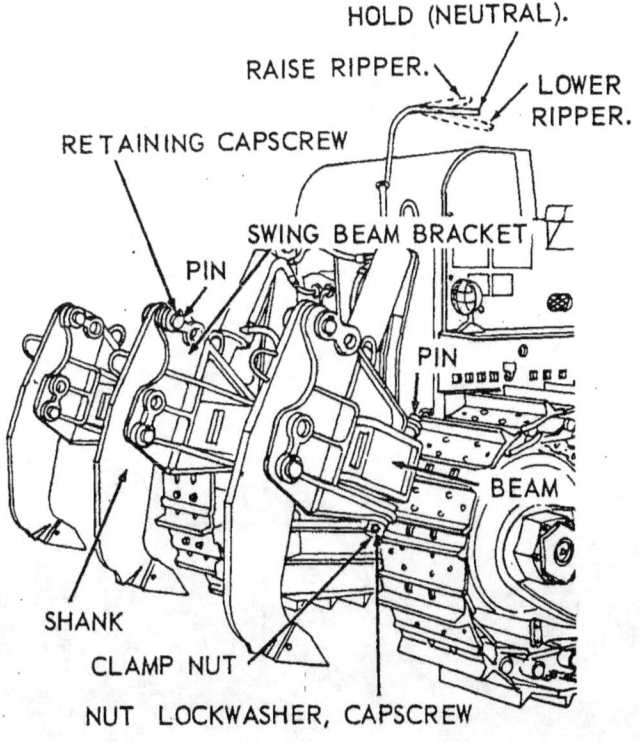

CAUTION: WHEN RAMS REACH THE END OF THEIR STROKE, RETURN THE CONTROL LEVER TO "HOLD" POSITION IMMEDIATELY.

Figure 6.— Ripper and control lever positions.

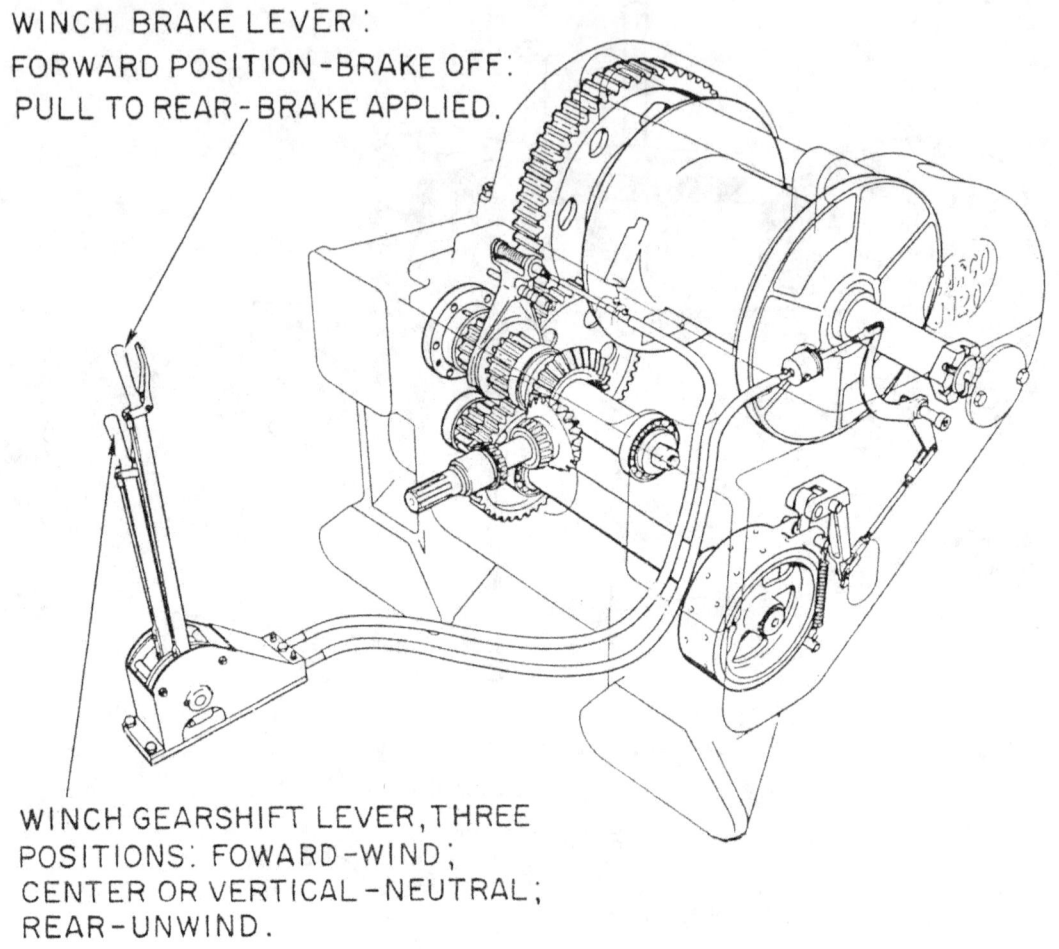

Figure 7. — Winch and winch control levers.

Figure 8. — Crawler tractor drawn scraper.

Figure 9.—Four-wheel tractor pulling scraper.

rather slow speed because of steep grades, poor haul routes, or poor ground conditions.

Scrapers towed by crawler-type tractors are used for short to medium hauls ranging up to 1,500 feet.

Scrapers towed by wheel-type tractors are employed when maximum use can be made of tractor speed. This combination requires good hauling conditons, including grades, surfaces, and hauling distances of 900 to 5,000 feet, to develop high average rates of speed. A pusher tractor is generally required to assist the prime mover (crawler or wheel tractor) in loading the scraper. Your greatest utilization of scrapers will be in making cuts and in hauling material from the borrow pit to the fill area.

SIDE-BOOM CRANE

The side-boom crane attachment shown in figure 10 can be used for any type of general hoisting, but it is used most frequently on pipe-laying projects. This attachment is equipped with one winch for raising and lowering the boom and another for hoisting and lowering the hook-block assembly. To prevent the weight of heavy loads from tipping the tractor, counterweights are attached to the opposite side of the boom to counterbalance the loads being handled.

TOWED ROLLERS

A towed roller is one which is towed by either a crawler or rubber-tired tractor. The principal types are the tamping roller and the grid roller.

A TAMPING roller contains one or more cylindrical drums which revolve on a shaft mounted on a box-type towing frame. The towing frame is equipped with a towbar or tongue for hitching to the drawbar of the prime mover. Each drum is studded with projections, called feet, which usually run from 7 to 9 1/2 inches in length. Figure 11 shows a tamping roller with tapered feet, each of which has an enlarged, off-center sole, called a sheepsfoot.

Tamping rollers are used mainly for compacting loose fill other than sand, gravel, or crushed stone. On the first pass, the feet will gradually begin to "walk" themselves upward,

Figure 10.—Side-boom crane attachment.

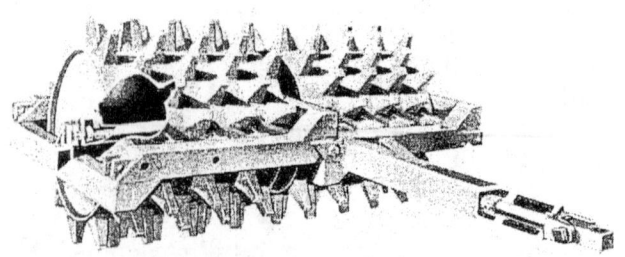

Figure 11.—Tamping roller.

until finally, when maximum compaction is attained, they will be almost entirely atop the ground.

Many tamping rollers can be ballasted for extra weight by filling the drum with sand or water. Some have containers for ballast mounted on the towing frame.

After ripping old bituminous material, GRID rollers (fig. 12) are used to break up and compact this material when it is to be used as a base course. They can also be used to crush such materials as sandstone, soft limestone,

Figure 12.—Grid roller.

coral, and cinders. Grid rollers are mounted in towing frames similar to those on the towed roller previously described. They are usually heavily ballasted with large blocks of concrete, set in containers mounted on the towing frame.

II. CAPABILITIES, GROSS LIMITS, AND UTILIZATION OF TRACTORS AND ATTACHMENTS

Fundamental to most construction projects and certain ground maintenance jobs is the requirement to lower high ground areas and raise low ground areas to meet a common grade. Removal, disposal and/or placement of dirt, rock and impediments; treatment of earth fill; and numerous related operations are within the special province of earthmoving equipment designed to reduce the cost, time, and complications of this type of work. The following kinds of jobs are typical of tractor and attachment applications:

1. Clearing, stripping, pioneering, and ripping.
2. Short and long haul excavating and push loading.
3. Sloping, filling, backfilling, compacting, and finishing.

Dozers will handle all short-haul excavations up to 300 feet. For long-haul excavations over 300 feet, crawler or rubber-tired tractors and scrapers should be used.

The speed of clearing depends on the type of clearing, output of equipment, and methods used. Production rates of equipment under normal operating conditions are used for determining the total time required for the job. Knowing the area and type of clearing and the production rates of available equipment, the time can be estimated and a job schedule prepared.

The productive capacity of tractors and attachments, when used in construction and maintenance operation, is given in table 1, which serves as a guide only, and not as a table of production capacity to be expected on every job.

III. OPERATION OF TRACTORS AND ATTACHMENTS

The sole source of complete and authentic information on tractor and attachment operations is the operator's manual provided by the manufacturer of the tractor or attachment concerned.

The information given in this section describes the prestart checks, starting and operating procedures, during operations checks, and securing methods which are typical of tractors and attachments used.

PRESTART CHECKS

The procedure for making prestart checks is similar with most types of tractors and attachments. However, the location of items to be checked differs from one type of tractor and attachment to another.

In making a prestart check of a CRAWLER TRACTOR equipped with a dozer blade of the type shown in figure 1, you should check the lubricating oil, radiator coolant, batteries, fuel, hydraulic oil, and rear frame oil.

Check the lubricating oil level with the bayonet gage provided. The level should be between the upper ("H") and lower ("L") marks on the "Engine Stopped" side of the bayonet gage. If it is necessary to bring the oil level up to the "H" mark on the gage, add a sufficient amount of the recommended type of lubricating oil.

Check the water level in the radiator. The correct level should be 1 inch above baffles; if below this level, add proper coolant.

After making sure the hydraulic dozer blade is resting level on the ground and the control handle is in the "Hold" position, remove the filler and level plug from the hydraulic reservoir located at the rear of the tractor. Check the level of hydraulic oil in the reservoir. If the oil level is low, add the specified type of hydraulic oil to bring the level up to the plug opening.

TRACTORS AND ATTACHMENTS

Table 1. — Productive Capacity of Tractors and Attachments

Equipment Used	Rate-Units Per Hour	Unit	Conditions
CLEARING AND GRUBBING			
Crawler Type Tractor with Dozer	0.25	Acre	Medium Clearing
Crawler Type Tractor with Dozer	1.00	Acre	Light Stripping
EXCAVATION			
Crawler Type Tractor with Dozer	44	Cu Yd	300 feet level haul
Crawler Type Tractor with Angledozer	86	Cu Yd	Sidehill Cut 50 feet Common Earth
Rubber-Tired Tractor with Dozer	66	Cu Yd	300 feet level haul
Crawler Type Tractor with Scraper 12 cu yd	74	Cu Yd	1,000 feet level haul
Rubber-Tired Tractor with Scraper 12 cu yd	120	Cu Yd	1,000 feet level haul
EMBANKMENT			
Crawler Type Tractor with Angledozer	300	Cu Yd	Spreading Material
Crawler Type Tractor with Towed Roller (sheepsfoot)	250	Cu Yd	9-inch layers, 8 passes
SUBGRADE PREPARATION			
Crawler Type Tractor with Towed Roller (sheepsfoot)	650	Sq Yd	6-inch layers, 8 passes
BASE COURSE CONSTRUCTION			
Crawler Type Tractor with Angledozer	300	Cu Yd	Spread Material

CAUTION: Always loosen the filler and level plug slowly, in case there is still some pressure in the system.

Check the water level in the batteries. You will find four 6-volt negative-grounded batteries connected in series, two mounted under the operator's seat and two mounted to the left of the operator's seat.

Now open the fuel tank drain valve, located at the bottom of the tractor fuel tank, to allow moisture to drain from the tank prior to starting.

As you continue, check the rear frame oil level. The rear frame oil level gage and filler pipe are located to the left of the operator's seat. The level should be at the upper ("FULL") mark on the "Engine Stopped" side of the bayonet gage. If it is necessary to bring the oil level up to the "FULL" mark on the gage, add a sufficient amount of the specified type of oil.

Note: Never operate the tractor if the level of the oil is at or below the "LOW" mark on the rear frame oil level gage.

Check the tractor headlights, panel lights, and rear lights by turning on the light switch and observing whether the lights are burning. Have someone observe the rear lights.

In making a prestart check of the RUBBER-TIRED TRACTOR equipped with a dozer blade of the type shown in figure 2, check the lubricating oil, radiator coolant, batteries, fuel, hydraulic oil, and air cleaner filter.

Check the lubricating oil level with the dipstick provided. The level should be at the "FULL" mark on the dipstick. If it is necessary to bring the oil level up to the "FULL" mark on the dipstick, add a sufficient amount of the recommended type of lubricating oil. The dipstick is located on the left side of the tractor engine.

Check the water level in the radiator. The correct level should be 1 inch above the baffles; if below this level, add proper coolant.

After making sure the hydraulic dozer blade is resting level on the ground and the control handle is in the "HOLD" position, remove the filler cap and dipstick from the hydraulic reservoir located on the right side of the operator's compartment. Check the level of the hydraulic oil in the reservoir. If necessary add the specified type of hydraulic oil to bring the level up to the "FULL" mark on the dipstick.

Check the water level in the batteries. You will find two 12-volt negative-grounded batteries connected in series and mounted on the right side of the tractor behind the hydraulic reservoir.

Inspect the air cleaner filler cartridge. Clean or replace, as required. The air cleaner is located on the right side rear of the engine compartment.

Now drain approximately 4 ounces of fuel from the fuel strainer and a similar amount from the fuel filter through the drain cocks provided for this purpose. The filter and strainer are located on the front right side of the engine.

Check the fuel in the fuel tank. See that the tank is full and the vent is open. The fuel tank is located on the left side of the operator's compartment.

When checking the wheels, tires, and horn on the rubber-tired tractor, follow the procedures described for equipment in previous chapters of this manual.

STARTING CHECKS

After starting the engine, but before putting a tractor into operation, a few additional checks are necessary. Major items to be covered in a starting check of the CRAWLER and RUBBER-TIRED TRACTOR are given below.

Crawler Tractor

The crawler tractor ammeter indicator should register a positive charge reading within the "RUN" range when the engine is operating faster than low idle speed.

The engine oil indicator should register in the "IDLE" range immediately upon starting. When full engine load speed is applied, it should register in the "RUN" range. If little or no pressure is indicated, stop the engine and notify the maintenance shop.

Observe the engine coolant heat indicator. The pointer of the indicator should register in the "RUN" range after the engine has operated a sufficient length of time and should remain there during regular operation.

Check the transmission clutch oil pressure indicator, which should register in the "RUN" range. If the gage indicates in the "CHANGE FILTER" range, stop the engine and service the suction and pressure filters.

Observe the transmission lubricating oil pressure indicator. The indicator should register in the "RUN" (green) range. If the indicator pointer moves into either of the red ranges, stop the engine and service the suction oil filter.

Check the torque converter oil temperature indicator. The pointer of the indicator must register in the "RUN" range (green area) after the engine has operated a sufficient length of time. If the indicator registers in the "CHECK" range, make the following checks:

1. Be sure the transmission clutch oil pressure indicator is registering in the correct range.
2. Stop the engine. Check the oil level in the rear frame as indicated in the prestart section of this chapter.
3. Be sure the transmission oil cooler (mounted on the front of the radiator) is not restricted.
4. Service the transmission and torque converter filters in the following sequence: pressure filter, safety filter, and then the suction filter.

Rubber-Tired Tractor

The rubber-tired tractor ammeter should show a reading in the charge range whenever the engine is running at medium speed. If the ammeter registers well into the discharge range during engine operation, the batteries are not receiving the correct charging current. Stop the engine and investigate the cause of the malfunction.

The engine coolant temperature gage should range between 160° to 185°F under normal operating conditions.

NOTE: A warning buzzer sounds when coolant reaches 210°F.

As you check your instruments further, observe the engine oil pressure gage. As the engine warms up at idling speed, the oil pressure should read between 30 and 60 psi on the gage. When registering lower than the prescribed pressures or if no oil pressure is indicated on the gage, stop the engine and notify the maintenance shop.

Check the transmission oil temperature indicator. The temperature should not exceed 250°F. If the temperature rises above 250°F, stop the tractor immediately and check the transmission for external oil leaks, pinched or obstructed lines. If no leaks or obstructions are evident, operate the engine at full rpm. The temperature should drop in about 15 seconds. If the temperature does not drop, stop the engine and notify the maintenance shop.

NOTE: A warning buzzer will sound when the temperature exceeds limits.

Check the transmission oil pressure gage for a constant reading between 110 to 120 psi on the gage. Erratic reading indicates low oil level or other trouble. If the oil is at proper level and pressure still remains erratic, stop the engine and notify the maintenance shop.

NOTE: A warning buzzer will sound when pressure exceeds limits.

Now check the air pressure gage. The brake air pressure system gage should always read in excess of 60 psi while the engine is running at fast idling speed or full governed speed. If pressure remains low, check the airbrake system for trouble such as air line leaks, broken air lines, or air reservoir drain cocks open. DO NOT operate any equipment with low brake air pressure. Notify the mechanics immediately.

DURING OPERATION CHECKS

Although all indicators on the tractor can be registering within the specified range during operation, there are additional symptoms by which a malfunction can be identified. Symptoms in addition to those discussed in chapter 5 of this manual are given below.

Steering Trouble

Besides your eyes, ears, and nose, your sense of touch will relay symptoms of mechanical failure to you. For instances, if you are operating a rubber-tired tractor, your hands on the steering wheel will tell you if the machine pulls to the right or left when the brakes are applied. When you feel the tractor pull to one side, stop and check the tires. Your hands on the wheel will also tell you if the tractor turns hard and if play in the steering wheel is excessive. You will also feel vibrations caused by unbalanced wheels.

When a crawler tractor is equipped with steering clutches, these clutches should engage and disengage positively.

Brakes

When the pivot brakes on the crawler tractor are too tight, this condition will cause the tractor to creep to one side. When this happens,

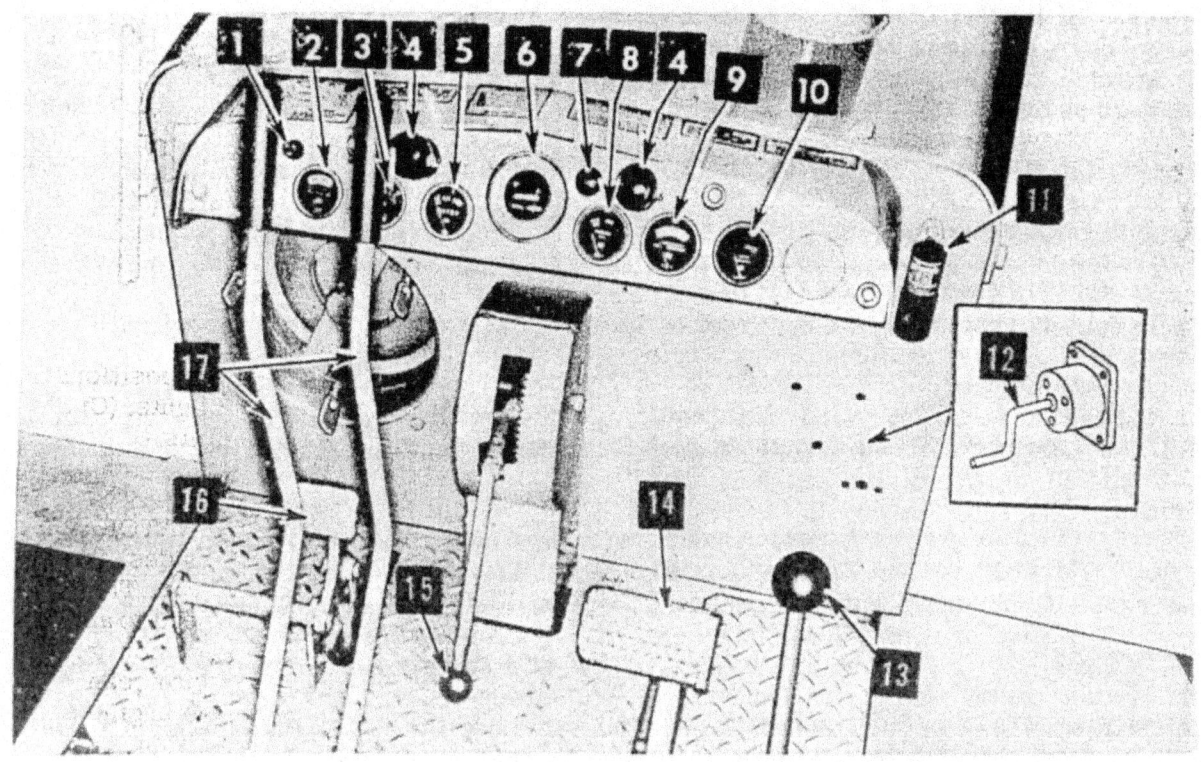

Figure 13.—Indicators and controls, TD-20B series.

adjustment is needed. Let the mechanic perform the necessary adjustment. After adjustments have been made, the tractor must be checked out in actual operation for proper functioning.

Clutches

If the tractor is equipped with a hand-operated master clutch lever, this lever should engage with a distinct snap over center. If this is not the case, a clutch adjustment must be made.

OPERATING CRAWLER TRACTOR

The safe and efficient use of a crawler tractor requires skill and alertness on the part of the operator. For earthmoving operations, the crawler tractor is especially suited for sidehill excavations and where maximum power is required at relatively slow rates of speed.

Let's take a look at one particular model of crawler tractor to familiarize you with the instruments and controls, as well as operational capabilities. The information given is on the International Harvester TD-20B series crawler tractor, and applies ONLY to this machine. This information will give you an idea of how one of the several types of crawler tractors used in industry and commerce is operated.

Before operating the crawler tractor, you should first become familiar with its different indicators and controls (fig. 13). The purpose of the various indicators and controls is explained below; the numbers in parentheses correspond to those used in figure 13 to indicate the location of indicators or controls.

The FUSE HOUSING (1) protects the panel lights, head lights, and rear lights.

The TORQUE CONVERTER OIL TEMPERATURE INDICATOR (2) registers the temperature of the fluid in the torque converter.

The AMMETER (3) indicates the rate at which the battery is being charged or discharged.

An ENGINE COOLANT HEAT INDICATOR (5) shows the temperature of the coolant circulating through the engine.

TRACTORS AND ATTACHMENTS

An ENGINE HOUR METER (6) records the actual hours of engine operation. It eliminates guesswork when determining proper lubrication and maintenance periods.

An ENGINE OIL PRESSURE INDICATOR (8) shows the pressure at which the lubricating oil is circulating through the engine.

A TRANSMISSION LUBRICATING OIL PRESSURE INDICATOR (9) registers the pressure of the lubricating oil in the transmission.

A TRANSMISSION CLUTCH OIL PRESSURE INDICATOR (10) registers the pressure of the oil being delivered to the clutch packs in the transmission.

The AIR CLEANER SERVICE INDICATOR (11) has a green signal band which telescopes a red signal band when a pressure drop (vacuum) between the air cleaner and the engine occurs. After starting the engine the green band may rise sufficiently, exposing part of the red band. (THIS MUST NOT BE MISTAKEN AS A SIGNAL FOR ELEMENT SERVICE.) During operation, the green band will gradually rise in the window as dirt accumulates in the filter element. When the filter element reaches the maximum allowable restriction, the green band is out of view and automatically locks in this position. (The red band will remain fully exposed even after stopping the engine. When this happens, filter element service is required.) After servicing the element, reset the indicator by pressing the reset button.

The RADIATOR SHUTTER CONTROL HANDLE (12) controls the movement of the radiator shutter. Turn the handle to the right to open the shutter, and to the left to close it.

The TRANSMISSION "HI-LO" SHIFT LEVER (13) is used to select the "HI" or the "LO" transmission gear range to provide two speeds forward and two reverse.

The BRAKE PEDAL (14) is used to stop the tractor by mechanically applying the pivot brakes. The brake pedal is also used as a parking brake.

The ENGINE SPEED CONTROL LEVER (15) is used to increase the engine speed by pulling the lever "up;" pushing the lever "down" decreases the speed. When you move this lever all the way down, it cuts off the fuel supply which stops the engine.

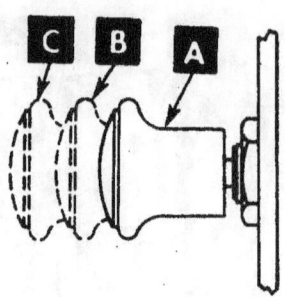

Figure 14.—Light switch positions: (A) Off. (B) Headlights and panel lights. (C) Headlights, panel lights, and rear lights.

Depressing the DECELERATOR PEDAL (16) slows the engine and overrides the setting of the engine speed control lever. The decelerator pedal will slow the engine speed to approximately low idle so that the transmission gears can be shifted easily and the tractor can be started in motion gradually, with the engine speed lever remaining in its original position.

The right- and left-hand STEERING LEVERS (17) are used to steer the tractor by engaging or disengaging the power flow from the transmission to either track.

The instrument panel lights are operated by the LIGHT SWITCH (7). The light switch has three positions, as shown in figure 14.

The STARTING SWITCH BUTTON is shown in view A, figure 15. To crank the engine, press the button to complete the electrical circuit between the batteries and the cranking motor.

The ELECTRICAL SYSTEM MASTER SWITCH illustrated in view B, figure 15 must be pulled and turned to either "OFF" position to cut-out the electrical system, or to the "ON" position to close the electrical system. (NOTE: Keep switch ON while the engine is running.)

The BRAKE PEDAL LOCK is shown in view C, figure 15. To lock the brake pedal, depress the pedal as far as possible and lift up on the lock lever as shown in figure 16; then remove your foot from the brake pedal, and the lock will hold the pedal in the locked position. To release the footbrake, depress the pedal and the lock will automatically disengage.

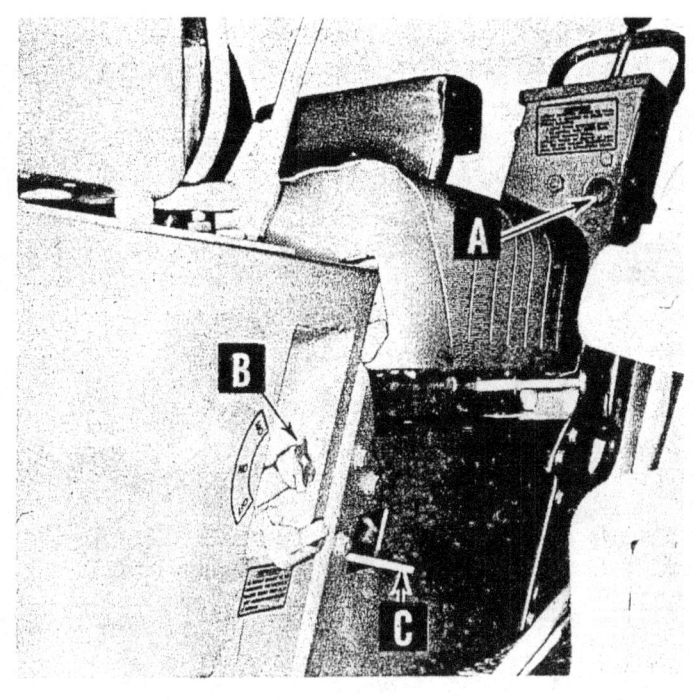

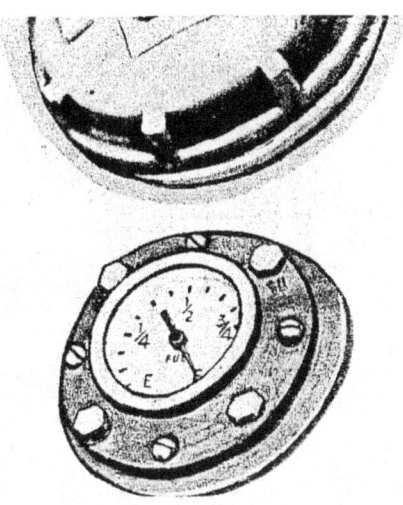

Figure 17.—Fuel tank level gage.

A FUEL TANK LEVEL GAGE, shown in figure 17, is located on top of the 86-gallon, fuel tank and registers the amount of fuel.

The TRANSMISSION GEAR SELECTOR LEVER, shown in view A, figure 18, is used to select the various transmission gear ranges.

Figure 15.—(A) Starting switch button. (B) Electrical system master switch. (C) Brake pedal lock.

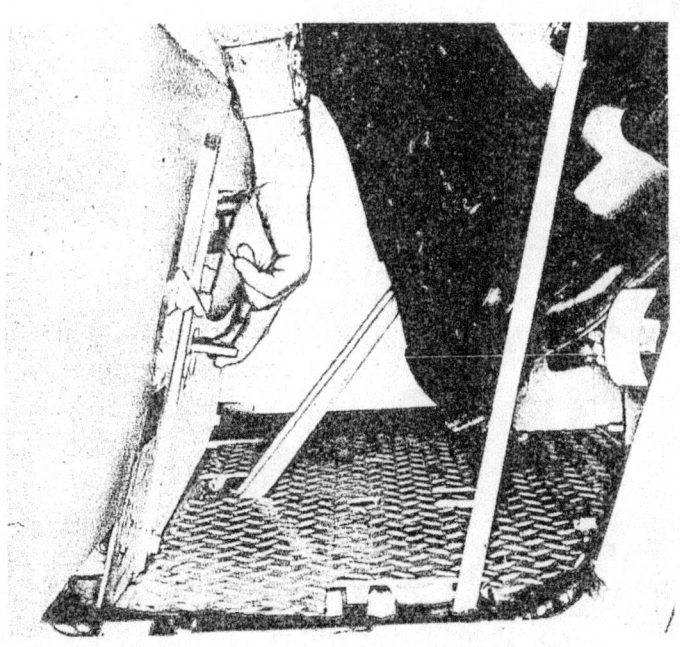

Figure 16.—Engaging the brake pedal lock.

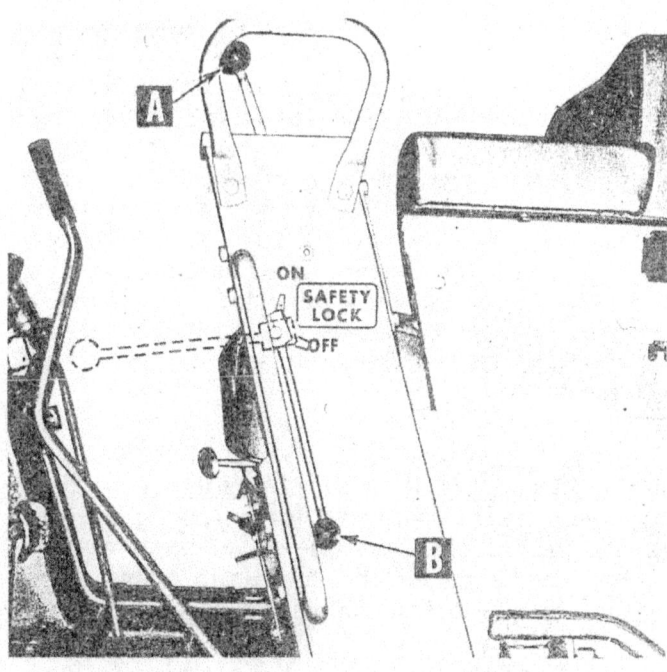

Figure 18.—(A) Transmission gear selector lever, (B) Selector lock lever.

Figure 19.—Seat adjustment.

The TRANSMISSION SELECTOR LOCK LEVER, shown in view B, figure 18, is used to lock the transmission gear selector lever in the NEUTRAL position.

The SEAT ADJUSTMENT, illustrated in figure 19, is accomplished by pressing down on lever (A), and sliding the seat back and forth to any one of five positions. When the seat engages the slide rail notch in the desired position, release the lever. Turn knob (B) to raise or lower the bottom seat cushion to any one of the four positions provided. Pull up on the adjuster rod (C), one on each side, and move the back seat cushion to any one of three positions.

When pulled toward the operator, the AUXILIARY CONTROL LEVER (A), figure 20, engages the hydraulic valve for engaging dozer blade operation. Pushing the lever away from the operator engages the hydraulic valve for engaging scraper operation control levers.

The HYDRAULIC CONTROL LEVER (B), figure 20, controls the dozer blade operation. Pull the control lever toward you for left-hand blade tilt; push the control lever away from you for right-hand blade tilt; release the lever

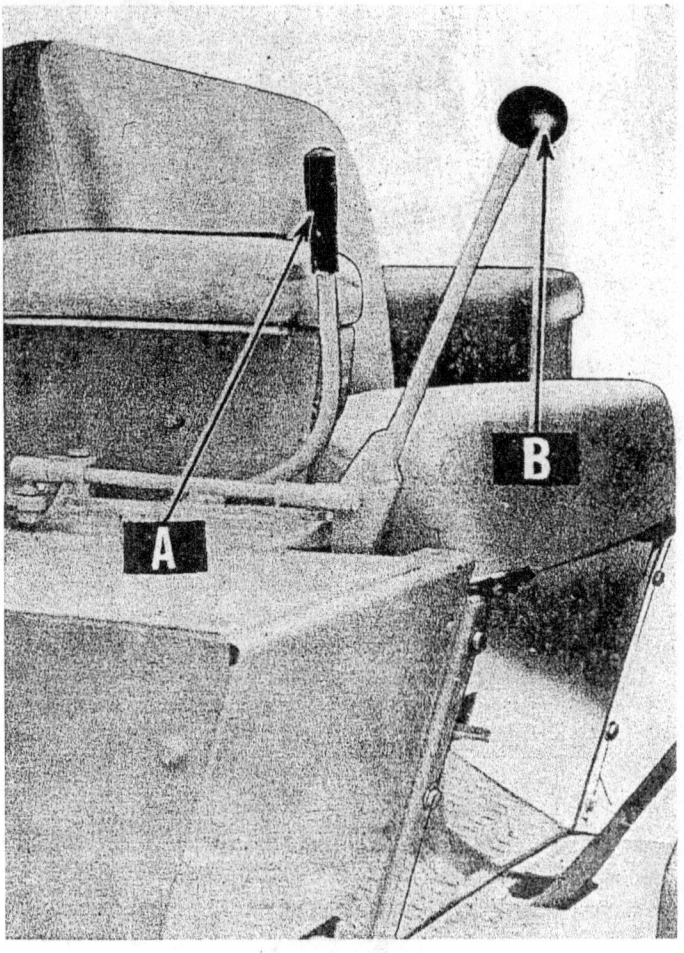

Figure 9-20.—Hydraulic valve control levers.

and it returns to "hold" position. The lever is pulled back to raise the dozer blade and pushed forward the lower the blade. To place the dozer blade in "float" position, the lever is pushed forward as far as it will travel.

Starting The Engine

The numbers in parentheses below correspond to those numbers listed in figure 21 showing the starting sequence of the TD-20B series crawler tractor engine.

Apply and lock the footbrake (1) and turn the electrical system master switch (2) to the ON position.

Now turn the radiator shutter handle (3) clockwise to open the shutter; counterclockwise to close it. Once the engine is warm, regulate

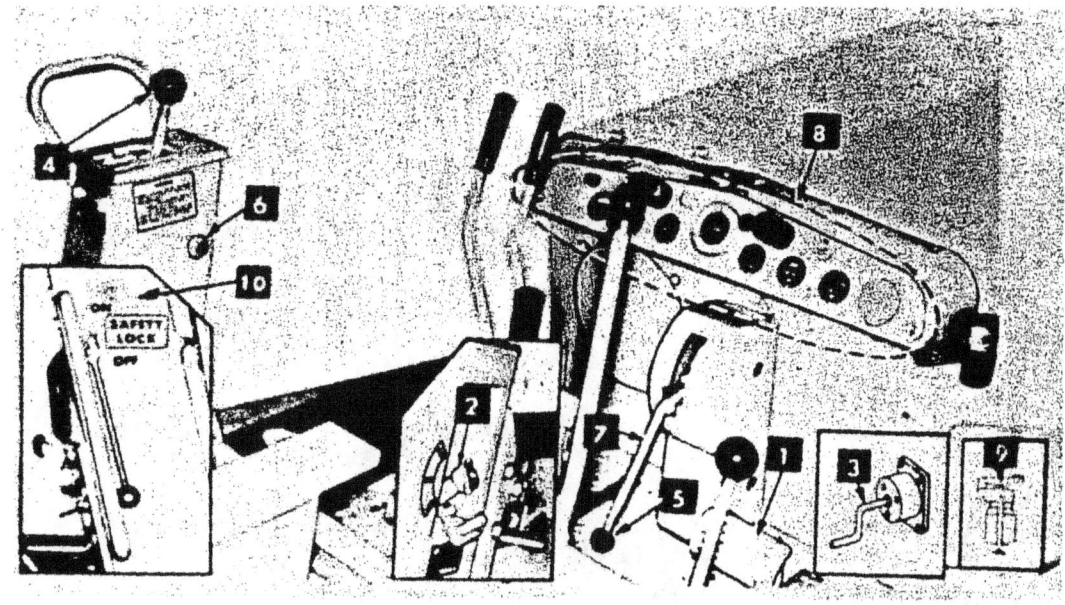

Figure 21.—Starting the engine.

the shutter as required to hold the needle of the engine coolant heat indicator in the center of the RUN range. The shutter must be left open in warm weather operation.

Lock the power shift transmission gear selector lever (4) in NEUTRAL by engaging the transmission selector lock lever to the ON position (10).

Move the engine speed control lever (5) all the way up, then return to half throttle (approximately fourth notch from bottom).

Crank engine as follows:

a. NORMAL START— Press the starting switch button (6).
b. COLD WEATHER START— Press the starting switch button (6), and simultaneously depress the injector lever (9). After starting, release injector lever.

After the engine starts, reduce engine speed to approximately 800 rpm (first or second notch (7).) Then check all indicators (8) for proper engine operation prior to operation of the crawler tractor.

NOTE: Crank the engine for 30 seconds at a time; if it does not start, allow the cranking motor to cool for 2 to 3 minutes before cranking again.

This engine cannot be started by towing, pushing, or coasting the tractor.

Steps For Operating

The numbers in parentheses below correspond to those in figure 22 showing the operating steps for the TD-20B series crawler tractor.

Place the engine speed control lever (1) in the high position.

Depress the decelerator pedal (2) to decrease engine speed to low idle.

Shift the HI-LO shift lever (3) from neutral (N) to the desired position.

Unlock the gear selector lever (4) and move it to the desired position.

Release the brake pedal (5) and gradually release the decelerator pedal (2).

Steering the tractor is accomplished by two steering levers; each lever functions in three positions as shown in figure 23. To turn to the right or left, pull the steering lever back on the side toward which the turn is desired. Pull the lever back just enough to make the desired turn. To make a pivot turn, pull the lever all the way back. When both steering levers are simultaneously pulled all the way back, the braking action "locks" both tracks.

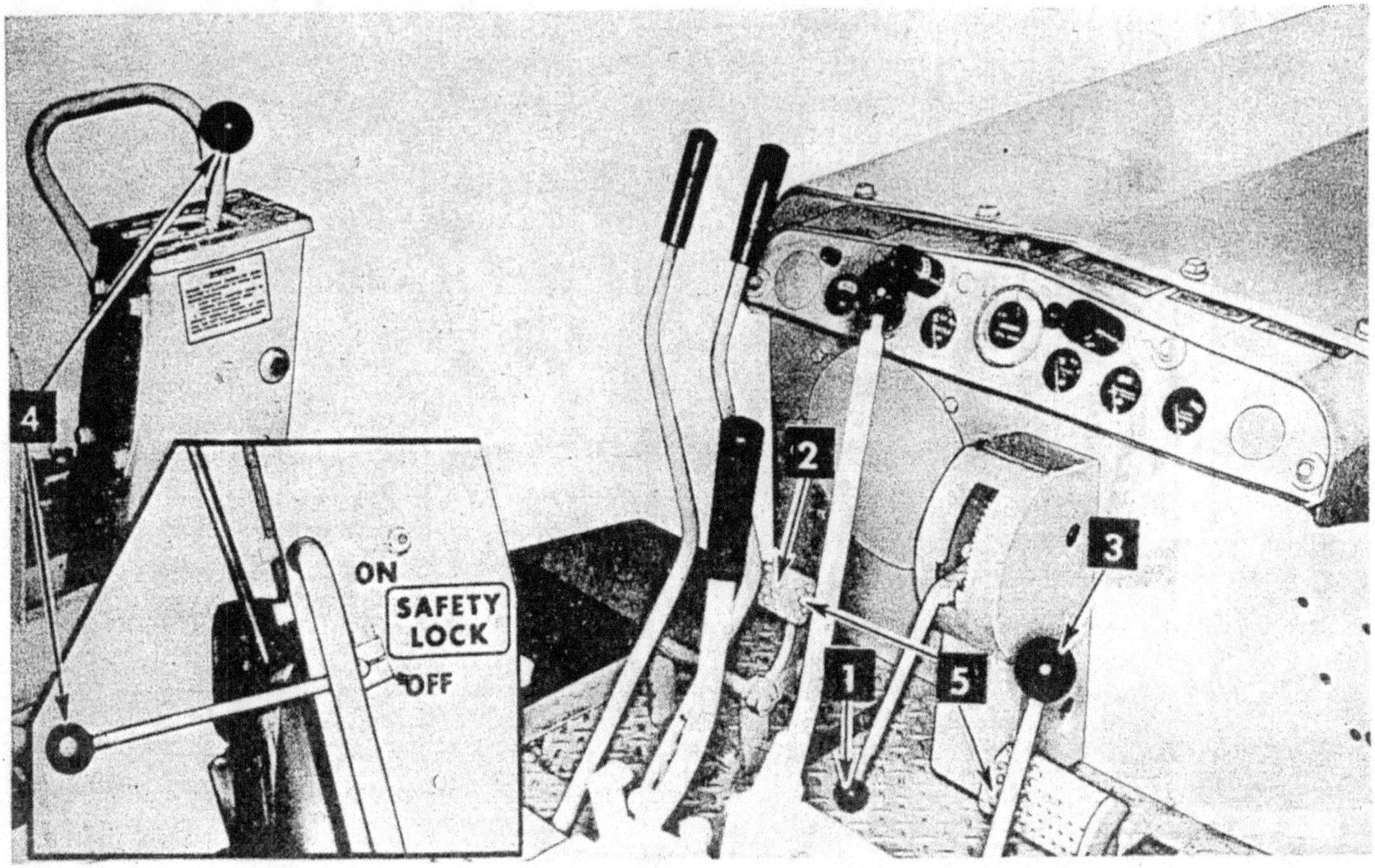

TRACTORS AND ATTACHMENTS

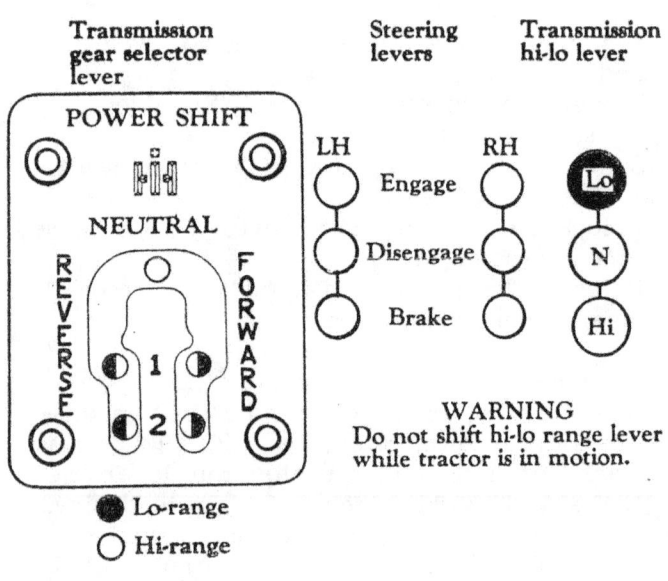

Figure 22.— Operating the tractor.

Figure 23.— Shifting patterns.

NOTE: Never pull both steering levers all the way back to stop the tractor unless the tractor is moving very slowly. Use the footbrake to slow or stop the tractor.

The transmission has a LO speed range for heavy work, and a HI speed range for normal work and traveling. Remember: selecting the proper HI or LO speed range will depend upon ground conditions and the type of material being handled. Before shifting to either HI or LO speed range, the transmission gear selector lever must be in neutral.

To shift the transmission gear selector lever within the HI or LO speed ranges, the tractor must be stopped. There are two power shift speed ranges, "1" and "2", as shown in figure 22. These speeds are available in both forward and reverse, and are power shifted with the gear selector lever. To operate in either HI or LO range, place the gear selector in range "1." If you want an "on-the-go" increase in tractor

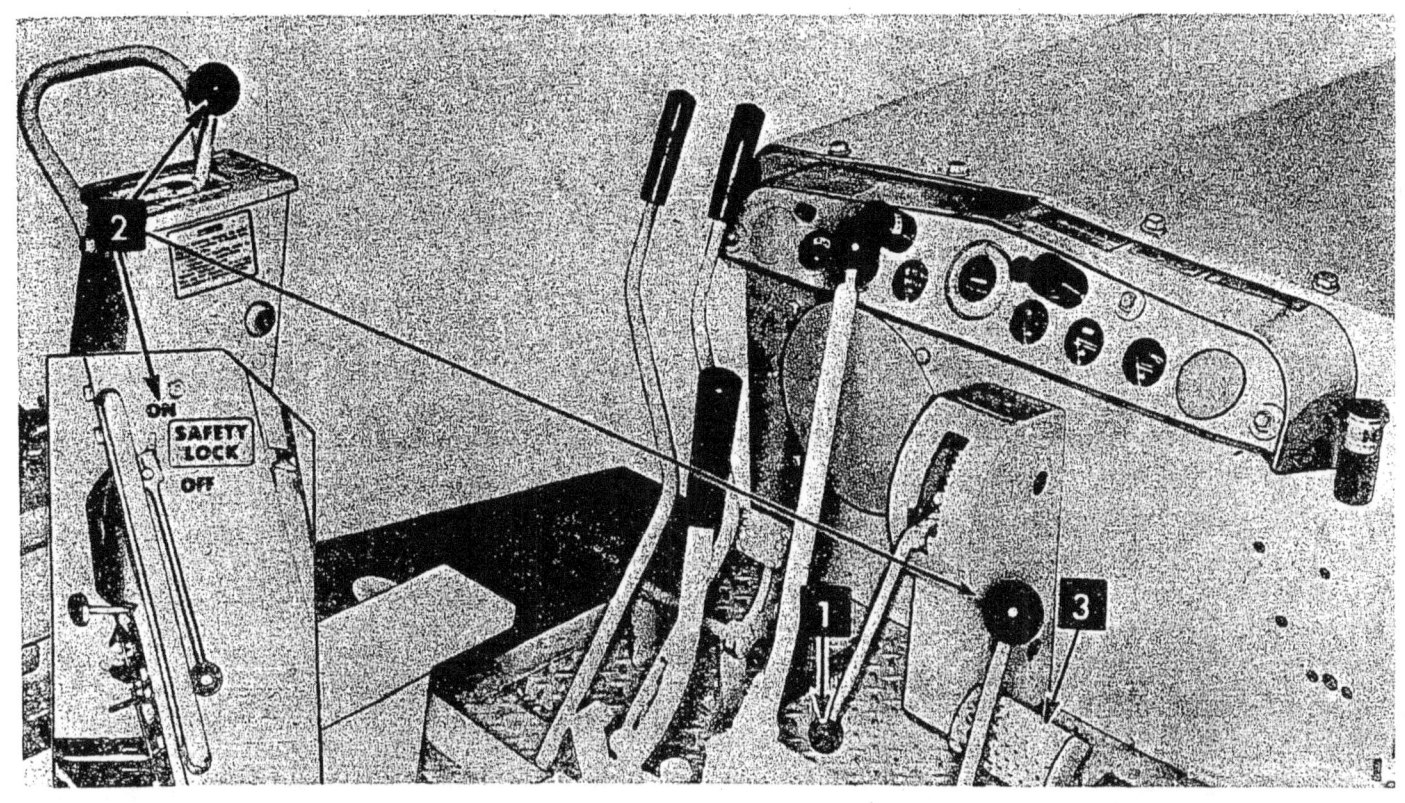

Figure 24. — Stopping the tractor.

speed, move the selector lever to range "2." When operating in range "2," and you want an "on-the-go" track power increase, shift the selector lever into range "1."

Stopping The Tractor

The numbers below correspond to those in figure 24 showing the sequence in stopping the TD-20B series crawler tractor.

Set the engine speed control lever (1), down to idle speed; DO NOT STOP THE ENGINE. Then place and lock the transmission gear selector lever in neutral and place the "HI-LO" shift lever (2) in neutral. As the last step, place foot on brake (3) and lock.

Stopping The Engine

The numbers below correspond to those in figure 25 showing the sequence in stopping the engine of the TD-20B series crawler tractor.

Operate the engine at low idle (1) for 3 to 5 minutes.

Figure 25. — Stopping the engine.

TRACTORS AND ATTACHMENTS

NOTE: Serious damage can result to the engine and turbocharger if the above step is neglected.

Move the engine speed control lever (2) down to the shut-off position.

Turn the electrical system master switch (3) to the "OFF" position.

Operation Capabilities

In operating the tractor, start all jobs, when possible, from relatively level ground. If necessary, level an area large enough to provide sufficient working space for the tractor. This prevents back-and-forth pitching of the tractor and will result in easier digging.

Avoid track spinning whenever possible; this wastes effort and only converts a relatively smooth working area into ruts and piles of material that pitch and tilt a tractor. In cold weather this material will freeze and cause additional difficulty the following work day.

Crossing ditches, ridges, rocks, or logs should be done slowly and, if possible, at an angle. This procedure slows the fall, lessens the danger of upsetting the tractor, and reduces the fall jolt which can be harmful to both the operator and tractor.

Always feed the blade into the ground gradually until the desired depth of the cut is obtained. When selecting the gear range and determining the depth of the cut, allow for an increase in resistance as the load increases. When raising the blade at the end of a cut, do so gradually to avoid an abrupt ridge or bump in the path of the tractor. Move your material down-grade whenever possible to gain reduced effort.

A sidehill cut can be started easier if a small bench cut is first made as shown in figure 26. Then, when digging, as in figure 27, keep the inside (uphill) surface slightly lower to gain greater tractor stability. Tilting the blade will provide this type of cut with little effort on the part of the operator. Always cut the shelf wide enough to provide solid support for equipment that will be using it later. If possible, move the material downhill to gain the advantage of gravity, reduced effort, and increased tractor stability. In addition to the method described above, side casting of material can be employed as well.

Soft soil or shallow slopes may allow the sidehill cut to be made as shown in figure 9-28. Increased stability is realized by running the

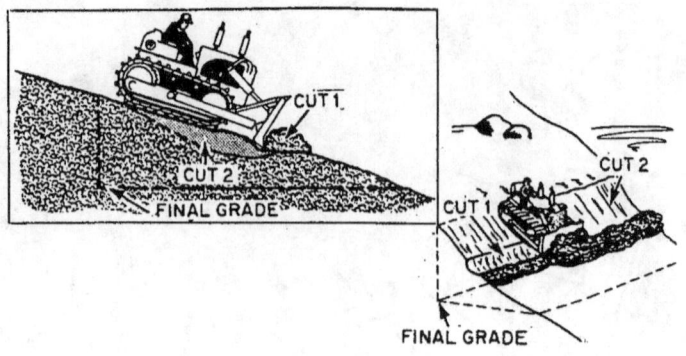

Figure 26.—Bench cut.

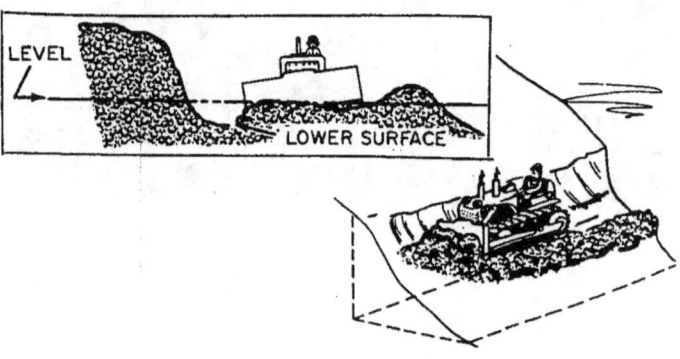

Figure 27.—Sidehill cut.

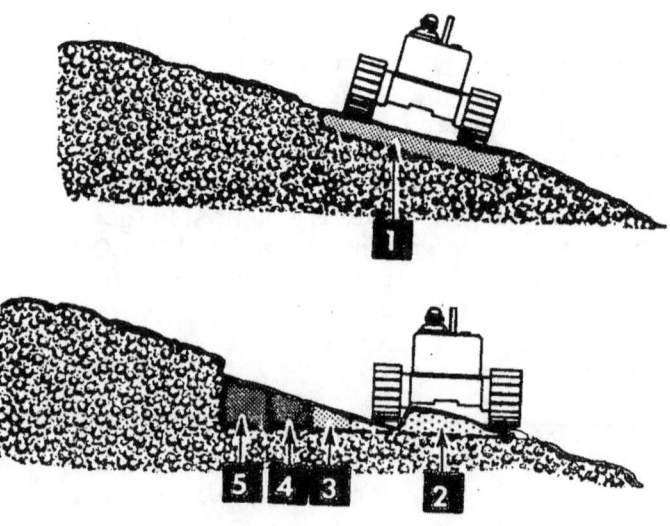

Figure 28.—Shallow slopes.

Figure 29.—Drifting material over embankment.

Figure 30.—Removing rock.

uphill track inside the ridge left by the first cut. Cuts 3, 4, and 5 illustrate the completion of the shelf. Once again, pushing the loosened material to the lower side of the slope will normally reduce time. Do not push material beyond the point required to retain firm track support as shown in figure 29. When backing up, do not raise the blade as this puts extra weight on the front idlers, thus causing greater track penetration. Let the blade float as you back away from the edge of soft fills.

When clearing a rocky area, remove the small and loose rocks first; then large and solid rocks can be loosened and moved with less difficulty. When loosening large solid rocks, tilt the blade and pry under the rock with the lower edge of the blade. Lifting rock with the blade while pushing will increase traction and reduce track spinning. Figure 30 shows the proper positioning of the blade for removing rocks. (After working in rock, check cutting edges, end bits, and bowl face for damage.)

When using your tractor as a pusher, aiding scraper operation as shown in figure 31, be sure you control your tractor. Excessive "push" effort can cause the scraper unit to "jackknife," resulting in injury to you or damage to the scraper. On turns, be sure the blade of your tractor does not cut the rear tires of the scraper, resulting in downtime and costly tire replacement.

Bulldozers are ideal for spreading fill material brought in by trucks or dump wagons. Your blade should be kept in a straight positon so the material is drifted directly under the cutting edge. Figure 32 illustrates this procedure.

When finishing in non-solid materials, such as earth, drag your blade backwards as shown in figure 33 for a smooth job. Rock, of course, may damage the blade base; therefore, dragging your blade backwards is not recommended where abrasive material is being placed.

Angling your blade is ideal for widening fills. Travel a foot or so from the slope side of the fill, allowing the material to spill off your blade and over the side of the slope, as illustrated in figure 34.

Figure 31.—Pusher.

TRACTORS AND ATTACHMENTS

Figure 32.—Spreading material.

Figure 33.—Finishing (back drag).

Figure 34.—Spilling material.

OPERATION OF RUBBER-TIRED TRACTOR

In the preceding section, we discussed the International Harvester TD-20B series crawler tractor. Now let's turn our attention to the M.R.S. model I-110 rubber-tired tractor. The information presented will give you an idea of how one type of rubber-tired tractor used by the Navy is operated.

Before operating the rubber-tired tractor, you should first become familiar with its controls and different instruments (fig. 35). The purpose of some of the individual controls and instruments is explained below; the numbers in parentheses correspond to those used in figure 35 to indicate the location of controls and instruments.

The AMMETER (1) is mounted at the top left hand side of the instrument panel. It indicates the charge and discharge rate of the battery.

The ENGINE SHUTDOWN CABLE (2) is located on the left-hand side of the control panel to the left of the steering column. This cable, when pulled, will place the fuel injector rack in the "no fuel" position.

The EMERGENCY STEERING CONTROL (4) is located on the forward side of the steering column. This pushbutton controls the electric motor driven hydraulic pump for the emergency front steering in case of engine failure. The front wheel steering control valve automatically reverts to a manual steering system.

The TRAILER BRAKE CONTROL LEVER (5) is mounted on the front side of the steering column directly under the steering wheel. It is used to operate the brakes of the trailing vehicle independently of the tractor wheel brakes.

The TRANSMISSION OIL TEMPERATURE GAGE (6) is located on the upper center of the instrument panel above the transmission oil pressure gage. It indicates the temperature of the transmission oil.

The TRANSMISSION OIL PRESSURE GAGE (7) is located on the lower center side of the instrument panel below the transmission oil temperature gage. It indicates the transmission main clutch oil pressure.

There are two LIGHT SWITCHES (9) located on the right-hand side of the instrument panel.

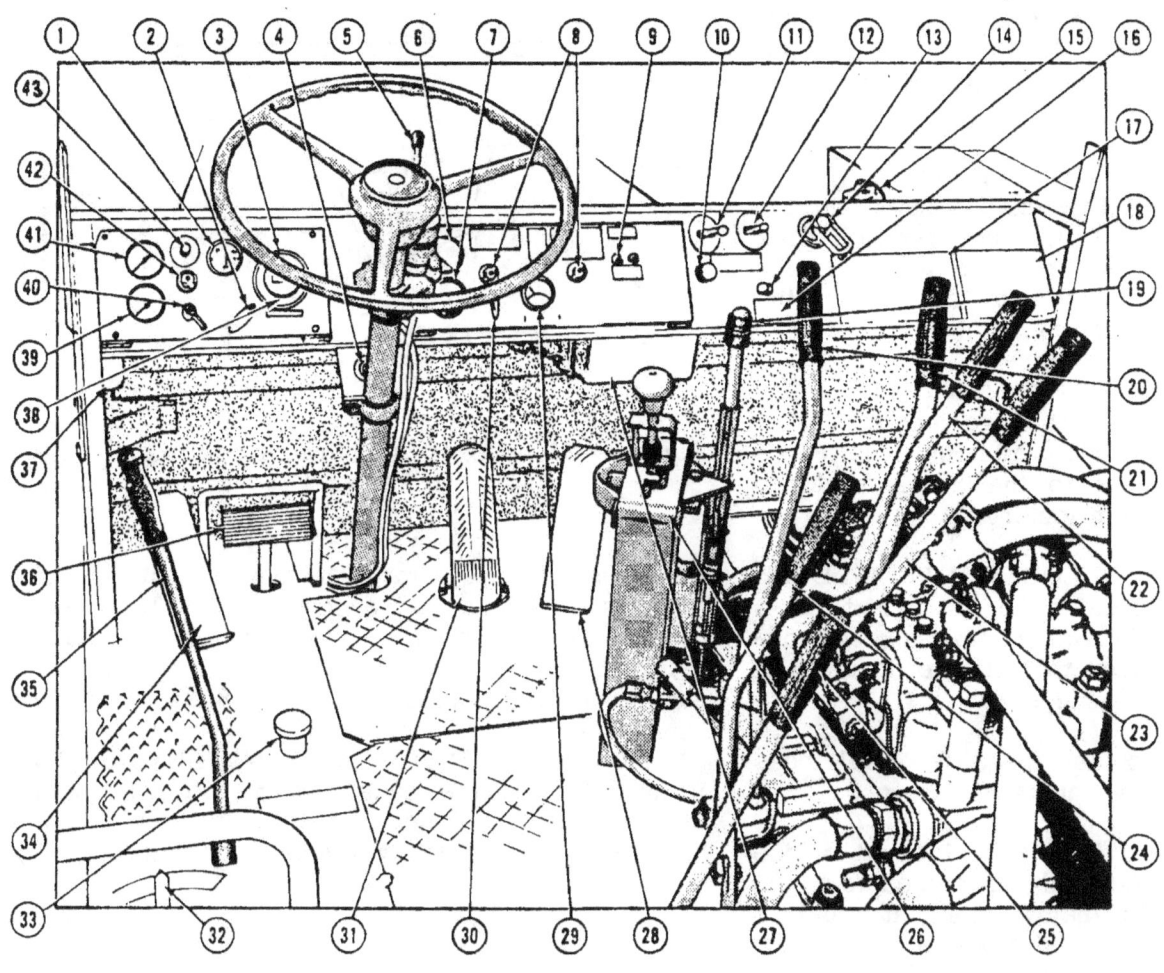

1. Ammeter
2. Engine Shutdown Cable
3. Hourmeter
4. Emergency Steering Control
5. Trailer Brake Control Lever
6. Transmission Oil Temperature Gage
7. Transmission Oil Pressure Gage
8. Panel Lights
9. Light Switches
10. Windshield Wiper Control
11. Thermatic Fan Control
12. Tractor Protection Valve
13. Differential Lock Control Lever
14. Cold Weather Starting Aid
15. Air Cleaner Restriction Indicator
16. Differential Lock Data Plate
17. Control Valve Instruction Plate
18. Transportation Data Plate
19. Parking Brake Lever
20. Dozer Tilt-Raise Lever
21. Bowl Lever
22. Apron Lever
23. Ejector Lever
24. Dozer Pitch Lever
25. Winch Control Lever (when installed)
26. Transmission Shift Lever
27. Generator Regulator
28. Accelerator
29. Air Pressure Gage
30. Emergency Stop Cable
31. Footbrake Treadle
32. Rear Steering Position Indicator
33. Brake Reservoir Dipstick
34. Rear Steering Control Pedal
35. Rear Steering Lever
36. Converter Brake (Retarder) Pedal
37. Warning Buzzer
38. Tachometer
39. Engine Coolant Temperature Gage
40. Ignition Switch
41. Engine Oil Pressure Gage
42. Panel Light
43. Starter Button

Figure 35. — Controls and instruments.

TRACTORS AND ATTACHMENTS

The left-hand switch controls the panel light, taillight, and left-hand headlights. The right hand switch controls the right-hand headlight, rear work light and stop light.

The THERMATIC FAN CONTROL (11) is a toggle action control valve located on the right-hand side of the instrument panel. This valve controls the air pressure to the engine fan allowing the operator to disconnect the fan during fording operations.

The TRACTOR PROTECTION VALVE (12)- is a toggle action control valve located on the right-hand side of the instrument panel. This valve controls the air to the trailer brake to prevent the brakes from locking.

The DIFFERENTIAL LOCK CONTROL LEVER (13) is centrally located on the instrument panel. It is integral with the two compressed air control valves and is used to shift the differential locks into and out of engagement.

CAUTION: Do not use the differential locks above second speed range.

The ENGINE PRIMER (14), located on the right side of the tractor dash, is used as a cold weather starting aid (below +40F.) It requires an ether bulb-type cartridge which is inserted into the primer body, punctured and discharged into the engine air intake.

The PARKING BRAKE (19) is used to apply the tractor parking brake. Its knurled handle also is used to adjust tension on the parking brake cable.

The DOZER BLADE TILT CONTROL LEVER (20) is mounted on the control valve forward of the dozer pitch lever. It is used to control the tilt and the raising or lowering of the dozer blade. (See fig. 36.)

CAUTION: Before operating the dozer be sure the travel lock bar assemblies are released (fig. 37).

The scraper operation is controlled by three levers: a SCRAPER BOWL CONTROL LEVER (21) which controls the bowl raise and lower functions; a SCRAPER APRON CONTROL LEVER (22) which controls the apron raise and lower functions; and a SCRAPER EJECTOR CONTROL LEVER (23) which controls the raise and lower

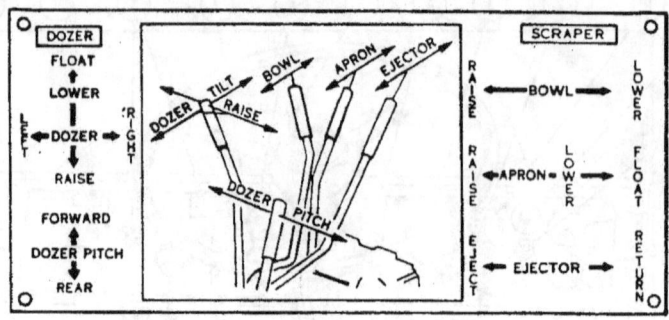

Figure 36.—Dozer and scraper operation control levers.

functions of the ejector. The power control unit is constructed so that each control will return to the neutral position when released. Each lever is moved toward the operator for raise; away from the operator for lower. (See fig. 36.)

The DOZER PITCH CONTROL LEVER (24) is mounted on the control valve to the right of the operator's seat. It is used to control the pitch of the dozer blade. (See fig. 36.)

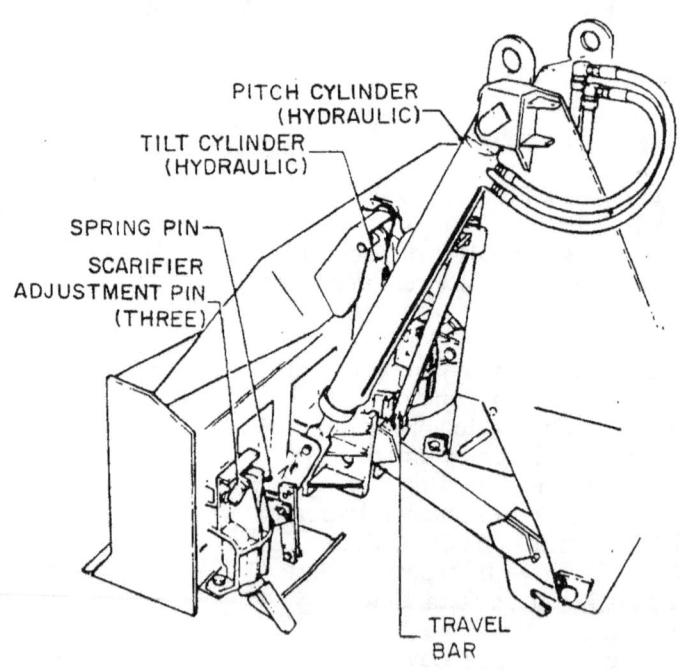

Figure 37.—Dozer blade attachments.

The TRANSMISSION SHIFT LEVER (26) is located to the right of the operator's seat and provides the selection of 6 forward speeds and 2 reverse speeds.

The ACCELERATOR PEDAL (28) is mounted on the front floorboard to the right of the service brake pedal. It is used to control engine speed.

The AIR PRESSURE GAGE (29) is located at the bottom center of the instrument panel. It indicates the air pressure in the airbrake system.

The EMERGENCY STOP CONTROL (30) is located near the lower center of the instrument panel. It is pulled out to stop the engine when normal shutdown procedures fail.

NOTE: After using the emergency stop control, the valve on the blower must be reset manually before restarting the engine.

The SERVICE BRAKE TREADLE (31) is mounted on the front floorboard to the left of the accelerator pedal. It is used to apply brakes to all four wheels of the tractor and to a trailing vehicle when connected.

The REAR STEERING DIRECTIONAL INDICATOR (32) is immediately to the rear of the rear steering lever. It is mechanically linked to the rear wheel steering arm and indicates the steering attitude of the rear wheels.

The REAR STEERING PEDAL (34) is mounted on the left side of the tractor front floorboard. It is mechanically linked to the rear steering hydraulic control valve and is used to steer the tractor rear wheels.

The REAR STEERING LEVER (35) is located immediately to the left of the operator's seat. It is attached to the rear steering hydraulic control valve and is used as a hand control to steer the tractor rear wheels only.

The CONVERTER BRAKE PEDAL (36) is mounted to the left of the steering column. A stirrup is mounted over the pedal to prevent accidental actuation of the converter brake (retarder) pedal.

The ENGINE COOLANT TEMPERATURE GAGE (39) is located in the lower left hand corner of the instrument panel directly under the engine oil pressure gage. It indicates the temperature of the engine coolant.

The IGNITION SWITCH (40) is in the lower left-hand quarter of the instrument panel. Its purpose is to provide an ON and OFF control for electric current to the instruments and to the starter pushbutton switch.

The ENGINE OIL PRESSURE GAGE (41) is in the upper left hand corner of the instrument panel. It indicates engine oil pressure.

The STARTER PUSHBUTTON SWITCH (43) is located near the upper left-hand corner of the instrument panel above the ignition switch. It is used to start the engine.

Starting The Engine

In starting the M.R.S. model I-110 rubber-tired tractor engine under normal conditions, follow the step by step procedure given below.

(1) Be sure the transmission shift lever is in neutral (N) position. If the transmission shift lever is not placed in neutral, the interrupter switch prevents starting the engine.
(2) Place the parking brake lever in the applied position.
(3) Make sure the emergency stop control is all the way in against the dash.
(4) Turn the ignition switch clockwise to the ON position.
(5) Depress the accelerator pedal to the half-way position.
(6) Depress the pushbutton starter switch until the engine starts; then release the pushbutton and ease off on the accelerator pedal.

As soon as the engine starts, observe the gages on the dash for proper readings. Run the engine at part throttle and no load for approximately 5 minutes allowing the engine to warm up. Once again check all instruments prior to operation.

In starting the M.R.S. model I-110 rubber-tired tractor engine under cold weather conditions, or whenever other circumstances make starting difficult, proceed as follows:

(1) Perform steps 1 through 4 as in normal starting.
(2) Unscrew the cap from the ether primer. Insert an ether primer cartridge with its neck forward and screw the cap down on the body of the primer.
(3) Depress the accelerator pedal, approximately three-quarters of the full distance.

TRACTORS AND ATTACHMENTS

(4) Press the starter button. After the starter motor has brought the engine up to cranking speed, discharge the pressure primer bulb by swinging the actuating lever through 180° to the opposite side of the primer. The primer cartridge takes about 15 seconds to discharge fully.

(5) Observe the instruments for proper reading.

> NOTE: Crank the engine for 30 seconds at a time; if it does not start, allow the cranking motor to cool for at least 60 seconds before cranking again.

This engine cannot be cranked by towing. If battery output is insufficient to start the engine, connect an external source of 24 volt direct current to the tractor electrical system by means of the electrical receptacle on the right side of the tractor.

Steps For Operating

Observe the following operating steps for placing the M.R.S. rubber-tired tractor in motion after the engine has been started:

(1) Set the tractor engine at idle speed.
(2) After air pressure is obtained, shift the transmission range lever to the speed range desired (six forward, two reverse).
(3) Release the parking brake.
(4) Depress the accelerator pedal slowly until desired speed is reached.

An automatic front wheel drive selector will engage the front wheel drive when the transmission range lever is in the first and second ranges of forward and reverse. This automatic front wheel drive selector will disengage when the tractor is shifted to third range, forward.

Stopping The Tractor

When bringing the tractor to a stop, proceed as follows:

(1) Release foot pressure from the accelerator pedal.
(2) Apply foot pressure to the service brake pedal.
(3) Shift the transmission range lever to neutral.
(4) Apply the parking brake; this action locks the transmission in neutral.
(5) Lower the dozer blade to the ground.

Stopping The Engine

To stop the tractor engine, here are the steps to follow:

(1) With no load on the engine, decrease engine speed and allow the engine to idle at half speed or less for 4 to 5 minutes (always allow the engine to idle for this period before stopping to permit gradual and uniform cooling).
(2) Pull the engine shutdown cable control to place fuel injectors in the no fuel position.
(3) After engine stops, place ignition switch in the OFF position.

> NOTE: Be sure the ignition switch is turned off before leaving the tractor. The constant drain of the current to the instruments will discharge the battery if the ignition switch is left on.

If the normal shutdown procedures fail to stop the engine, pull the emergency stop control handle out as far as it will go. This will stop the engine by cutting off the combustion air supply from the blower.

After the engine has stopped, push the emergency stop handle all the way in against the dash.

After using the emergency stop control, the valve on the blower must be reset manually before restarting the engine.

> NOTE: Be sure to notify the field mechanics if the engine's normal shutdown equipment is no longer operational.

Operation Capabilities

Operating techniques which were described in previous sections as to the operation of the crawler-type tractor also apply basically to the rubber-tired tractor. As pointed out below, there are some differences, however, in the application of the dozer blade and attachments when it comes to dozing techniques.

With the model I-110 tractor, the dozer blade control lever (number (20) fig. 35) is used not only for raising and lowering the blade, but also for tilting the blade. An additional control lever, known as the dozer blade pitch control lever (number (24) fig. 35), is used to pitch the dozer blade forward or rearward, depending upon the condition of the ground. Generally, the blade is pitched back for soft ground and forward for hard ground.

Other attachments on the dozer blade (fig. 37) include three scarifiers for backripping operations. In addition, travel lock assemblies are mounted on the front of the radiator guard to hold the blade in the travel position. Before moving the tractor, be sure to raise the dozer blade to its extreme travel; also, remove the two pins and use them to attach the lock assemblies to the travel lock bracket provided on the push frame.

> CAUTION: Always release the travel locks before operating the dozer controls.

The M.R.S. model I-110 rubber-tired tractor is designed to stop, start, and negotiate a 30-percent longitudinal slope. For slope operation, the tractor is capable of loading a scraper on a 20-percent side slope.

If the grade is short, the tractor may be worked from the bottom directly up the slope; if the grade is comparatively long, it must be worked from above. Care must be taken that the tractor is steered directly down the slope — not diagonally. A diagonal course down a steep slope may cause the tractor to overturn.

For sidehill cuts, be sure to adjust the bank side of the dozer blade lower than the outer side. This will greatly aid in holding the tractor against the bank and securing a satisfactory and controllable cut. Work down from above the cut to start a shelf. Work from this self along the slope line, digging with one corner of the blade and swinging away from the hill side. Keep the downhill side of the cut high. Build a shelf along in front of the tractor as it travels forward.

Keep in mind that the M.R.S. model I-110 tractor is not designed primarily as a bulldozer; but as a prime mover for a rubber-tired scraper.

HAND SIGNALS ·

A uniform system of hand signals must be used on all tractor operations of a similar nature. While the authority for giving signals must be assigned to only one person under normal working conditions, the responsibility for giving an emergency signal belongs to anyone in the vicinity who believes such a signal is necessary. The person giving the signals must be located so as to be clearly visible to the operator at all times. The hand signals used in tractor and attachment operations are depicted in appendix I. It is important that you not only recognize and understand these hand signals when operating equipment, but also be able to give them when called upon to act as a signalman on a construction project.

SECURING

When securing a crawler tractor, position the attachment for traveling, drive the tractor to the designated securing area, and position the machine in a safe manner. After the machine has stopped, lower the attachment to the ground, set the brake lock, and place the transmission in neutral position. Then allow the engine to throttle down to slow idle (no load) for 3 to 5 minutes before moving the engine speed control lever to shut-off position and stopping the engine. After the engine stops, place the electrical system master switch in the "OFF" position.

When securing a rubber-tired tractor, position the attachment for traveling, drive the tractor to the designated securing area, and position the machine in a safe manner. After parking the machine, lower the attachment to the ground, set the parking brake hand lever, and place the transmission shift lever in neutral position. Then allow the engine to throttle down to slow idle (no load) for 4 to 5 minutes before pulling the engine shutdown cable control and stopping the engine. After the engine stops, place the ignition switch in the "OFF" position. Drain the air tanks by opening the drain cocks.

IV. OPERATOR'S MAINTENANCE

The procedures used in an operator's maintenance inspection of the various components of tractors are the same as described in previous portions of this manual for vehicles and materials-handling equipment, and need not be repeated here. These components include brake systems, fuel systems, ignition and electrical systems, cooling systems, and lubricating oil systems. Items such as fan belts, batteries, transmissions, and wheels and tires were also discussed.

In addition to the above, the tractor has two other components, the hydraulic system and the air cleaner system, which will be covered below.

HYDRAULIC SYSTEM

When inspecting the hydraulic system, ensure that the proper level of hydraulic oil is maintained in the hydraulic reservoir. Be sure to add the

TRACTORS AND ATTACHMENTS

type of hydraulic oil recommended by the manufacturer. This is especially important because some hydraulic systems are equipped with natural rubber packing seals and others with synthetic rubber packing seals. And unless the recommended hydraulic oil is used, the packing seals will deteriorate quickly and cause the system to leak. Check the hydraulic lines for leaks, and if any are found, tighten hose connections. In addition, check the hydraulic cylinders to ensure that they hold the load. If they fail to hold the load, tighten the cylinder packing nuts.

AIR CLEANER SYSTEM

Most tractors are usually equipped with some type of an air cleaner service indicator. This device will normally actuate as dirt accumulates in the filter element and reaches the maximum allowable restriction. When this happens, the filter element must be removed and cleaned, either by washing or with compressed air. Washing is the preferred method as it removes more dust and soot and restores the element to an almost new condition. It is suggested that a spare element be available for use while the serviced element is drying. This will reduce downtime to only a few minutes and will allow sufficient time to service the restricted element properly.

Cleaning the element with compressed air is not considered an entirely satisfactory method. Some dust will remain in the element causing more frequent servicing. Use this method only as a temporary measure until sufficient time is available to clean the element by washing.

CAUTION: Never wash elements in fuel oil, gas or solvent. DO NOT OIL ELEMENTS. Do not attempt to take elements apart. Do not tap the element against a hard surface; this will damage the element.

LUBRICATION

The life and performance of a tractor depends on the care that it is given. Proper lubrication, performed at definite intervals, will aid greatly in prolonging the life of the tractor and in reducing operating expense. The type of work being done, loads handled, ground and weather conditions, are all factors to consider in determining the frequency of lubrication. It may be necessary to lubricate more frequently when working under severe operating conditions such as heavy dust, low engine temperature, intermittent operation,

excessively heavy loads with high oil temperatures, or when diesel fuel with a high sulphur content is used. However, the time intervals between lubrication periods must never exceed those indicated on the lubrication chart.

A lubrication guide for the International Harvester model of crawler tractor is presented in figure 38. The guide shows a lubrication chart indicating the points on the crawler tractor to be lubricated and the lubrication intervals. A specification and capacity chart showing the type and amount of lubricant to use is presented in figure 39.

A lubricating guide for the M.R.S. model rubber-tired tractor is presented in figure 40. This guide indicates how often to lubricate, what to lubricate, and what lubricant to use. The lubricating chart shown in figure 41 indicates the points on the rubber-tired tractor to be lubricated and provides a key to the symbol, type, application, and specification of lubricant to use.

ADJUSTMENTS

In this discussion, information as to the procedures for checking and adjusting track tension on the International Harvester model TD-20B series crawler tractor will be covered.

Checking Track Tension

Improper track tension will cause damage and premature wear to the track. In checking for track tension, here is the procedure to follow:

1. Place a wooden block, approximately 1 foot in height, under the foremost track shoe lug.
2. Start the engine and move the tractor forward just enough so that the sprocket drive tightens the track chain along the ground and around the sprocket.
3. Apply and lock the brake; stop the engine.
4. Place and lock the transmission gear selector lever in the "NEUTRAL" position.
5. Stand on the track between the track idlers; this will pull the track chain tight around the idlers and accumulate all the slack at this point.

NOTE: ALL DOTTED SHAFT ARROWS INDICATE POINTS THAT MUST BE LUBRICATED ON BOTH SIDES OF TRACTOR.

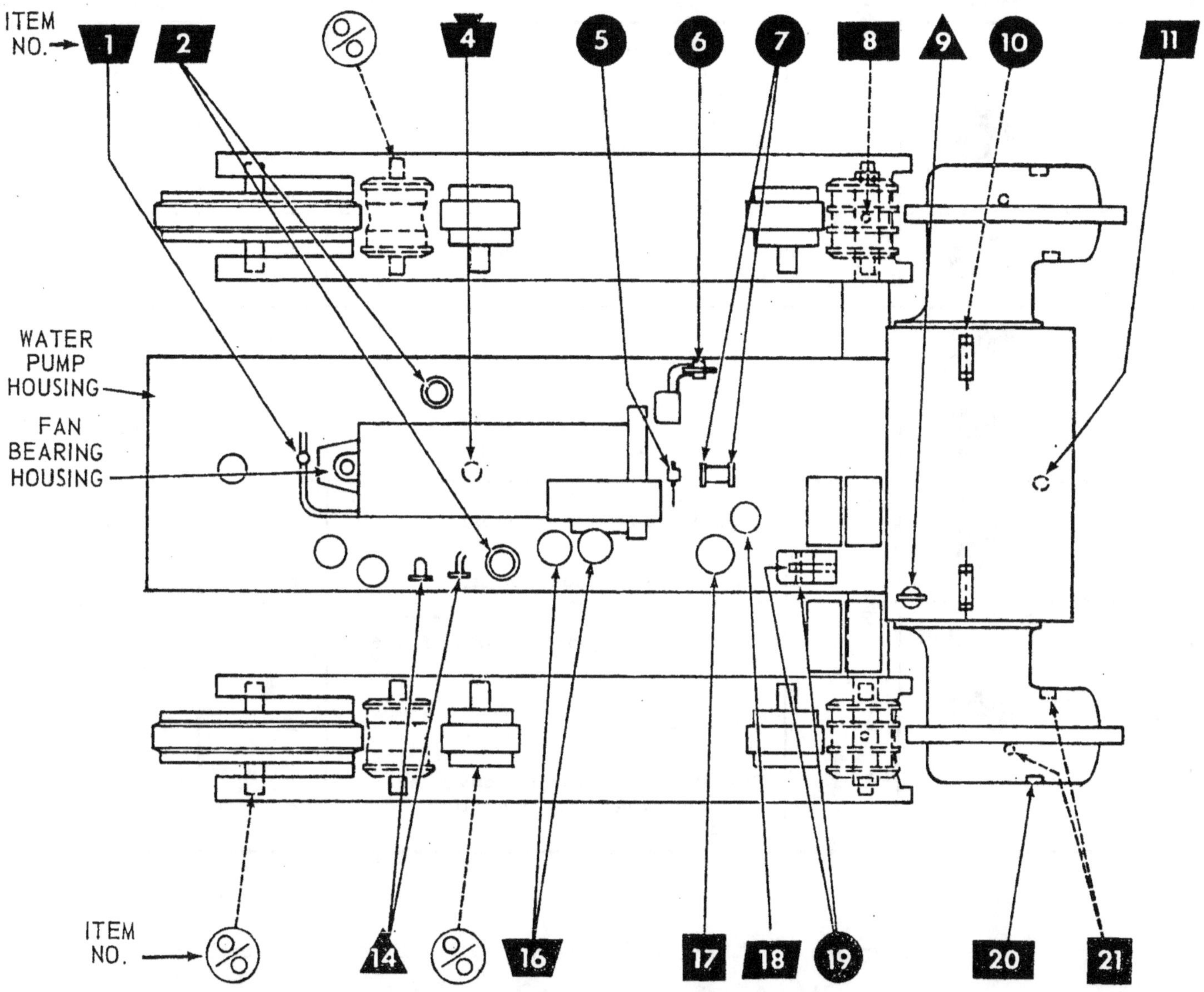

FRONT IDLERS, TRACK IDLERS AND TRACK ROLLERS ARE LUBRICATED FOR LIFE WITH A GRADE-30 ENGINE OIL WHEN ASSEMBLED AND DO NOT REQUIRE ADDITIONAL LUBRICATION EXCEPT WHEN RE-CONDITIONED, THEN INSTALL (SERIES 3 OR MIL-L-45199A) GRADE-30 ENGINE OIL.

Figure 38.—Lubrication chart for crawler tractor (TD-20B series).

TRACTORS AND ATTACHMENTS

LUBRICATION INTERVAL	ITEM NO.	POINT OF LUBRICATION	LUBRICANT	REMARKS
Every 10 hours ▲	9	Rear frame oil level	EO	Check
	14	Crankcase oil level	EO	Check
Every 50 hours ●	5	Governor control upper and lower bell crank	MPG	Grease
	6	Brake pedal	MPG	Grease
	7	Universal joint	HTG	Grease
	10	Steering brake shaft	MPG	Grease
	19	Upper and lower shifter bell crank shafts	MPG	Grease
Every 100 hours	4	Crankcase oil	EO	Change
Every 200 hours	1	Front engine support	MPG	Grease
	16	Lubricating oil filter elements	- - -	Change
Every 250 hours ■	8	Track frame pivot shaft housings	MPG	Grease
	20	Sprocket drive housing oil level		
Every 500 hours ■	17	Transmission, torque converter and steering booster pressure filter element	- - -	Change
	21	Sprocket drive housing oil	MPL	Change
Every 1000 hours	2	Transmission, torque converter and steering booster safety filter element	- - -	Clean
	11	Rear frame oil	EO	Change
	18	Transmission, torque converter and steering booster suction filter element	- - -	Clean

Figure 38.—Lubrication chart for crawler tractor (TD-20B series)—Continued.

6. Place a straightedge on the track and check the slack as shown in figure 42. If the clearance is less than 3/4 inch or more than 1 inch, adjust the track tension.

Adjusting Track Chain Tension

Before attempting to adjust track chain tension, you should first become familiar with the location and functions of the hydraulic track adjuster. Figure 43 shows the hydraulic track adjuster of the International Harvester model TD-20B series crawler tractor.

Track chain tension is adjusted by hydraulic pressure. The front idler is forced forward for track adjustment by chassis lubricant under pressure with the standard type bucket or hand lubricator. The pressure in this system is held by the socket head screw and a check valve under the lubricating fitting. NEVER loosen the socket head screw more than ONE turn, and NEVER remove the socket head screw under pressure.

Ensure that you remove the scraper, then connect the lubricator nozzle to the fitting under

		ANTICIPATED AIR TEMPERATURES		
LUBRICATION POINT	CAPACITY	Above +32°F	+32°F to -10°F	Below -10°F
LUBRICANT KEY: EO - Engine Oil MPG - Multi-purpose Grease MPL - Multi-purpose Type Gear Lubricant HTG - High Temperature Grease				
Crankcase:		EO - SERIES 3 or MIL-L-45199A.		24 qts. Grade-10 Diluted w/ 3 qts. Kerosine
With filters drained	25 qts.	Grade-30	Grade-10	
With filters changed	27 qts.			
Rear Frame ⊕	40 gals.	EO - SERIES 3 or MIL-L-45199A. Grade-10		MIL-L-10295A or DEXRON ATF
Hydraulic System (tractor equipment):		EO - MIL-L-2104B, Sup. 1, DEF. 2101C, SERIES 3 or MIL-L-45199A. Grade-10		
Model D-1 or D-3 (equipped with hydraulic tilt)	3 gals.			
Model D-2 or G-2 (equipped with hydraulic tilt)	28 gals.			
Model D-2 or G-2 (not equipped with hydraulic tilt)	26 gals.			
Track Roller (each) ⊘	2-1/4 pts.	EO - SERIES 3 or MIL-L-45199A. Grade-30		
Track Idler (each) ⊘	3 pts.			
Front Idler (each) ⊘	2 pts.			
Sprocket Drive Housing (each)	28 qts.	MPL - IH B-22 Grades 132H EP, 134H EP or MIL-L-2105B		MIL-L-10324A
		Grade-90 ⊕	Grade-80 ⊕	
Water Pump Housing	1/2 oz.	MPG - I.H. 251H EP or equivalent		
Fan Bearing Housing	2-1/2 oz.			
Pivot Shaft Housing (each)	2 qts.			
Cable Control Unit:		EO - SERIES 3 or MIL-L-45199A		
MODEL 110 (gear case)	4-1/2 qts.	Grade-50	Grade-30	
MODEL 260 (main housing)	9 qts.			
MODEL 260 (transfer case)	1 qt.			
MODEL 260S (main housing)	8 qts.			
All lubrication fittings	Fill as instructed	HTG - MIL-L-3545 or MIL-G-3545A as indicated on the "LUBRICATION GUIDES"		

⊕ - Common reservoir for planetary steering, hydraulic steering boosters, torque converter and transmission.

⊕ - A multi-grade 80-90 may be used at temperatures between -20°F and +90°F. A Grade-140 may be used at temperatures above +90°F.

⊘ - Front idlers, track idlers and track rollers are lubricated for life.

Figure 39. — Specification and capacity chart for crawler tractor (TD-20B series).

TRACTORS AND ATTACHMENTS

the opening and add lubricant to obtain the proper track chain tension. It is advisable to move the tractor forward and backward slightly to be sure the correct tension has been obtained.

To reduce track chain tension, loosen the socket head screw one full turn. This will allow the check valve ball to unseat and furnish a relief passage for the pressurized lubricant. When the proper tension has been obtained, tighten the socket head screw.

When the tractor chain tension adjustments have been completed, install and fasten the scraper.

> CAUTION: When working tracked equipment in materials such as sand or snow, the tracks tend to further tighten.

V. TRACTOR TIRES

Inspecting, checking, and maintaining tractor tires is a primary responsibility of the EO. Inspection of tires consists of checking for missing valve caps, leaking valves, cuts, breaks, abrasions, and imbedded foreign matter. Some punctures can be repaired without removing the tire. When major damage or a blowout occurs, or normal wear limits have been reached, the tire must be removed. Size alone makes the removal and replacement of tractor tires difficult. In addition, the nature of the terrain over which tractors operate, and locations of many operations, often cause conditions to be far from ideal. Certain tools are necessary to change these large tires. Hand tire tools and hydraulic tire tools are specifically designed to break the beads, for easier removal of the tire.

Figures 44 through 47 indicate procedures for demounting and mounting tractor tires (on machine), and mounting, as well as demounting tires (off machine).

For your safety—remember, an inflated tire and the rim on which it is mounted can be very dangerous; under pressure it packs the explosive force of TNT.

In demounting a tractor tire, be sure to remove the valve core and exhaust ALL air from the tire. Next check the valve stem by running a wire through the stem to be sure it is not plugged. A broken rim part under pressure could blow apart and kill you the moment you remove the lugs on the assembly. Remove valve cores from BOTH tire assemblies if so equipped.

Use a clip-on chuck and extension hose long enough to allow you to stand to one side and NOT in front of the tire assembly while inflating.

Be careful to clean all dirt and rust from the lockring gutter. This is important to allow the lockring to secure in the proper position. Inspect the rim base and lockring gutter for cracks. Any cracked, damaged, or sprung rim bases or lockrings should be replaced.

Bead breakers and rams apply pressure to bead flanges. KEEP YOUR FINGERS CLEAR. Slant a bead breaker about 10 degrees to keep it firmly in place. If it slips off, it can fly with enough force to kill. ALWAYS stand to one side when you apply hydraulic pressure.

When using a cable or chain sling, stand clear. It might snap and lash out.

Never attempt to rework, weld, heat, or braze wheel parts. Always replace with new parts of the same size, type, and make.

Spare tires mounted on demountable rims should only have enough air pressure to keep the rim parts in place. NEVER TRANSPORT A FULLY INFLATED TIRE. Inflate tires to correct operating pressure AFTER the tire and rim assembly have been fastened in place with all lug nuts properly torqued.

Be sure you note the following:

THE TRACTION DIRECTION ARROW ON THE TIRE TREAD IS TO POINT IN THE OPPOSITE DIRECTION AS THE ROTATION OF THE WHEEL.

It is recommended that clamp-on inflation hoses, safety chains, or some other safety device be used during inflation.

Inflation air lines should have traps to prevent airborne moisture or oil from getting into the tire and causing rim corrosion or tire deterioration.

VI. CHANGING FRONT-END TRACTOR ATTACHMENT

When it becomes necessary to remove the complete hydraulic or cable operated blade from the tractor, proceed as follows:

1. Place the blade on level ground and block up the ends of the C-frame or push arms which are closest to the trunnions. This will maintain a proper height for reassembly.

DESCRIPTION (NO. POINTS)	LUB.	HRS.	DESCRIPTION (NO. POINTS)	LUB.	HRS.
1. Pitch Cylinder (2 Pts.)	GAA	10	16. Steer. Cyl Pins (8 Pts.)	GAA	10
2. Check Coolant Level		Daily	17. Steering Knuckles (4 Pts.)	GAA	50
3. Fuel Filter		Daily	18. Tie Rod Ends (4 Pts)	GAA	10
4. Engine Oil Filter		Monthly	19. Drive Shafts (6 Pts.)	GAA	50
5. Air Cleaner		Daily	20. Check Strainer in Filler Neck		Weekly
6. Trans. Check (Dipstick)	OE	10	21. Rear Steer Ind. (1 Pt.)	GAA	25
7. Hyd. Oil Check (Dipstick)	OE	10	22. Brake Oil Check (Dipstick)	OE	10
8. Hydraulic Oil Filters		500	23. Trans. Shift Indicator (1 Pt.)	GAA	10
9. Hyd. Control Links (6 Pts.)	GAA	8	24. Rear Steer Pedal (2 Pts.)	GAA	10
10. Transmission Oil Filter		Monthly	25. Final Drive (4 Pts.)	GO	50
11. Batteries		Weekly	26. Engine Oil Check (Dipstick)	OE	10
12. Air Tanks		Daily	27. Front Axle Pivot Pin (1 Pt.)	GAA	10
13. Scraper Coup Ball (1 Pt.)	GAA	10	28. Lift Cylinder (4 Pts.)	GAA	10
14. Differ. Check Plug (2 Pts.)	GO	50	29. Tilt Cylinder (2 Pts.)	GAA	10
15. Pintle Hook (Jaws & Shaft)	GAA	10	30. Sliding Shoes (2 Pts.)	GAA	10
			31. Push Frame (4 Pts.)	GAA	10

Figure 40.— Lubrication schedule for rubber-tired tractor (M.R.S. I-110).

2. For a tractor equipped with a hydraulically operated blade, disconnect the hydraulic cylinder piston rods from the hydraulic jack brackets on the back of the blade. Retract the piston rods into the cylinders and secure the rods in this position.

3. For a tractor equipped with a cable operated blade, remove the capscrews and locknuts holding the lower sheave block universal mounting shaft; then remove the shaft, universal and sheave block from the blade or C-frame. Raise the lower sheave block, with universal, as far as possible and secure it in this position.

4. Remove the two capscrews, nuts, and shims from the left and right trunnion bearing caps located at the rear of the C-frame or push arms.

5. Back the tractor out and away from the C-frame or push arms.

6. Reassemble the trunnion bearing cap and shims to the C-frame or push arms to avoid loss or damage. If stored outdoors, coat the trunnion bearing cap and shims with grease to prevent corrosion.

VII. CHANGING REAR-MOUNTED TRACTOR ATTACHMENT

When it becomes necessary to disconnect a hydraulically operated scraper from the tractor, proceed as follows:

1. With the hydraulic system in operation, put the scraper in a transport position and insert travel lock pins.

TRACTORS AND ATTACHMENTS

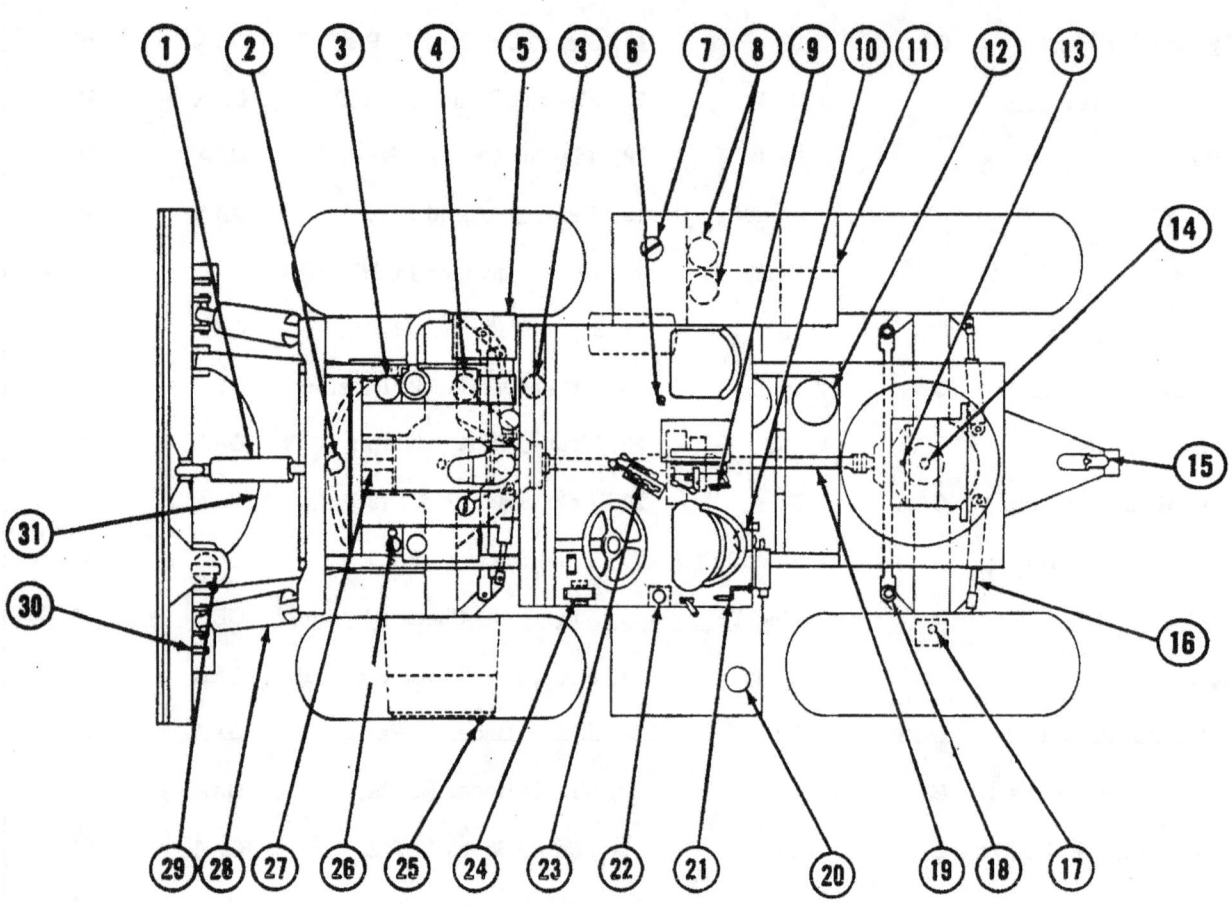

SYMBOL	LUBRICANT AND APPLICATION	TEMPERATURES	
		ABOVE +32°F	+32°F TO -25°
OE	OIL, Engine Engine Crankcase	SAE 30 MIL-L-2104	SAE 10 MIL-L-10295
	Transmission, Hyd.Tank, Brake Reservoir	SAE 10 MIL-L-2104	
GO	OIL, Gear Final Drive, Differential	SAE 90 MS GO-90 MIL-L-2105	
GAA	Grease, Automotive & Artillery All Pressure Gun Fittings	MIL-L-10924	

Figure 41. — Lubricating chart for rubber-tired tractor (M.R.S. I-110).

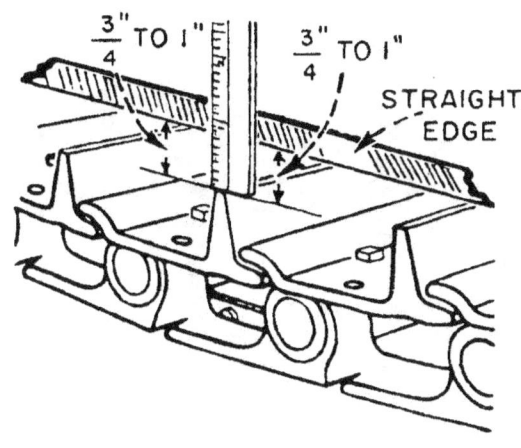

Figure 42. — Checking slack in track chain of a TD 20B series tractor.

2. Put ejector all the way down and close apron.
3. Screw jack for positioning headframe and scraper tongue. This will maintain proper height for reassembly.
4. Stop tractor engine.
5. Work all hydraulic levers in both directions to relieve hydraulic pressures.
6. Disconnect the hydraulic hoses from their respective openings in the manifold on the head frame of the tractor.

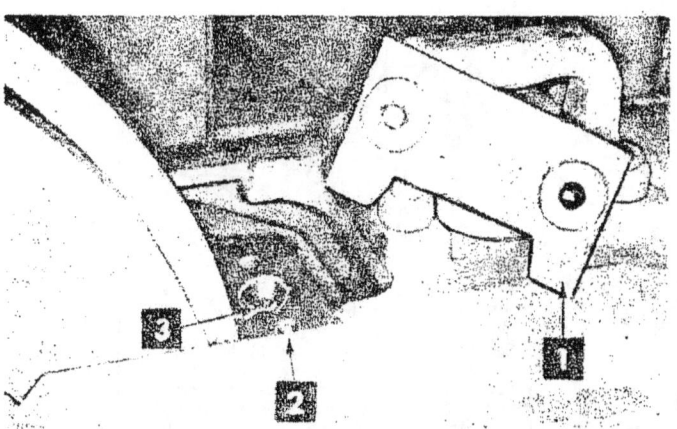

1. SCRAPER, FRONT IDLER.
2. SCREW, SOCKET HEAD.
3. FITTING, LUBRICATION.

Figure 43. — Hydraulic track adjuster of a TD 20B series tractor.

7. Pull the tractor drawbar pin from the scraper tongue.
8. Start the tractor engine and move the tractor away from the scraper unit.

VIII. SAFETY

Standard safety precautions applying to tractors follow:

1. Equipment must be operated at no greater speed than the maximum at which the machine can be kept under control at all times.
2. Navy safety regulations require that all dozers used in clearing operations be equipped with crankcase guards and radiator protectors. All dozers purchased by the Navy are equipped with these features, and they must never be used in clearing operations without the features in place.
3. When using a dozer for demolition, care must be taken to prevent falling objects from striking the operator or other personnel.
4. When felling trees with a dozer, the greatest care must be taken to avoid being struck by falling branches, or by the backlash of a branch or trunk. Whenever possible, it is highly advisable to erect an overhead guard, consisting of a framework of pipe or some similar structure, to protect the operator.
5. Men must NEVER ride the drawbars of tractors. This dangerous practice has been the cause of numerous accidents.
6. Operators of dozers and rippers should make every effort to learn the locations of any underground high voltage electric lines or gas lines which might be contacted by their equipment.
7. A tractor must not be operated near the edge of a cut; the edge may give way, overturning the machine. An overturning machine is very likely to crush its operator.
8. A steep incline should be climbed slowly. "Gunning" up a steep slope has often caused overturning.
9. Do not attempt a turn on a steep slope. Sliding sideways may not appear to be dangerous, but it can easily become so if the low side of the rig hits a solid rock or a stump.
10. Before starting a tow, carefully check the towing hitch. A runaway tow is a very dangerous hazard.
11. Chains, wire rope, and other makeshifts must not be used for towing. Always use a **towbar**.

TRACTORS AND ATTACHMENTS

1 With vehicle jacked up on the side which is to have the tire removed, and after fluid has been removed, remove rim nut and core housing to completely deflate. Push valve through valve hole.
Using a "bead breaking" tool and a heavy hammer, drive the tool between the tire bead and the rim flange, being careful not to damage bead area. Beads should be unseated on both sides of rim.

2 As an alternative to the procedure above, a bead unseating tool and instructions are available from Iowa Mold Tooling Company.

3 Thoroughly lubricate rim flange, tire bead and base of tube with a thin solution of vegetable oil soap in water or equivalent rubber lubricant recommended for this requirement. (Never use petroleum-base solution or silicones.)

4 Lock wheels by putting vehicle into gear with valve at top. Force outside bead at bottom into rim well. Insert long tire irons under bead at the top and pry bead over rim flange. Take short bites to avoid extremely hard prying and possible damage to tire bead.

5 After first section of bead is over rim flange, use one iron to hold that section over flange and use other tire iron to pry next section over flange. Do not attempt to pry too large a section over the rim flange at one time.
Safety Precaution — *Never release grip on either iron as they may tend to spring back.*

6 Pull tube out of casing. When only tube requires repair or replacement, this can be done without removing tire completely from rim.

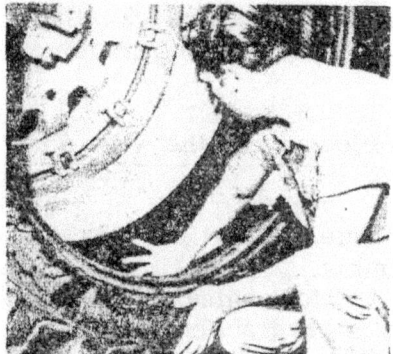

7 Thoroughly inspect inside of casing for foreign material or damage and remove moisture from inside of tire.

8 To remove tire completely from wheel, insert tire irons under the inside bead at side of tire. Pry rest of inside bead over rim flange. When starting this operation, be sure that the bead area on opposite side of tire is down in rim well.

Figure 44.—Demounting tractor tires (on machine).

Before mounting a tire on a used rim, be sure the flange area and partciularly the bead seat area is clean and smooth. Remove any buildup of rust, corrosion or old rubber with chisel or wire brush. Bent, cracked or otherwise damaged rims should be repaired or replaced.

Thoroughly inspect inside of casing for foreign material or damage.

Lubricate both beads with a thin solution of vegetable oil soap in water or equivalent rubber lubricant recommended for this requirement. (Never use petroleum base solutions or silicones.)

Note: Some steps of the following procedure may require two men on larger size tires.

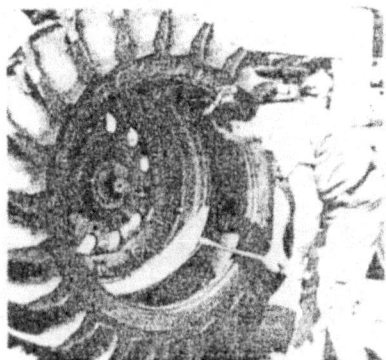

1 To put tire on wheel, place inner tire bead over flange at top. Be sure bead is not on bead seat but is guided into well as tire irons are used to work down either side, forcing rest of inner bead over flange. With first bead on rim, pull tire toward outside of rim as far as possible to make room for tube. Be sure inside of tire is completely dry.

2 Before inserting tube in tire, be sure that valve hole is at bottom of wheel. Align stem with valve hole and place tube in tire starting at the bottom. Place valve in valve hole and screw rim nut on stem to hold it in place. Be sure that tube is well inside rim before proceeding to next step.

3 Tube should be partially inflated and base area that contacts rim should be lubricated to prevent localized stretching.

4 Starting at top, use tire irons to lift outer bead up and over rim flange and down into rim well. Be careful not to pinch tube in the operation.

5 After getting first section of outer bead into rim well, place one hand against that section to hold it, and then pry remainder of bead over flange with tire iron in other hand. Do not attempt to pry large sections of bead over flange at one time.

6 Safety Precaution: *Centering the tire is extremely important to prevent broken beads. Remote control inflation equipment should be used. Never stand in front of assembly.*

With valve stem at bottom, lower the jack until tire is centered on rim. Inflate sufficiently to seat beads on rim at bottom.

7 Raise tractor; rotate tire to have valve at top. Inflate to 35 pounds pressure to fully seat beads.

Then remove valve core housing and completely deflate. Reinsert valve core housing and reinflate tire to recommended pressure. Note: If either bead should fail to seat at 35 pounds inflation, the tube may be pinched between tire bead and rim, or something else is interfering with proper mounting. *Do not increase inflation pressure to seat beads,* but remove valve core housing and completely deflate tube. Unseat both beads from the rim; relubricate both tire beads and rim bead seat areas; reinstall valve core housing, and reinflate tube to 35 psi. Repeat process until both beads are properly seated.

Reduce to operating pressure before putting tire in service.

Figure 45.—Mounting tractor tires (on machine).

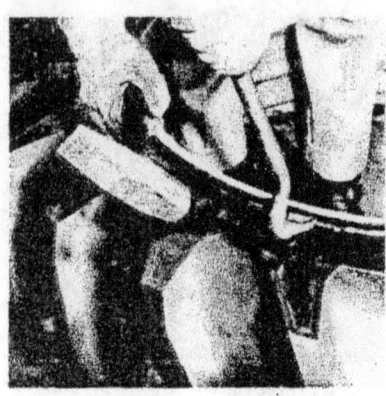

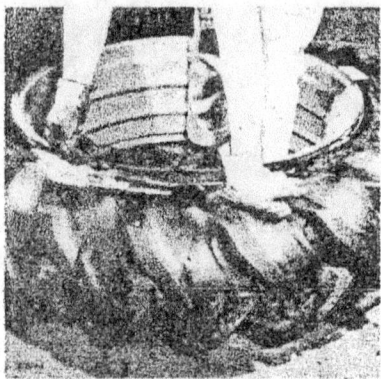

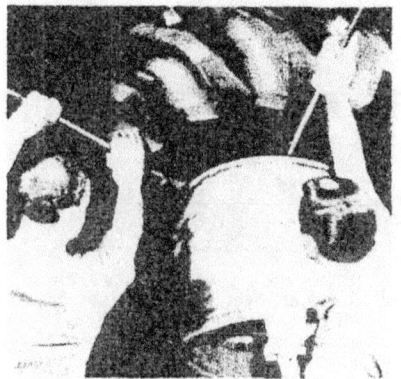

1. To dismount tire, completely deflate tube by removing core housing and remove rim nut. Using a "bead-breaking" tool and a heavy hammer, drive the tool between tire bead and rim flange, being careful not to damage bead area. After bead has been released completely around tire, turn tire and rim over and repeat above procedure with the second bead.

2. Thoroughly lubricate rim flange, tire bead and base of tube with a thin solution of vegetable oil soap in water or equivalent rubber lubricant recommended for this requirement. (Never use petroleum-base solution or silicones.)

3. With part of top bead forced into rim well, pry opposite side of bead over rim flange using two long tire irons. Continue until top bead is completely over the rim flange.

4. With weight of tire braced against a solid support, pull tube out of tire casing. When only tube requires repair or replacement, thoroughly inspect inside of tire casing for foreign material or damage and make sure inside of casing is dry before reinserting tube.

5. To completely remove tire from rim, with weight of assembly supported, be sure one side of bottom bead is in rim well and insert tire irons under opposite side of bead. With smaller size tires work bottom bead over rim flange by taking small bites with two tire irons.

6. Stand large section heavy tires on tread. With weight of assembly supported, and one man holding rim, the second man can work second bead over rim flange until rim drops out.

Figure 46.—Demounting tractor tires (off machine).

1 Before mounting a new tire on a used rim be sure the flange area and particularly the bead seat area is clean and smooth. Remove any buildup of rust corrosion, or old rubber with chisel or wire brush. Bent, cracked or otherwise damaged rims should be repaired or replaced. Rim should be laid on the floor with the valve hole on the top side. In the case of a deep well rim, the deep well must always be on top.

Inflate tube until it is rounded out and insert it in the tire with the valve on the top side before starting to mount tire on rim. Lubricate bottom tire bead and top rim flange with a thin solution of vegetable oil soap in water or equivalent rubber lubricant recommended for this requirement (never use petroleum-base solutions or silicones).

Push bottom bead over rim flange as far as possible. With the tire cocked on rim, screw rim nut finger-tight on valve stem to hold it in place.

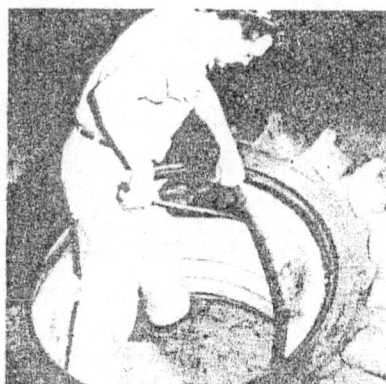

2 Using long tire irons, work first tire bead completely over rim flange.

3 Starting opposite the valve, use tire irons to lift top bead over the rim flange and down into rim well. Care must be used to avoid pinching tube with tire irons. When bead is well statred, lubricate remaining unmounted portion of tire bead and rim flange.

4 Tire bead must be forced into rim well when working tire bead over rim flange (lifting opposite side of bead may be required to do this). For small tire, stand on half of tire which is in rim well and work equally around both sides to spoon tire bead over rim flange until final section drops over at the tube valve. Do not attempt to pry large sections of bead over flange at one time.

5 With large section tires a second man may be required to hold tire bead in rim well — either with tire iron or by standing on the tire sidewall.

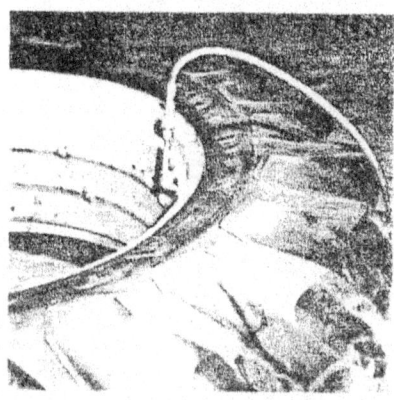

6 Safety Precaution: *Centering the tire is extremely important to prevent broken beads. Remote control inflation equipment should be used. Never stand over the assembly when inflating.*

Center the tire on the rim and inflate to 35 pounds pressure. Then remove valve core housing and completely deflate. Re-insert valve core housing and reinflate tire to recommended pressure. Note: If either bead should fail to seat at 35 pounds inflation, the tube may be pinched between tire bead and rim, or something else is interfering with proper mounting. *Do not increase inflation pressure to seat beads*, but remove valve core housing and completely deflate tube. Break both beads loose from the rim; relubricate both tire beads and rim bead seat areas; reinstall valve core housing, and reinflate tube to 35 psi. Repeat until both beads are properly seated.

Reduce to operating pressure before putting tire in service.

Figure 47.—Mounting tractor tires (off machine).

TRACTORS AND ATTACHMENTS

12. Coupling trailing equipment to the tractor is hazardous; be especially alert while this is being done. Whenever possible, it should be done with the tractor stopped and the clutch, if so equipped, disengaged.

13. When towing a heavy load downgrade, keep the tractor in low gear. Coasting is dangerous. A coasting tractor with a tow is very likely to jackknife.

14. At the end of a day's work, secure a dozer blade by lowering it to the ground. Do this also whenever dismounting from the tractor. Lowering the blade takes the weight of the blade off the power unit; more important still, it eliminates the possibility of the blade falling on someone. Whenever it is necessary to work on the dozer with the blade up, the blade must be securely blocked up to prevent accidental falling.

www.ingramcontent.com/pod-product-compliance
Lightning Source LLC
Chambersburg PA
CBHW082038300426
44117CB00015B/2531